The German Inflation of 1923

PROBLEMS IN EUROPEAN HISTORY:
A DOCUMENTARY COLLECTION

The German Inflation of 1923

EDITED BY

FRITZ K. RINGER

Indiana University
Bloomington

New York
OXFORD UNIVERSITY PRESS
London   1969   Toronto

FOREWORD

Problems in European History: A Documentary Collection has arisen out of a collective teaching experience. The series seeks to overcome a shortcoming which the authors believe persists in college history instruction. Certainly the restricting confines of the traditional textbook have been expanded as numerous collections of "readings" have appeared. But the undergraduate still remains at a distance from the historian's workshop. A compilation of heavily edited "significant documents" does not make for the sense of contact with the past that the study of history ought to promote. And the predigested selections from contending historians, neatly arrayed on either side of "classic" controversies, does not get the student to probe the underlying evidence; in fact, these academic disputations often leave him bewildered.

The conviction that students learned little of the way in which historians actually worked prompted a group of young Harvard historians five years ago to develop a new approach. The course that resulted—Social Sciences 3: Problems in Modern European History —represented an attempt to focus intensively on a small number of problems. Each problem would involve careful analysis of a wide variety of original source material. The student could develop the skills and understanding of historical explanation. In learning to compare evidence, make and test hypotheses, and judge critically earlier accounts, he would encounter some of the problems of historical research as experienced by the working historian.

In Social Sciences 3 eight studies in historical analysis are presented in a year. Our intention here is to make these documentary collections available, not necessarily as a series except in their underlying aim, but as separate problems that can be studied individually in connection with courses in European history. Each book has been edited and introduced with that purpose in mind. Thus the student can wrestle with the problems inherent in historical writing and judgment while he studies intensively a segment of the history of the country or period being taught.

Social Sciences 3 has developed over the past four years through the efforts of our collaborators, who share in the creation of these books beyond what we can gratefully acknowledge. Individual problems were prepared or substantially recast by the respective authors, but each case study was discussed and scrutinized by the entire staff of Social Sciences 3. To all of them, to the Committee on General Education of Harvard College, which has generously given of its time and efforts, and to our students—whose criticisms and suggestions were a fundamental guideline—we extend our thanks.

Cambridge, Mass.   RICHARD BIENVENU
August 1967   JOHN F. NAYLOR

PREFACE

The German Inflation of 1923 profoundly affected the social and political life of Germany during the Weimar Republic. It has been widely assumed that the financial crisis produced a kind of social revolution and that it alienated important segments of the German population from the young Weimar Republic. In this way, the inflation contributed to the eventual rise of National Socialism.

This book is intended to shed light on the connections between the economic facts of inflation on the one hand, and its social and political consequences on the other. While it is generally agreed that there were such connections, some questions remain about the exact nature of these links and about the types of evidence which can be brought to bear upon the problem. In the chapters which follow, readers will encounter the arguments of an economic historian. They will also deal with a number of contemporary impressions of the crisis, "eyewitness accounts" which reveal as much about the witnesses' mentality as about the events they describe. Finally, readers will have a chance to consider some samplings of statistical data.

The college course for which all these materials were originally collected had certain general objectives. The idea was to illustrate some of the historian's tools and procedures through practice and example; within the framework set by this general purpose, the present book was meant to include the use of statistical materials in social and political history. In a short book and a few classroom hours, this can only be done in a rudimentary way. It was not difficult, though, to provide occasion for a few of the satisfactions and many of the frustrations which the use of statistics typically entails. Thus the selections served their purpose: they occasioned reflection upon some of the historian's methods; the hope is that they will continue to be helpful in this way.

The final responsibility for the contents of this book rests with me. But I am intellectually in debt to my former colleagues in Social Sciences 3 for many of my ideas on the German Inflation of 1923. Like every other product of that course, this book evolved amidst frequent and very lively discussions among all the teachers of Social Sciences 3. For help in translating and editing, for constructive suggestions and salutary skepticism, I want to thank my friends Elizabeth Brown, Mack Walker and Philip Dawson, Richard Bienvenu and John Naylor, Robert Duggan, Thomas Gleason, and Charles Maier. Finally, I am grateful to Robert Grogg for help in the preparation of the final manuscript.

Bloomington, Indiana   F.K.R.
February 1969

CONTENTS

I   The Social and Political Background   3   •

Politics and Society under the Empire   3
The Political Parties in 1912   9
From Empire to Republic   15
The Parties in 1919 and 1920   28
Issues of the Early 1920's   34

II   The Economics of Inflation   40

German Economic Organization and Economic Conditions
before 1914   47
    Gustav Stolper: *The German Economy*   47
Origins of the Inflation during World War I (Stolper)   63
Economic Crisis of the Early Weimar Period (Stolper)   70
Explaining the Need for Inflation   90
    Hugo Stinnes: *On His Interview with the American Ambassador,*
    June 23, 1922   90
Defending the Policy of the Reichsbank   93
    Rudolf Havenstein: *Address to the Executive Committee of the*
    Reichsbank, August 25, 1923   93

III   Social Consequences of the Currency Crisis   97

The Report of an Expert Eyewitness   99
    Moritz Julius Bonn: *The Last Phase of Inflation*   99
The Complaints of Scholars   103
    Georg Schreiber: *The Distress of German Learning*   103
    Alfred Weber: *The Distress of the Intellectuals*   110
A Report on the Nation's Health   112
    Franz Bumm: *Speech before the Reichstag,*
    February 20, 1923   112

IV   The Inflation in the Experience of a German Family   119

Monetary Confusion and Moral Decay   120
    Pearl Buck: *How It Happens*   120
Family Crises and the Realities of Life (Buck)   130
Economic Contrasts and Political Choices (Buck)   138

V   Census Data and Election Returns   147

Occupations of Germans in 1907 and in 1925   155
German Elections, 1919-1932   161
The Elections of June 1920, May 1924, and December 1924   162

VI   The Inflation and Hitler's Putsch of 1923   163

The Participant as Historian   164
    Konrad Heiden: *Der Fuehrer*   164
The Death of Money (Heiden)   165
War in the Ruhr (Heiden)   178
The Beer Hall Putsch (Heiden)   196

The German Inflation of 1923

I

THE SOCIAL AND POLITICAL BACKGROUND

The German inflation of 1923 had many of the characteristics of a revolution; it transformed the social structure and the political life of Germany. Why and how this was so will concern us in the following chapters. But it will be best to begin by considering the status quo ante, the historical situation of German society and politics during the decades before the advent of the currency crisis.

POLITICS AND SOCIETY UNDER THE EMPIRE

German society during the late nineteenth and early twentieth centuries was a curious mixture of modern and traditional elements. On the one hand, Germany experienced an extraordinarily rapid industrial expansion, chiefly during the decades after 1870. In a very short period, a relatively backward nation was transformed into one of the greatest industrial powers in the world. In politics, the conflict between industrial employers and workers suddenly became a dominant issue.

On the other hand, the change was uneven as well as abrupt. Primitive farm communities and sleepy provincial towns continued to exist side by side with huge industrial and metropolitan centers. In northeastern Germany, agriculture survived in the form of great landed estates, on which cereals and other crops were produced rather efficiently for the market. Here the Junkers, the landed aristocracy of Prussia, tried to perpetuate a nearly feudal style of life. In the subalpine regions of the south and southwest, small and unspecialized farms struggled for subsistence, even while factories

3

mushroomed along the Rhine and Ruhr in the west and northwest and in the central states of Saxony and Thuringia. There were religious differences too; for the Catholic faith predominated in the south and in parts of the west and east, while the north was mostly Protestant. The politics of industrial conflict were thus confounded with much older forms of cultural and regional rivalry. The defenders of agriculture and of rural life challenged the claims of the cities, and painful contrasts arose between the established values of a pre-industrial culture and the new urban and technological civilization.

Every society is a mixture of heterogeneous elements. Contrasts were particularly violent in Germany, however, because modern developments had been so abruptly grafted upon a traditional context. Even after the industrial explosion was well under way, Germany continued to be dominated by groups that originated in a pre-industrial environment. The obvious case is that of the Junkers; but there are other examples as well. The aristocratic officer corps traditionally ranked very near the top of the German social hierarchy. The government bureaucracy, the actual ruling class of the nation, regarded the new industrial and commercial elites with jealousy and contempt. The old educated upper middle class, the officials, clergymen, professors, secondary teachers, doctors, and lawyers, showed little sympathy and much disdain for the new entrepreneurial middle class. Officials and professional men had formed a kind of mandarin caste in Germany before the advent of high industrialization. Their social standing and their influence in local and national politics had been based upon their education. At a time when only a very small fraction of the population studied at the universities, the minority of the "cultivated" had enjoyed special distinctions and privileges. But all this was changed when wealth and economic power began to rival and even to replace older sources of social influence and esteem.

One way to describe the whole transformation is to draw upon the distinction between "class" and "status." The modern concept of class refers primarily to a man's wealth or to his objective place in the industrial economy. Status, by contrast, suggests a place of social honor and a certain style of life which is based upon convention, and upon the "subjective" estimates of one's contemporaries. The great German sociologist Max Weber argued that during periods of economic stability, class and status ranks would tend to coincide; for rich families would eventually become "good families" as well. During periods of rapid socio-economic change, however, class patterns would at least temporarily conflict with the established hierarchy of status. This is exactly what happened in Germany during the late nineteenth and early twentieth centuries. Before the industrial boom, status had been conferred to a large extent by education, by official titles and functions, and by such pre-democratic sources of influence and esteem as "nearness to the throne." But economic change threatened to submerge the traditional status configurations in a flood of money, of economic power, and of other class criteria.

Of course there were business classes in Germany well before 1870. One thinks particularly of the old merchant oligarchies of Hamburg, Lübeck, Frankfurt, Augsburg, and Nürnberg. These originally commercial groups had long fortified their class positions with elements of status; they had become "old" families, "cultivated," sometimes titled, well connected, and well married. They had little in common with the new industrial upstarts of the Ruhr cities, of Düsseldorf, Dortmund, and Essen. Nor was the conflict between class and status confined to the upper reaches of the social hierarchy. The provincial pharmacist or postmaster was a traditional notable in his own way. The ordinary burgher, the owner of a small store or of an artisan establishment, too, represented "old wealth" on a small scale. In any case, he had reason to resent the new wholesaler or shop foreman, along with the whole world of large-scale enterprise which threatened his social place as well as his livelihood. Thus the antagonism between industrial management and industrial labor, which appeared rather suddenly upon the

German scene after 1870, cut across an even more deep-seated ten-
sion between the rising manufacturing classes and the old society of
pre-industrial or early industrial Germany.

The antithesis between modern and traditional groups profoundly
affected the cultural life of the nation; for it inevitably raised questions of value. What made an old family "good," and when was an
educated person a "cultivated" man? What happened when the
newly rich streamed into the universities to learn a bit of Greek
before settling down to run their enterprises? If that wasn't "cultivation," what was? And more generally, how should the new world
of technology and economic power be evaluated in the scale of
established cultural norms and goals?

In politics, industrialization led to overt class conflict. During the
early nineteenth century, German political parties had still essentially been assemblies of notables. Many parliamentary politicians
had been officials, academics, or other members of the educated
elite. Parties had been very loosely organized, and individual deputies had considered themselves autonomous political leaders, rather
than passive representatives of their constituencies' interests. All
this changed after 1870. A workers' party now made its appearance, which drew its strength from the immense number of its
voters, and which agreed always to vote as a bloc in parliament. It
meant to make the economic interests of labor as great as possible
an influence in national affairs. In the meantime, industrialists and
even landowners and farmers had also formed great associations to
lobby in their behalf. Entrepreneurs bought mass newspapers to
influence the popular vote, so that economic power became an increasingly important weapon in the politics of economic competition. Clever politicians continued to cloak their clients' demands in
the conventions of "idealistic" and, above all, nationalistic rhetoric;
but this fooled only the innocent. In any case, the old status elites
recognized that their traditional leadership was threatened by the
new conditions. They responded with a moralistic attack upon
"materialism," upon the influences of "the masses" in national
affairs, and upon all forms of "interest politics."

The legal and institutional framework of German political life was itself a very odd mixture of modern and traditional elements, which only added to the existing social tensions. To begin with, Germany was not a fully integrated state before 1919. In the Constitution of the new German Empire (*Reich*) of 1871, the "federal," decentralizing tendencies almost predominated over the unitary, centralizing elements. In some sense Germany remained a confederation of twenty-five semi-autonomous states, some of which continued to be ruled by their own royal or ducal families. The states managed most of their own internal affairs; the Reich had no centralization administrative organization which extended all the way down to the local level. The main unifying element in Otto von Bismark's Constitution was the domination of Germany by Prussia, the largest and most powerful of the states. The King of Prussia, William II after 1888, was also German Emperor; and the offices of German Chancellor and Prussian Prime Minister were combined in one person as well.

Prussia was a constitutional monarchy with a bicameral legislature. The upper house was utterly dominated by the Junkers and by conservative officials, who were often younger sons of the landed aristocracy. The lower house, the Diet, was a little more democratic, since it was elected on the basis of a special three-class suffrage. The rule was that the small upper crust, those who paid one-third of the taxes in large individual amounts, were entitled to elect one-third of the deputies. Another third of the Diet was elected by the middle bracket of taxpayers, who paid the second third of the taxes. All the rest of the population, voting in the third class, chose the last third of the deputies. At the same time, law and custom guaranteed the Junkers' control of the Prussian juridical and administrative system on the local level. This was true at least in the old northern and eastern provinces of Prussia, though the situation was a little more complicated in Prussia's newer provinces in the industrial northwest.

The *Reichstag,* the lower house of the national legislature, was elected on the basis of universal and equal suffrage, though women were not given the vote. Candidates competed in single-member electoral districts, and there were run-offs if no candidate achieved a majority on the first ballot. Electoral districts were never redrawn after 1871, so that the new urban populations were in fact under-represented in the Reichstag. The Federal Council, the upper house of the national legislature, was really an executive organ of government, chaired by the Chancellor. All the states of the Empire sent delegations to it, Prussia having the largest vote with seventeen delegates. The Prussian Prime Minister instructed and headed the Prussian delegation. The Bavarian delegation, the second largest contingent in the Federal Council, was the potential leader of any resistance to Prussia by the smaller states.

There were no Reich ministries at all. Instead, the important government departments of the central administration were headed by Secretaries of State, who were responsible to the Chancellor. As of 1914, there were Reich departments for the Interior, Foreign Affairs, the Navy, the Treasury, Justice, and Colonial Affairs. The army was controlled by a Prussian ministry; but Prussia in turn had no foreign office of its own. The Chancellor of the Reich, and therefore the whole Reich government, was not responsible to the Reichstag. The Chancellor, who had the power to dissolve the Reichstag and to call new elections, was appointed and dismissed at the will of the Emperor. Ordinarily, legislative proposals were originated in the offices of the Reich Secretaries, and then proposed to the Reichstag by the Chancellor or by a Secretary acting as his deputy. After negotiation and passage, the bills went to the Federal Council, which reviewed them principally from the point of view of existing state and federal law, and which then sent the new regulations to the appropriate ministries of the states with instructions for their promulgation and execution.

This institutional pattern assigned a decisive role to the state and national bureaucracies. It also tied the affairs of the Reich very firmly to Prussia. The reactionary Prussian lower house was in a position to check the initiative of the Reichstag. The Prussian Junkers, the Prussian officer corps, and the Prussian bureaucracy exercised a disproportionate influence over the affairs of the nation as a whole. Finally, the ambiguous position of the Reichstag produced a whole series of painful contradictions. Here was a democratically elected legislature which had only very limited powers over the budget. The Chancellor needed majority support in the Reichstag to achieve his program; but he was not responsible to the legislature or to the voters. Inevitably, the parties in the Reichstag fell into a primarily passive role. They could accept or reject what the Chancellor proposed, and they were in an ideal position to obtain petty concessions for their constituencies. But they had no integral responsibility for the government, because it in turn did not depend upon them. Thus a façade of democratic mass politics and all too obvious interest bargaining was propped up before a traditional system of government which was fundamentally illiberal at the core.

THE POLITICAL PARTIES IN 1912

The German Social Democratic Party (SPD) had its place at the extreme left of the German political spectrum as of 1912, the year of the last elections held under the Empire. In its origins, the party dated back to the 1860's. Two small worker parties arose at that time, both of them affiliated with early trade union movements. One of them was founded by Ferdinand Lassalle, who hoped to obtain the help of the Prussian state against the liberal middle classes. The other proletarian party, led by Wilhelm Liebknecht and August Bebel, had little confidence in the paternalism of the Prussian monarchy. Unlike Lassalle, Liebknech and Bebel were anti-Prussian, anti-militarist, and internationalist in their outlook. Their followers came increasingly under the influence of Karl Marx and Friedrich Engels.

In 1875 these two early workers' parties were united. Their new joint program was to some extent a compromise, though the Marxist elements in it gradually became predominant. Then, from 1878 to 1890 the party was subjected to all sorts of harassment under Bismarck's anti-socialist law of 1878. Bismarck combined this legal persecution with social insurance schemes, which were designed to protect the workers against the worst hazards of industrial labor, and incidentally, to wean them away from their party. The experiment failed. The unions continued to grow despite the legal restrictions under which they were placed. Nor could the expansion of the party itself be stopped, though much of the leadership was in exile. The real result of the whole episode was that the party became more thoroughly committed to the goal of socialist revolution.

Nonetheless, the Social Democratic platform which emerged from the party congress of 1891 at Erfurt was still a compromise of radical and reformist elements. The theoretical spokesmen of the new Marxist orthodoxy insisted that there could be no real improvement of the workers' condition under capitalism. The laws of capitalist production ensured that the laborer would receive a decreasing share of the wealth he produced, even while competition and recurrent crises of overproduction continued to force more marginal capitalists into the ranks of the proletariat. In an effort to avoid the consequences of this process, the capitalists would seek to exploit foreign markets and foreign labor, thus provoking imperialist conflicts. The party of the proletariat ought therefore to repudiate the existing regime entirely, to cultivate the class-consciousness and international solidarity of all workers, while looking ahead to the final crisis of capitalism and the socialist revolution.

While the Erfurt program enshrined some of the leading propositions of the emerging orthodoxy, however, it also left room for political and trade union activity which would protect the workers' interests even under capitalism. The only theoretically consistent defense of this reformist tactic was Eduard Bernstein's revisionism. Bernstein held that there was nothing inevitable about the increasing misery of the proletariat under capitalism, as long as the workers united to force an improvement in their lot. The weapons of political democracy and collective bargaining could, according to Bernstein, be used to affect a gradual transition from capitalism to socialism. Violent revolution might still be necessary, but only against reactionary attempts to reverse the democratic movement toward a just society.

In practice, the conflict between radicalism and reformism within German Social Democracy was the difference between the leaders of the trade unions and the orthodox intellectuals of the party. The unions were daily engaged in bargaining for higher wages. Many of the party officials also saw the advantages of electoral cooperation with honest reformers among the bourgeois liberals in the Reichstag. It was easy to fall into reformist tactics, even for those who repudiated revisionist theory. One can distinguish a radical, a centrist, and a revisionist branch within German Social Democracy in 1912. But frank defenders of theoretical revisionism were almost as small a minority as the determined radicals. Most of the center of the party combined lip service to theoretical orthodoxy with the tactics of reform.

The party's unanimity rule bound Social Democratic deputies to vote as a bloc in the Reichstag. But it became increasingly difficult to maintain the unity of the movement in fact. One of the most diversive issues around 1912 was the conflict between nationalism and social internationalism. In the era of international conflict which culminated in the First World War, German socialist leaders found it increasingly difficult to stifle patriotism and enthusiasm in their constituency and even in themselves. This, more than any other issue, was eventually to precipitate overt divisions in the party. But as of 1912, unity was formally maintained despite painful disagreements. Outwardly, the party had never looked more powerful than it did in 1912. In the elections of that year, the Social Democrats gained 110 seats in the Reichstag and thus became the strongest political party in Germany.

One of the reasons for the Social Democratic electoral success of 1912, which was achieved despite the retrograde delimitation of voting districts, was an alliance in the run-off elections between Social Democrats and the German Progressive Party. The Progressives, who obtained 42 seats in 1912, represented the left of the middle-class liberal spectrum in German politics. The liberal movement as a whole had suffered a serious decline of vitality in Germany during the later nineteenth century. Once an optimistic philosophy of social progress and civic and political freedom, German liberalism had been weakened by the shortcomings of Bismarck's constitutional settlement, by middle-class nationalist and militarist enthusiasms, and by the appearance of proletarian socialism on its flank. Even the Progressive Party of 1912 was really a coalition of splinter groups; some Progressives were constitutionally liberal but indifferent or hostile to social legislation, while others favored social reform but hesitated to oppose illiberal measures which were defended on nationalist grounds.

Still, compared with other German parties, the Progressives were relatively firm in their defense of civic and constitutional rights. They were free traders, relatively internationalist in outlook, suspicious of the bureaucracy and of militarism, and anxious to make liberalism as attractive as possible to the workers. During the 1860's the Progressives Max Hirsch and Franz Duncker had begun a small cluster of trade unions which remained affiliated with the left wing of the liberal movement in politics. As of 1912 the Progressives were determined above all to force a democratic suffrage upon Prussia, to make the Chancellor responsible to the Reichstag, and thus to transform the German government into a truly liberal parliamentary regime. For the sake of this objective, the party was prepared to cooperate with the Social Democrats, as in the elections of 1912.

As might be expected, the Progressive Party received little support from the entrepreneurial bourgeoisie. Some analysts have distinguished between commercial and industrial capitalists. Merchants engaged in foreign trade with developed countries are likely to be interested in low tariffs and in international cooperation. They have nothing to gain from government expenditures for heavy armaments, and they are not as directly involved in wage disputes as the manufacturers. Thus it is possible to imagine Progressive voters among the merchant patriciate of the northern ports. The Progressive Party also had a certain following among the old middle and lower middle classes, particularly in the southwest, in the states of Baden and Württemberg, where a strong tradition of burgher liberalism dated back to the eighteenth century. Finally, the left wing of the German academic intelligentsia, though rarely Social Democrats, often voted for the Progressives.

To the right of the Progressive Party, the National Liberals gained forty-five seats in the election of 1912. Though still formally committed to the principles of constitutional liberalism, this party had lost most of its reforming zeal during the decades since 1870. When Bismarck or his successors in the German chancellorship wanted to gain support in the Reichstag, they found four tactics particularly useful. The first was a campaign against the cultural and educational programs of German Catholics. This was the strategy of the *Kulturkampf* (cultural conflict) of the early 1870's. It brought Protestant liberals and conservatives alike into the fold of the government majority. The second tactic was the attack upon socialism which produced the anti-socialist law of 1878. The third government strategy was tariff protection for German industry and agriculture, which caused middle-class liberals to forget their principles for the sake of their interests. Finally, there was a whole complex of legislative proposals which could raise the "national issue," whether it was a question of armaments, of the colonial budget, or of military discipline. The national issue was always an effective weapon against the Social Democrats and sometimes against the Progressives as well. Whenever any of these four favored issues arose, the National Liberals found it difficult to maintain their libertarian scruples. Slowly and painfully, they were drawn into the position of a government party, often cooperating with Junker reactionaries and ready to tolerate many of the illiberal aspects of German social and political organization. Like the Progressives, the National Liberals probably had the support of some professional people. A segment of the bureaucracy and of the academic elite undoubtedly voted National Liberal as well. But in the main, the National Liberal Party of 1912, the party of tariff protection and armaments spending, was the agent of heavy industrial and entrepreneurial interests.

The Center Party, which sent ninety-one deputies to the Reichstag of 1912, is hard to place in the political scale from left to right. On some questions, chiefly civic and cultural matters, it stood vaguely to the right of the National Liberals. But on other issues, and increasingly during the early twentieth century, it should really be placed between Progressives and National Liberals. The Center was the party of German Catholicism, in many ways a product of the *Kulturkampf*. All the other German parties, to some extent even the Social Democrats, were predominantly Protestant. Under attack during the early 1870's, German Catholics drew together in the Center Party. Henceforth, the party looked after Catholic interests in education, in family law, in questions of censorship, and in other civic and cultural matters.

Catholicism was particularly strong in Bavaria and in southern Germany generally. This was predominantly a region of petty agriculture and small provincial towns. Even when big cities contained large Catholic populations, urban life tended to make confessional attachments seem less important than social and political allegiances. The Center therefore drew much of its support from rural and provincial Germany. At times, it played the role of a conservative party, siding with the Junkers in support of agrarian tariffs and in the defense of rural against industrial and commercial Germany. Its cultural policies also made it a potential ally of conservative Protestants in defense of religion, the family, and public morality. But there was also a small cluster of trade unions affiliated with the Center, and the party was capable of asserting the interests of Catholic workers and tradesmen against the politics of the Junkers, entrepreneurs, and officials. Under the leadership of Matthias Erzberger, this progressive tendency within the Center Party came to the fore during the first decade of the twentieth century. Erzberger and his followers were capable of cooperating with the Social Democrats. They could be quite critical of bureaucratic arrogance, German colonial policies, heavy armaments budgets, and the excesses of German militarism and imperialism.

Finally, at the far right of the political spectrum, two Conservative parties jointly gained 57 seats in the election of 1912. The Conservatives represented the interests and the outlook of the Prussian Junkers. Almost all Conservative politicians were Prussians, and the majority were either owners of aristocratic estates or younger sons of Junker families in the officer corps and in the bureaucracy. A few great industrialists, assuming the role of a new court nobility, supported Conservatives. Much of the bureaucracy and many academics voted Conservative as unquestioning supporters of the Prussian monarchy. A small splinter party allied to the Conservatives even attracted some lower middle-class support through anti-Semitic propaganda.

Still, the main object of the Conservatives was the defense of Junker predominance in German politics and social life. The demand for export subsidies and tariffs on grain was probably the most important plank in the Conservative platform. It led the party into alliances either with the Center or with the National Liberals, who agreed to a joint campaign in behalf of industrial and agricultural protection. The Conservatives played a tougher and more successful game of interest politics than any other party. Yet they were also most adept in the use of moralistic and nationalistic rhetoric in electoral conflicts. The three-class suffrage gave them almost undisputed control of the Prussian legislature. Their influence in Prussian local government, at court, in the officer corps, and in the higher ranks of the administration made them the chief beneficiaries and the most intransigent defenders of the existing social and political system.

FROM EMPIRE TO REPUBLIC

Germany was not alone responsible for the failure of diplomacy which led to the outbreak of the war in 1914. The arrogant, vacillating, unreasoned foreign policy of the German leadership, however, was certainly a serious obstacle to international stability. German imperialism was not primarily the product of a capitalist need for colonial markets. If there was a specific connection between the interests of German industrialists and German foreign policy, that link is to be sought chiefly in the armaments program. German industrial interests campaigned openly and vehemently for armament expenditures and for the naval expansion which strained Anglo-German relations. On the other hand, officials, academics, and professional people played as prominent a role in the fleet agitation as the industrialists themselves. The cult of nationalism became particularly rabid in Germany because the national issue was so often used as a political substitute for domestic reform. There is no reason to suppose that the industrialists were the only ones to have an interest in this falsification of Germany politics. In some respects, the old pre-industrial ruling elites were even more likely to profit from it.

Whatever the reasons, large segments of the German upper and middle classes were gripped by the fever of nationalism before and during the First World War. While German armies stood in Russia and in France, German Junkers and industrialists, officials and academics, joined in developing a staggering program of German war aims. They called for extensive territorial annexations on Germany's eastern and western borders, and for German suzerainty over much of central and eastern Europe. These demands were supported by the military leadership, which assumed almost dictatorial powers in domestic affairs as well as at the front. Civilian leaders who tried to reduce German war aims to somewhat more moderate limits simply could not assert themselves against their more rabid colleagues, against the clamor of the ultra-annexationist lobby, and against the all-powerful Quartermaster General Erich Ludendorff.

Many Germans, especially within the mandarin elite of officials, academics, and professional people, interpreted the war as a profound conflict between German ideality and the materialism of the west European democracies. They contrasted German culture with the shallow commercial and technological civilization of England and America. They praised German loyalty to the community, arguing that west European democracy was based on the political egotisms of individuals and of classes. Some of them spoke of a "German socialism" which would not be materialistic or in any way utilitarian, but in which class hatreds would be forgotten and a spirit of national community would prevail. They were delighted that upon the outbreak of war, German workers forgot all their grievances and internationalist theories in an outburst of patriotic enthusiasm.

Nevertheless, a number of prominent intellectuals and politicians realized that neither the ideological defense of German culture nor the nationalist fervor of 1914 could permanently take the place of needed political and social reforms. Even before the war, it had become increasingly difficult to obtain a Reichstag majority which would put up with the three-class suffrage in Prussia and with the Chancellor's lack of responsibility to the Reichstag. It seemed reasonable to hope that the wartime spirit of solidarity would lead to reforms in these areas. A few liberal academics and politicians also urged moderation in the German war-aims program, knowing that the workers would not gladly give their lives in a blatantly aggressive war. It was only when such good advice was not heeded that the enthusiasm of 1914 gave way once again to bitterness and internal division. There was no evidence of declining morale at the front; but the strain began to show among the political parties at home.

A split in the ranks of the Social Democrats became overt in 1916 and deepened in 1917, partly under the influence of the Russian Revolution. The two radical minority factions which now emerged on the left wing of the German socialist movement were the Spartacus League (Spartacists), and the Independent Social Democratic Party (Independents, USPD). The issues which separated these two groups from the rest of the Majority Social Democrats (SPD) were rooted in the ambiguities of the Erfurt Program. The theoretical and tactical divisions which had begun to agitate

German socialists around the turn of the century were aggravated during the World War, primarily because the moderate majority of the party abandoned socialist internationalism. In 1914, breaking established precedents and relying on the unanimity rule, the majority leadership asked Social Democratic deputies in the Reichstag to support the government in its need for financial credits to finance the war effort.

The Majority Social Democratic Party, as it emerged from the schisms of 1916 and 1917, was no longer committed to revolutionary socialism. It did not immediately or fully adjust its doctrinal to its tactical position. But it fell increasingly under the influence of revisionist theory, while its practice became more and more frankly that of a reform democratic party. It continued to demand the complete liberalization and democratization of the German political system. It also called for thorough social reforms, for the nationalization of important industries, and for trade union participation in industrial organization and in all economic decisions. In foreign policy, the party favored a peace without extensive annexations. But it no longer denied the patriotic sentiments of its members, and it permitted union leaders to cooperate with the authorities in the management of war production.

The Independent Social Democrats, by contrast, continued to adhere to socialist revolution, at least as an ultimate goal. What really separated them from the majority group, however, was their determined opposition to the war. They considered the European conflict a product of capitalist imperialism and militarism, a tool in the hands of the old class society. The members of the USPD felt deeply committed to socialist internationalism. Nothing did more to alienate them from the SPD than the majority's repeated votes for war credits between 1914 and 1916. The Independents urged a more determined opposition not only to extensive annexations, but to the war itself. Some of them had wanted to use mass demonstrations and strikes to prevent the opening of hostilities in 1914. Eduard Bernstein himself had favored such energetic opposition, showing that at least on the issue of nationalism, tactical radicalism could be combined with theoretical revisionism—and vice versa. In any case, the USPD represented a rather broad range of doctrinal positions, from Bernstein to the old orthodox party leadership, and even further to the left.

The Spartacus League was not sharply separated from the USPD at first; the memberships of the two groups initially overlapped to some degree. Yet the Spartacists, led by the young radicals Rosa Luxemburg and Karl Liebknecht, in fact represented the extreme left wing of German socialism. They saw imperialism, and therefore the World War, as the last defense and the last fatal crisis of capitalism. Accordingly, they meant to do more than just oppose it. Using the dislocations and the popular unrest which it engendered, they hoped to overthrow the capitalist system and thus to secure the immediate triumph of socialism. Rosa Luxemburg disliked Lenin's idea of revolution imposed by a disciplined minority. She was prepared to use political mass strikes and even violence to defeat capitalism. But she wanted socialist leaders to be guided by the desires of the proletarian masses in all their tactics, which made her revolutionary doctrine more democratic than Lenin's. Until 1919 it was Luxemburg's brand of democratic revolutionism which chiefly inspired the German Spartacus League.

While German socialism divided into rival factions, the liberal parties in the Reichstag drew together in defense of moderate war aims and parliamentary reform. A coalition between Majority Social Democrats, Progressives, and the Center Party made up a new parliamentary majority. Under the leadership of Matthias Erzberger, the left wing of the Center, which represented Catholic trade unionists and segments of the lower middle class, asserted itself against agrarian and conservative elements in the party. This prepared the ground for the new liberal Reichstag coalition, which was to outlast the Empire itself. Majority Social Democrats, Progressives, and liberal Centrists agreed in their desire to reform the Prussian electoral system and to increase the powers of the Reichstag. The first tactical success of the new alliance, however, was the Reichstag peace resolution of July 19, 1917, which called for a moderate war-aims program and a negotiated peace.

Unfortunately, the peace resolution produced no decisive results. The Reichstag was simply not in a position to carry out a close and continuous supervision of the German government and diplomatic service. The military leadership exercised almost dictatorial powers, and it would have taken much more determined opposition from the Reichstag to change that. Such opposition was not forthcoming, particularly since the fortunes of war seemed temporarily to favor Germany in late 1917 and early 1918.

Russia withdrew from the conflict after the Bolshevik revolution. On March 3, 1918, Germany was able to impose the very severe peace of Brest-Litovsk, which stipulated huge territorial annexations and German suzerainty over much of central and eastern Europe. Meantime, even before the treaty was signed, contingents of German troops could be transferred from the eastern to the western front, where the Germans launched a major offensive in the spring of 1918. Despite temporary successes, however, this last German effort in France was a military failure; the Allied defense lines were weakened but not broken through. Fresh American troops began to appear at the front in increasing numbers, and the Allies were able to check the German drive during the summer and to start a great counteroffensive in August. In September, Austria-Hungary sued for peace after the collapse of the Balkan front.

Even though German troops were still deep within French territory, the German case was really hopeless by the summer of 1918. Yet the German military leadership concealed the true state of affairs from the public and the civilian leadership until October. Then, suddenly, Ludendorff announced that the army needed an immediate armistice under any conditions. He would accept no delays for the purpose of bargaining for terms with the Allies. Leaving to others the tasks of suing for peace and of organizing the retreat, he resigned his command. Ironically, it was he who later launched the vicious legend that disloyal and defeatist civilians had stabbed a victorious German army in the back.

Germany's only hope under these conditions lay in President Wilson's Fourteen Points of January 1918, which proposed a settlement on the principle of national self-determination. Because it seemed clear that the Allies would be more likely to make a favorable peace with a new and liberal government, the German Empire was abruptly transformed into a parliamentary regime. On October 3, Prince Max von Baden became Chancellor. Supported by the established coalition of Center, Progressives, and Social Democrats, Max von Baden initiated the overdue reforms in the powers of the Reichstag and in the Prussian suffrage. He also asked for an immediate armistice. The first answer he received, a note from American Secretary of State Lansing, demanded unconditional surrender and hinted that the German Emperor should be removed. A later Allied note of November 5 promised that the ultimate settlement would be based on the Fourteen Points, but added that Germany would have to pay for war damages suffered by the civilian populations of Allied nations.

In any case, Germany now had to accept whatever terms were proposed by the Allies. The military situation was clearly hopeless; the Allied blockade resulted in an ever more acute food shortage, and there was increasing political unrest as well. Socialist ideas were making some converts among the troops at the front; but disaffection was most marked among recent recruits still stationed at home, and among the sailors of the fleet, which lay idle in the North Sea ports. Many of the workers in the big cities, too, began to think of socialist revolution. Their language, at any rate, was often vaguely socialist; their real objectives probably had less to do with the dictatorship of the proletariat than some of the radical leaders believed. Above all, they wanted peace. They had been told that the war was lost, and they wondered what or who prevented an immediate end to the fighting. They were also determined to rid themselves of the Emperor and of the whole clique of aristocratic officers, Junkers, and bureaucrats which had misgoverned the Empire. Some of them meant to overthrow the capitalist system. Even those who knew little about Marxism were attracted by the language of socialism. But the class revolution they meant to make was in fact directed against the traditional caste and status system of an early capitalist society.

On October 23, a mutiny broke out among the sailors at Kiel. They had been asked to undertake a further expedition which seemed to them pointless. The revolt quickly spread to Hamburg and to other cities. Max von Baden, among others, hoped that the constitutional monarchy as an institution could be saved, if William II abdicated in favor of his heirs. Events now moved too fast for the constitutional monarchists, however. While William vacillated, Max von Baden announced the Emperor's abdication. He then handed the chancellorship to Friedrich Ebert, the leader of the Majority Social Democrats. Finally, responding to the spread of revolutionary disorder and wishing really to check further radicalization and political chaos, the SPD leaders Friedrich Ebert and Philipp Scheidemann decided almost reluctantly to abandon the monarchical system. On November 9, 1918, the Republic was proclaimed by Scheidemann in Berlin. Two days later, an armistice finally ended the First World War.

There now followed two months of near-anarchy. What central government there was could not assert itself in the provinces. In Bavaria, a republic had been proclaimed as early as November 7. The outcome of scattered and frequent political disorders all over Germany was dictated by local conditions and by the strength of locally organized groups. Military units, returned from the front or informally reorganized, asserted their influence. Trade unions also played a role, along with the revolutionary Councils (or Soviets) of Soldiers and Workers. The central government in Berlin, a sort of coalition cabinet of Majority Social Democrats and Independent Social Democrats, was styled the Council of People's Representatives.

While there was little doubt that the mass of Germans desired thorough social as well as political changes, the socialist leaders could not agree how far to carry the revolution. Under Ebert's leadership, the SPD opted for the democratic republic and for social reform within the capitalist system. This choice was supported by moderate elements within the Councils, particularly among the Soldiers' Soviets. The trade unions also backed Ebert's group. They demanded—and eventually obtained—the eight-hour work day and the institution of shop councils to represent the workers' interests in all industries. Above all, the Majority Social Democrats proposed to hold general elections on January 19, 1919, to convene a National Assembly and thus to leave the question of Germany's future constitution to a democratically elected parliament, which would operate under the established ground rules of the liberal tradition.

This was the point at which all the disagreements among socialist factions came to focus. The Independent Social Democrats wanted to postpone the elections, so that the revolutionary Councils would have more time to destroy the ruling institutions and elites of the old system. They felt particularly adamant about the traditional army and officer corps. They wanted time to revolutionize the masses and to transform the established patterns of agrarian and industrial ownership and organization. The Spartacists, who founded the German Communist Party (KPD) on January 1, 1919, did not believe in democratic elections and parliamentary rule at all. They opted more and more openly for minority rule through the most radical branches of the system of Soviets. Accordingly, Spartacist formations took to the streets to prevent the elections by force.

Against this threat, Friedrich Ebert and Gustav Noske, the Majority Social Democratic defense minister in the central cabinet, called on elements of the old army. This caused the USPD to break with the SPD leadership in the central government. A series of bloody engagements then took place between Spartacist formations and other radical worker groups on the one hand, and army units and Free Corps on the other. The Free Corps were informally organized paramilitary formations, often made up of unemployed former soldiers and officers. They helped to make the street-fighting which preceded the elections of 1919 particularly fierce and brutal. In one of the clashes, Rosa Luxemburg and Karl Liebknecht were murdered. This robbed the radical wing of German socialism of its most brilliant leaders and helped to convert the newly formed Communist Party into a nearly passive instrument of Moscow's policies.

The elections, which were boycotted by the Communists, made the Majority Social Democrats by far the strongest party in the National Assembly. But the SPD alone did not obtain a majority of the seats. It was also weakened by the rupture with the USPD, which would not join a coalition with its former party comrades. As a result, the new Weimar Constitution was written by the so-called Weimar coalition of Majority Social Democrats, Democrats, and Center Party. The new German Democratic Party (DDP), which in some ways continued the traditions of the old Progressive Party, played a particularly important role in the coalition. It held the balance of power between the SPD and the Center, and it commanded the services of several distinguished jurists and political scientists from the left wing of the German academic community.

The Weimar Constitution, which was completed by August 11, 1919, created a truly democratic parliamentary regime in Germany. One important innovation had already been made before the elections to the National Assembly. Women were given the vote; the voting age was reduced from 25 to 20; and a system of proportional representation was introduced. By 1920, the rule was that 60,000 votes from any electoral district were enough to elect a deputy from that district. Any votes left over after seats thus earned had been distributed were proportionately assigned to national slates put up by the various parties. In place of the Emperor, a popularly and directly elected President became the head of state. It was he who appointed the Chancellor, asking him to form a parliamentary coalition government. The President was also supreme military commander; he could dissolve the parliament and call elections, as well as plebiscites on specific questions. Finally, the President was given emergency powers to rule by decree and to suspend constitutionally guaranteed civil liberties under certain specific conditions. The Chancellor's government was responsible to the democratically elected legislature, which continued to be named the Reichstag. The old Federal Council (*Bundesrat*), which represented the governments of the several states, became the *Reichsrat;* but its legislative veto could now be overridden by a two-thirds majority of the Reichstag.

Altogether, the Weimar Republic became a much more centralized polity than the old Empire had been. The number of states was reduced, and the competence of the central government was increased. On the other hand, the state bureaucracies continued to control local affairs; cultural and educational matters remained in the hands of the states; and the anomalously large state of Prussia was not broken up. Next to Saxony and Thuringia, Prussia became the most reliable stronghold of Social Democracy and of republicanism generally, because the loss of some of the old agrarian provinces left Prussia as a whole a predominantly urban and industrial state.

Friedrich Ebert became the first President of the Weimar Republic. Philipp Scheidemann, the first Chancellor, headed a government supported by the Weimar coalition from February until June, 1919. But even before the Constitution was completed, the new liberal regime faced a whole series of crippling difficulties. Perhaps the most serious of these political obstacles was the Treaty of Versailles.

Germany was not asked to participate in the peace negotiations which began in Paris on January 18, 1919. The treaty which was signed at Versailles on June 28, 1919, imposed very harsh terms on the defeated nation. This was not a peace according to the principle of national self-determination. It would have been very difficult to impose a purely Wilsonian settlement in any case. Wartime agreements among the Allies militated against it, as did the French presence in the Rhineland before the negotiations began. Wilson did what he could to restrain French expansion into western

Germany. But he could not totally ignore or overrule France in its determination to acquire securities against a resurgence of German military might. He consoled himself with the idea that the League of Nations would help in the just and peaceful arbitration of conflicting national claims during the years of international understanding for which he hoped.

Germany at Versailles lost one-seventh of its prewar territory and one-tenth of its population. In the north, a part of the province of Schleswig went to the Danes. In the south, sections of the Austrian Tyrol were ceded to Italy. In the west, Alsace-Lorraine was returned to France. The left bank of the Rhine was demilitarized and occupied by France for fifteen years as a military guarantee. The French were also given the right to occupy and to exploit the coal resources of the Saar region for fifteen years, after which the future of the region was to be settled by plebiscite. Germany lost land in the east, especially to Poland. The so-called Polish Corridor absorbed much of the provinces of West Prussia and Posen, and a slice of East Prussia as well. Upper Silesia was to be divided after a contested plebiscite in 1921, which assigned 60 per cent of the province and most of its industry and coal to Poland. In the dismemberment of Austria-Hungary, German-speaking minorities were incorporated into Czechoslovakia, as France tried to create a cluster of client states hostile to Germany on her eastern border. The rump of German Austria was forbidden to seek incorporation (*Anschluss*) into Germany. The German colonies were lost; the German fleet and army cut to token size. Finally, an enlarged definition of Germany's reparations obligations made her liable not only for losses suffered by Allied civilian populations but for more broadly conceived war damages and costs as well. The huge reparations bill which resulted was formally justified in the famous war guilt clause, which made Germany solely responsible for the conflict.

Inevitably, the treaty provoked a storm of protest in Germany. Henceforth, the agitators of the nationalist right had a powerful weapon in the memory of Versailles. Responsible politicians, who knew that Germany had no choice but to accept the settlement, could easily be made to look like traitors. Indeed, the task of signing the treaty was too much for the Scheidemann government, which divided and fell in June 1919. The Weimar coalition survived to support two other ministries until June 1920, but the peace treaty added greatly to the coalition's difficulties, which in any case were very great throughout 1919 and early 1920.

The mild social reformism of the Majority Social Democrats in the government provoked intense dissatisfaction among the followers of the USPD, while the Spartacists continued in their determination to create a revolutionary soviet regime. A short-lived Soviet Republic in Bavaria in April 1919 was put down by right-wing Free Corps. Strikes and Spartacist uprisings took place in many German cities, and the old conflict between radical workers and the military in the Ruhr led to the formation of a revolutionary "red army" in March 1920. At the same time, the anti-republican right continued to gain in strength, especially after the Treaty of Versailles. The Free Corps and other paramilitary organizations thrived, and something like a tradition of political murder became established among the young rowdies and fanatics of the nationalist opposition.

During the early months of 1920 the leaders of the right-wing parties in the Reichstag launched a general campaign of slander and vilification against Matthias Erzberger, the leader of the Center Party's progressive wing. Erzberger was hated because he had dared to undertake a thoroughgoing reform of the German tax system in 1919. He had increased the revenues of the central government, which had previously been dependent upon contributions from the states. He had also introduced some direct taxation, which affected the wealthier segments of German society. His main accuser was Karl Helfferich, who had been Reich Secretary of the Treasury during the war, and whom Erzberger had charged with irresponsibility in that office. Helfferich became a leader of the parliamentary right-wing opposition to the Republic after the war. He stressed Erzberger's role in the peace resolution of 1917, his criticism of the German military leadership during the war and since, and his willingness to sign the Treaty of Versailles. While Helfferich thus mobilized the radical nationalists against Erzberger, he also accused him of personal dishonesty. Erzberger brought a libel suit, in which he was technically vindicated. But testimony at the trial did not remove all questions about his conduct, so that he was politically discredited. Shortly after the beginning of the trial, an unsuccessful attempt was made on Erzberger's life. A jury gave the would-be assassin one and one-half years in jail, citing his "idealistic motives" as mitigation.

The resurgence of the right-wing extremism, which became visible during the Erzberger process, culminated in the Kapp Putsch of March 1920. A nationalist Free Corps invaded Berlin and installed a reactionary junta under Wolfgang Kapp. The regular Reich government fled. The regular army, under Chief of Staff Hans von Seeckt, refused to fight against former comrades in the Free Corps and maintained an ominously neutral stance. Kapp's regime, which met some passive resistance from the government bureaucracy, was brought down after four days by the socialist and trade union leaders, who called an extremely effective general strike. When radicals in the Ruhr attempted to convert this victory of labor into renewed revolution, the army recovered its willingness to act. In the civil war which ensued, the radical workers' "red army" was defeated. Thus the institutions of the liberal Republic barely survived the trials of 1919 and early 1920. It remained for the elections of June 6, 1920, to show how seriously the new regime had lost ground among the voters.

THE PARTIES IN 1919 AND 1920

A good insight into the politics of the early Weimar period can be obtained from a comparison of election returns for 1912, January 1919, and June 1920. The elections of 1912 returned the last Reichstag of the Empire. In January 1919 voters sent deputies to the constituent National Assembly which created the Weimar Re-

THE SOCIAL AND POLITICAL BACKGROUND

public. In 1912, about 7.2 million voters, 84.5 per cent of those eligible to vote, elected 397 deputies. In 1919, some 30.4 million voters, 82.7 per cent of the eligible, elected 421 representatives. In 1920, about 28.2 million voters, 79.1 per cent of those eligible, elected 459 deputies to the Reichstag. The results, in percentages of the total vote and in Reichstag seats obtained by the major parties, are described in Table 1.

Table 1
The Elections of 1912, 1919, and 1920.

Parties	1912		Parties	1919		1920	
	Per cent	Seats		Per cent	Seats	Per cent	Seats
Conservatives	12.6	60	Nationalists	10.3	44	15.1	71
Center	16.4	91	Center	19.7	91	13.6	64
			Bavar. People's P.	—	—	4.2	21
Nat. Liberals	13.7	45	Ger. People's P.	5.1	23	14.8	69
			Democrats	18.6	75	8.4	39
Progressives	12.3	42	Social Dems.	37.9	163	21.6	102
Social Dems.	34.8	110	Independents	7.6	22	18.0	84
			Communists	—	—	2.0	4
Other	10.2	48	Other	0.6	3	2.3	5

The 1912 figures for the Conservatives include 0.4 per cent and 3 seats for the anti-Semitic Christian-Social Party. The results listed for the German People's Party (DVP) for 1919 and 1920 include, respectively, 0.7 per cent (4 seats) and 0.8 per cent (4 seats) for the middle-class Economics Party and the Bavarian Farmers' League, which were allied with the DVP. The large category "Other" for 1912 includes 32 seats for national and regional minority parties of Poles, Danes, Welfs (Hannoverians), and Alsatians. These qualifications, particularly the large representation of splinter parties in 1912, should be kept in mind during the interpretation of results for the old and "new" parties of 1919 and 1920.

The German National People's Party (Nationalists, DNVP) was one of several new political formations which emerged after the collapse of the Empire. It officially acknowledged the democratic parliamentary regime as a political framework. But especially during the early years of the Weimar period, it was in fact the most determined right-wing enemy of the Republic and of the new demo-

cratic society. As the heir of the Conservatives, it had the support
of the old ruling elites, the agrarian magnates, army officers, and
bureaucrats of the Empire. Its membership also included many
university professors and secondary teachers, some conservative
industrialists, and certain lower middle-class elements who were
attracted by reactionary and anti-Semitic doctrines.

As the voting returns suggest, some of the bitterest reactionaries
stayed away from the polls in 1919, whether from timidity or dis-
gust. Many of them continued to have vague hopes of a restored
monarchical or authoritarian regime long after 1919. But the dema-
gogic successes of Helfferich's DNVP, along with the general atmosphere of reaction in late 1919 and early 1920, brought these
extreme opponents of the Republic back into the electoral arena
as Nationalist voters. A few former right-wing National Liberals probably helped to elect DNVP deputies in 1919 and 1920.
Among the northeastern districts lost by Germany in the Treaty of
Versailles, several had been former strongholds of Conservatism.
One therefore has to regard the elections of 1920 as a considerable
success for the DNVP, perhaps particularly among middle-class
voters. In the main, though, the reactionary Nationalists of 1920
were identical with the Conservatives of 1912.

The continuity of German political groupings between 1912 and
1920 is even more marked in the case of the Center Party, which
was led by Erzberger until 1920. It continued to represent Catholic
voters, especially in the rural and provincial south and southwest.
The party gained some support between 1912 and 1919, perhaps
partly among Catholic trade unionists. Soon after the elections of
1919, Erzberger led his followers into the Weimar coalition. This
policy alienated elements on the right wing of the party. Inevitably,
the Erzberger trial in early 1920 also disturbed many voters. Disaffection with the Center's relatively liberal course was particularly
marked in Bavaria, where a right-wing separatist and monarchist
movement profited from traditional suspicions of Prussia, from
popular dislike of Social Democratic Berlin, and from a general
reaction against the short-lived Soviet Republic. Before the elections

of 1920 former members of the Center Party in Bavaria created the Bavarian People's Party (BVP) as an organ of monarchist and Catholic separatism. In cultural and religious questions, the new party proposed to act in alliance with the Center; but it stood politically to the right of its parent party. After 1920, the Center itself ran in Bavaria only during the elections of May 1924.

The National Liberals and Progressives jointly captured about 26 per cent of the popular vote in 1912. In 1919 and again in 1920, between 23 per cent and 24 per cent of the popular vote fell to two new middle-class liberal parties, the German Democratic Party (Democrats, DDP), and the German People's Party (DVP). The Democratic Party was in fact the only genuinely new political grouping formed after the war. The sociologist Alfred Weber was one of its founders. Another important early supporter was Walter Rathenau, a progressive industrialist, the organizer of German raw materials rationing during the war, and something of a social and political visionary. The DDP also attracted most of the progressive and socially reformist minority within the German academic community. All these intellectuals felt that the old political parties of the Empire were either discredited by their militarism or lacking in original and constructive ideas for the new society. The Democrats were committed to constitutional liberalism. They also thought it possible to cooperate with the Social Democrats in behalf of thorough social reform, even though they had no faith in Marxist socialism or in the dictatorship of the proletariat.

In 1919, under the influence of revolution and general disenchantment with the old regime, the new DDP received 18.6 per cent of the popular vote. It clearly attracted former Progressives; but it also received support within the former constituency of the National Liberal Party. Its voters came from broad segments of the educated, professional, and mercantile classes, though probably less from entrepreneurial and industrial groups. Parts of the old burgher class of artisans and tradesmen also elected Democratic deputies, particularly in the traditionally liberal southwest. Indeed, the DDP might have succeeded in uniting almost all former National

Liberals and Progressives had it not been for Gustav Stresemann.

Stresemann was a young National Liberal who came to prominence during the last years of the Empire. Because of his vigorous nationalism before and during the war, the founders of the German Democratic Party hesitated to give him a leading role in their new political union. In reaction, Stresemann reconstituted a sector of the old National Liberal Party as the German People's Party. The men who supported him in this tactic generally came from the right and center of the National Liberal Party. They were particularly representative of entrepreneurial and industrial interests. They objected more to the social reformism than to the constitutional principles of the Democrats, and they were generally more vociferous in their nationalism than the DDP as well. After 1920, Stresemann developed into a responsible though not enthusiastic republican and an advocate of a realistic foreign policy. Seeking a gradual and essentially diplomatic revision of the Versailles settlement, he sought to curb the pointlessly provocative and politically decisive rhetoric of the hypernationalists. Ironically, his political rationality increasingly alienated those in his own party who had originally encouraged him to break with the Democrats.

Treating the votes of the Democrats and those of the People's Party as a single unit, one sees little change between 1919 and 1920. The shift in the relative position of the two parties, however, is a striking symptom of the Republic's early difficulties. The Democrats were the main authors of the Weimar Constitution and a key partner in the Weimar coalition of Social Democrats, Democrats, and Center. All three members of the coalition suffered serious losses in the elections of 1920; but the Democrats were most decisively punished for assuming the responsibility of government in a period of crisis. The social conflicts of 1919 and 1920 polarized the electorate. While the Majority Social Democrats lost ground to the Independents and Communists, middle-class voters abandoned the Democratic Party for the more reliable anti-socialism of the People's Party.

The story of the three German socialist parties has already been briefly told. As a group, they received 34.8, 45.5, and 41.6 per cent of the popular vote, respectively, in 1912, 1919, and 1920. Even before the war, the Social Democratic electorate was apparently not restricted to blue-collar workers in industry and commerce. The jump in the Social Democratic vote in 1919 was nonetheless remarkable. One has to take into account the enlargement of the electorate for the 1919 election, and the disappearance of the national and regional splinter parties of 1912. One also has to remember that over 15 per cent of eligible voters stayed at home during each of the three elections we are comparing. It is possible to imagine a good turnout of Social Democratic voters coupled with widespread abstention among non-socialists in 1919. Even after all such explanations have been considered, however, the figures still suggest at least a mild shift toward the Social Democrats among middle-class and lower middle-class voters, perhaps especially among former Progressives. The decline of the socialist vote between 1919 and 1920 might reflect the return of these middle-class voters to their former politics.

On the other hand, there are certainly other good reasons for the 10 per cent drop in the electoral strength of the socialist parties after 1919. This was a period of intense rivalry and mutual distrust among the various factions of the socialist camp. In 1919 voters clearly supported the Majority Social Democrats (SPD) in their choice of parliamentary democracy. The Independent Social Democrats (USPD) received only 7.6 per cent of the popular vote, while the Spartacists boycotted the elections entirely. After January 1919, however, many German workers became increasingly dissatisfied with the moderate policies of the SPD. They had expected more far-reaching social changes, and they were upset by the government's use of troops against the proletariat in the Ruhr and elsewhere. As a result, the Majority Social Democrats fell from 37.9 to 21.6 per cent of the popular vote between 1919 and 1920, while the representation of the Independents climbed from 7.6 to 18.0 per cent.

Meantime, the German Communist Party (Communists, KPD) began to participate in Reichstag elections in 1920, earning 2 per cent of the vote. The Communists chose to use the electoral process for purposes of protest only, and their tactics in the Reichstag were purely obstructionist. Communist votes thus inevitably weakened the liberal coalition in the Reichstag; in the short run, they actually increased the influence of the right-wing parties. Because most leaders of the USPD were troubled by this dynamic, they chose to rejoin the SPD in January 1922. They hoped at one and the same time to preserve democracy against its reactionary opponents and to strengthen socialist sentiment within the SPD. As we shall see later in this book, the constituency of the USPD did not fully accept the tactical decision of the party leaders. The movement of voters away from the parties most loyal to the Republic certainly did not end in 1920.

ISSUES OF THE EARLY 1920'S

In sum, the elections of 1920 constituted a serious electoral shift to the right of the political spectrum. The Weimar coalition no longer had a majority in the Reichstag. It could continue in power only as a minority government. Another possibility was a minority coalition between the DDP, the Center, and the DVP, which depended upon the tolerance of the SPD. Finally, there was the option of the so-called great coalition from the Social Democrats to the People's Party. Obviously, none of these combinations could be achieved or maintained without serious strains and dilemmas. The cabinets which succeeded each other between June 1920 and November 1922 functioned as minority governments. Then, from November 1922 until August 1923, Heinrich Cuno headed a nonpartisan ministry of experts to deal with the pressing issues of reparations payments and monetary inflation. Though nominally neutral, the Cuno government stood closest to the People's Party. It thus reflected the political shift to the right, the trend away from progressive social policies which inevitably followed upon the e'ections of 1920.

Outside the Reichstag too, the right gained in strength during the early 'twenties. In fact, reactionary and nationalist extremism reached violent proportions. Erzberger fell victim to a second attempt on his life in August 1921. In June 1922 republicans were shocked by the murder of Walter Rathenau, who had been much abused by the extreme right for his loyalty to the Republic, his moderate course as German Foreign Minister, and his Jewishness. The Reichstag was sufficiently alarmed by the spread of violence on the right to pass an emergency law for the protection of the Republic which was designed to control extremist organizations and propaganda. This measure in turn precipitated a conflict between the central government and the state of Bavaria, which had become the foremost stronghold of armed reaction.

The fanaticism of the extreme German nationalists was stirred up again and again during the early 'twenties by the question of reparations. The whole period from 1920 to 1923 was filled with continual and heated international negotiations on this issue. The peace treaty had left open the final amount of reparations and the long-term schedule of payments. The Allied Reparations Commission was to settle these problems. The German government repeatedly appealed for a moratorium on payments already ordered, and for a reduction in the burden which was ultimately to be imposed. In the London Ultimatum of May 1921 the Allies set the total of the German obligation at 132 billion gold marks. They also demanded immediate payment of arrears on some initial reparations installments which had been stipulated at Paris. They threatened, in case of default, a renewed Allied blockade, coupled with military occupation of several towns in the Ruhr.

At this point Walter Rathenau entered a new German cabinet as Minister for Reconstruction, later as Foreign Minister, to carry out a "policy of fulfillment." His plan was to abandon the blatant and useless resistance to Allied reparations demands which had been the German tactic until 1921. He proposed instead to negotiate in good faith and to try honestly to meet the established schedule of payments. Rathenau felt that Germany's need for a partial moratorium on payments would be all the more clearly revealed by her genuine effort to pay. He also hoped to encourage the growing sympathy and support of the English and Americans, who were beginning to resent French intransigence toward Germany and to worry about French hegemony on the European continent.

The idea of approaching the reparations question from the purely matter-of-fact viewpoint of the economists led to the Genoa Conference of April 1922. But before the meeting took place, a left-liberal coalition in the French Chamber of Deputies was replaced by the conservative and nationalist government of Raymond Poincaré. As a result Genoa produced no substantive alleviation of the German burden. On the contrary, it provided the impetus for a Russo-German economic understanding, the Treaty of Rapallo, and for a new decline in Franco-German relations. The French were absolutely determined to protect themselves against a resurgent Germany. In the peace negotiations at Paris, France had been prevented from annexing the Rhineland. Instead, she had been given a defensive guarantee against Germany by England and the United States. But this pact became null and void when the American Congress refused to ratify the whole Treaty of Versailles. Even England was rid of its obligation to France because the wording of the guarantee made English support conditional upon American concurrence. France, alone and feeling cheated, began a desperate search for concrete securities against the Germans. She sought to create separatist movements in the German regions temporarily under her control, and she was in no mood to relax her demand for reparations. Rejecting English attempts to restrain her, she actually began to seek a conflict with Germany over the issue of reparations.

On January 9, 1923, French and Belgian troops invaded the Ruhr. Overriding English protests, they justified their action by pointing to rather minor defaults in German reparations payments. Their plan was to supervise the operation of German mines and factories in the Ruhr, and thus to extract reparations payments in kind from Germany by force. Poincaré had the support of French industrialists who needed German coal.

In Germany, the Cuno government decided to meet the French encroachment with a policy of "passive resistance." The workers and the management in the Ruhr industries and mines refused to cooperate in any way with the French. Railroads ceased to run; a kind of general strike was carried out. The central government did what it could to support the striking workers and to reimburse industrialists for the losses they incurred. The whole scheme worked rather well at first, as Germany was swept by a wave of patriotic enthusiasm. Difficulties soon began to show themselves, however. The French brought in their own people to run the factories and mines. Despite sabotage by German volunteers, the French managed to resume production in the Ruhr. They also created a small German separatist movement, which proposed the secession of the Rhenish provinces from the Reich. At the same time passive resistance imposed a severe strain upon the already precarious finances of the Reich. A runaway inflation soon made clear that the government could not long continue to resist the French.

From August 13 to November 23, 1923, Gustav Stresemann headed a government of the great coalition which abandoned the struggle in the Ruhr. Passive resistance ended on September 26, and the ground was thus prepared for the economic stabilization which followed. The French were still in the Ruhr, where they fomented separatist putsches in September and October of 1923. In the so-called Micum agreements, which terminated the conflict in the Ruhr, they had been given partial control of Ruhr production as a "productive guarantee" against future defaults in German payments. But strong English and American pressure and the convening of the Dawes Committee in January 1924 finally brought relief for the Ruhr and for Germany as a whole. The Dawes Committee, a panel of economic experts headed by the American banker Charles Dawes, submitted a comprehensive report on the whole reparations question in the summer of 1924. At another London Conference this plan was agreed to by the Allies. In return for German acceptance of the new scheme, the French agreed to withdraw from the Ruhr by July 1925. The details of the Dawes proposal need not concern us now. Suffice it to say that it contained improved terms for the Germans, that the French kept their promise in 1925, and that German reparations payments never after 1924 exceeded the amounts which flowed into Germany in the form of loans from abroad.

Before the Dawes Committee helped to launch this improvement of Germany's economic position, however, the Weimar Republic had to weather a whole series of nearly fatal crises in the fall and winter of 1923. There was much unrest among workers over wages. There was determined opposition to Stresemann from heavy industrialists and from rabid nationalists within his own party. The nationalists objected to what they considered Stresemann's renewed policy of "fulfillment." The industrialists, among them Hugo Stinnes, demanded firmer steps against strikes and worker unrest. In fact, German entrepreneurial groups now sought to reverse the decision favoring the eight-hour day, one of the main social reforms of the early Weimar period. At one point, Stinnes and his friends even asked the French to lengthen the work day in the Ruhr. Putschist ideas began to gain ground on the right wing of the People's Party. Stresemann's Minister of Economic Affairs was forced from office by conservative dissidents in his own party, along with Rudolf Hilferding, the Social Democratic Minister of Finance who had sought to reduce government compensations to the industrialists during the Ruhr conflict.

The new intransigence of the bourgeois right was in part a consequence—and in part a cause—of a resurgence of left-wing radicalism. In October 1923 a coalition of Communists and Social Democrats came to power in the state of Saxony, while left-wing socialism was also gaining strength in neighboring Thuringia. Proletarian guards were being organized, and a revolutionary soviet regime in central Germany seemed a distinct possibility. The threat caused the central government to use the army against Saxony, as well as against a Communist uprising in Hamburg. The Social Democrats in the Reichstag reluctantly agreed to these punitive measures; but they insisted that the government be equally firm in dealing with right-wing dissidents in Bavaria.

The hope for a separate Bavaria under its own restored dynasty had never ceased to grow in and around Munich during the early 'twenties. The Bavarian legislature was dominated by a coalition of the Bavarian People's Party and the German National People's Party. A professor of forestry at Munich University had organized a Bavarian Home Guard, which was eager to fight for Bavarian autonomy against Prussians, socialists, and Democrats. The Bavarian authorities tolerated all kinds of extremist organizations of the anti-republican, nationalist, and anti-Semitic right. Munich was the early home of Hitler's National Socialists.

When the Reich government called an end to passive resistance in the Ruhr, the Bavarian reactionaries found their opportunity. Gustav von Kahr, a monarchist and a leader of the Bavarian People's Party, declared a state of emergency and assumed dictatorial powers. His position was ultimately based upon the power of the Home Guard. General Otto von Lossow, the commander of the Reich army units in Bavaria, joined the rebellion. He refused to carry out the central government's instruction to forbid the *Völkischer Beobachter,* the newspaper of the National Socialists. There was much mutinous talk of marching against Saxony and on to Berlin. On November 3 President Ebert asked Seeckt whether the Reich army could be trusted to put down the Bavarian rebellion. The answer he received was as "neutral" and unsatisfactory as Seeckt's position in the Kapp Putsch.

This was the background of Hitler's famous Beer Hall Putsch of November 8, 1923. It will form the subject of a later chapter. Fortunately for the Republic, it was a failure. Gustav Stresemann's government fell in a vote of no confidence on November 23. The right thought Stresemann too internationalist and too liberal, while the Social Democrats could not forgive him for moving against Saxony and not against Bavaria. Stresemann stayed on as Foreign Minister. In this position, he helped to lead Germany into a short period of national and international stability between 1924 and 1929. For a time, the Republic seemed on the way to recovery. But the social and political damage done by the great inflation was never fully repaired.

II

THE ECONOMICS OF INFLATION

It will now be necessary to consider the economists' view of the German inflation. Our chief interest is in the social and political consequences of the currency crisis, not in its economic causes and dynamics. But we must understand, at least roughly, how prices can be affected by fiscal and monetary policies, by banking practices, and by the problems of international trade and finance.

Putting it generally, the introduction of additional currency into the economy will cause prices to rise unless there is a proportionate increase in the quantity of goods produced. In the long run, an equilibrium will establish itself between (1) the total amount of money in circulation, multiplied by the average speed of transaction; (2) the quantity of goods available for exchange, multiplied by the level of prices. Thus prices will tend to rise if, other factors remaining constant, there is a decrease in the quantity of goods, or an increase in the velocity of buying and selling, or (most important) an increase in the amount of currency in circulation.

Governments can affect this equation in several ways. They withdraw money from circulation by borrowing from their citizens or by taxing them. They bring currency back into circulation by spending money on goods and services of various kinds. As long as government income equals government expenditure, the price equation is not affected. But the situation changes as soon as the government takes either more or less money out of circulation than it puts back in. It can take more out by accumulating a budget surplus; it can put more back by way of deficit spending. That is the basic relationship between fiscal policy and prices. One should add that mild and controlled inflationary or deflationary policies are by no means *inherently* harmful. There is no absolute standard of what a currency is or should be worth. Government policy in this field can be judged only in terms of its total effect upon the economy and the society. Indeed, many modern economists argue that a mildly inflationary trend best achieves the objectives of economic productivity, full employment, and social progress.

If a government has a surplus, it does not simply burn the excess currency; nor does it immediately print new money when it means to spend beyond its income. Instead, a central bank or system of banks is given the task of handling the currency and of serving as an intermediary between the government and the private economy. The several techniques available to the central bank in the fulfillment of its functions cannot now be discussed in all their complexities. They have varied, in any case, for different countries and periods. The German central bank (*Reichsbank*), as we shall see, was continually involved in the "discounting of Treasury bills." A bill is something like an IOU, except that it is generally dated in advance. A short-term bill upon the Treasury, for example, might read to the effect that the Treasury will pay one million marks (the *Mark* is the German currency unit) to the holder of the bill upon its maturity, say, in one year's time. Instead of directly printing currency for its deficit spending, the German Treasury periodically made out such bills and passed them on to the Reichsbank. In "discounting" the bill, the Reichsbank simply deducted a year's interest from the amount of the IOU and then advanced the remainder to the Treasury in banknotes. As a "bank of issue," the Reichsbank had the right to print its own banknotes. It could thus physically convert government deficits into new currency.

Even an ordinary bank, one without the right to issue its own banknotes, can create the equivalent of new currency. It can assume that only a part of the money deposited by customers will be withdrawn at any given time; the rest may be invested. Conversely, the bank may lend money beyond the amount of its original capital;

for only a part of the credit it extends will lead to immediate cash withdrawals, while repayments from earlier loans will help to finance later ones. If a bank invests in stock, or discounts a commercial bill, it acquires securities which can be used as collateral for further loans or investments. Thus even ordinary banks can stretch the available currency, create credit, or, in terms of our initial equation, increase the velocity of monetary circulation. This process cannot be extended indefinitely, of course. The bank will have to protect itself against sudden demands by its customers. It will want to distinguish between its "demand deposits," accounts which can be withdrawn without notice, and its more predictable liabilities.

Yet prudence alone has repeatedly been found an insufficient restraint upon the expansion of credit. That is why so-called coverage requirements are an important part of every modern banking system. It is possible to regulate the expansion of credit by restricting private banks to one of several specialized functions, perhaps that of making commercial loans, or that of investing depositors' funds in industrial shares. Such specialization limits the opportunities for stretching money. But even more effective restraints can be created by stipulating the amount and type of assets a bank must hold against its liabilities. The classic form of such "coverage requirements," which are naturally most important for banks of issue, demands that banknotes be "covered" by a stipulated minimum proportion of gold certificates.

It is *changes* in coverage requirements and credit regulations generally, not the established practices themselves, which can have inflationary or deflationary effects. This must be understood in studying the German inflation. The Reichsbank and the other German banks were rather unrestricted in their functions, and that made a difference. Even at the height of the currency crisis, the Reichsbank extended credit at very low discount rates directly to commercial enterprises, not just to other banks. The rapid depreciation caused its loans to exceed repayments in real value. Quite apart from the effect of easy credit on the velocity of monetary circulation, the Reichsbank thus in effect expanded the currency. But many of these practices became possible only because they were preceded by a general relaxation of coverage requirements and credit regulations.

Problems of international trade and monetary policy may also be pertinent to the economics of inflation. An unfavorable balance of trade, an excess of imports (and other expenditures abroad) over exports (and other earnings abroad), will tend to lower the international demand for the home currency and raise the demand for foreign currencies which are backed by export surpluses. The price of the home currency on the international market will therefore fall, unless the government chooses to maintain a constant rate of exchange between its currency and gold. In the latter case, the imbalance of trade will result in gold exports, which will persist until the home currency is formally revalued in terms of gold, or until the balance of trade is restored.

When a currency falls in value, relative to gold or to foreign currencies, exports from the home country are stimulated and imports are inhibited. This is true whether the domestic currency is formally devalued, or whether it is simply allowed to fall gradually in the international monetary market. The stimulus to exports and the inhibition of imports result from the fact that all domestic goods in effect become cheaper for foreign buyers, while domestic consumers find it more expensive to buy goods from abroad. In this way, the effects of devaluation may eventually restore the balance of trade, but at a new (and, for the home country, less favorable) set of monetary exchange rates.

The only other alternative available to countries facing a negative balance of trade, an import surplus, is to tax money out of domestic circulation or to engage in other measures of fical austerity. Such procedures may alleviate the need for devaluation by reducing domestic consumption—and imports—while yet depressing the prices of domestic goods and thus making them cheaper for foreign buyers.

If a country makes unilateral transfers of money abroad, if it pays reparations or gives foreign aid, the amount of such transfers must be counted as imports in its international account. Unless the country can bring the extra money back home by an export surplus in its ordinary commerce, it will face the alternative created by any passive (negative) balance of trade. This was the situation of Germany after the Treaty of Versailles, which demanded huge reparation payments from an economy already weakened by wartime deficit spending, by serious losses of territory and natural resources, and by the forfeiture of its merchant fleet and other "reparations in kind." German economists of the 1920's therefore had some reason to consider the reparations a source of inflation. Regarded as an ordinary government expenditure, reparations demanded heavy taxation or deficit spending. Regarded as a huge passive item in the balance of trade, the reparations required extensive export of gold, plus currency devaluation, or (again) heavy compensatory domestic taxation.

So impressed were German politicians and economists with the reparations as a cause of their economic difficulties that they completely ignored the role of deficit spending itself. They were encouraged in their one-sided interpretation by a curious circumstance. At certain phases in the development of the inflation, the mark seemed to lose value faster abroad than at home; that is, the foreign exchange rates moved ahead of other indices of depreciation. This helped to convince experts as well as ordinary Germans that the currency crisis actually originated on the international monetary market, where the German position had been undermined by reparations.

As early as 1931, Costantino Bresciani-Turroni, an Italian economist, effectively challenged this view of the inflation.* He called attention to anticipatory speculation as a source of difficulty for the mark on the international exchange. A careful examination of inflationary indices over the whole period of the currency crisis also enabled him to show that the phenomena which fascinated so many Germans appeared only briefly and under special conditions. Finally, Bresciani-Turroni discovered that reparations accounted

* Costantino Bresciani-Turroni, *The Economics of Inflation: A Study of Currency Depreciation in Post-War Germany, 1914–1923*, trans. M. E. Sayers (London: Allen & Unwin, 1937).

for only a fraction of the German government's deficit spending.

Some German officials and economists also liked to argue that the amount of currency in circulation at the height of the inflation was less, in real value, than it had been during periods of economic stability before the First World War. This comparison seemed to prove that domestic fiscal and monetary policies were not responsible for the inflation; but it completely neglected the tremendous increase in the velocity of monetary circulation during a period of rapid depreciation. In interpreting the attitude of German experts, it is well to remember that some of the analytical tools of modern economists were just being developed during the early decades of the twentieth century. Thus German contemporary accounts of the inflation might have been quite various mixtures of honest error, interested preference, and propagandistic purpose. Here the historian confronts a typical difficulty of interpretation, one of the many interesting problems posed by the German inflation of 1923.

The first of the three selections that follow is from Gustav Stolper's *The German Economy*. Stolper originally published his German economic history in 1940, in an American edition. German editions, edited and supplemented by Karl Häuser and Knut Borchardt, appeared in 1964 and 1966. The selected passages are taken from the latest American edition, which was translated from the German by Mrs. Toni Stolper in 1967.

The second selection is an excerpt from a memoir by Hugo Stinnes (1870–1924), a German businessman. Having entered his father's firm in 1890, Stinnes began his career as an independent entrepreneur in 1893 and eventually built an immense industrial empire during the First World War and the early 1920's. As Stolper points out, Stinnes was also active in the German People's Party. His memoir reveals that he was considered—and considered himself—a very important adviser to German policy makers. He defended the inflation as if it had been consciously planned, while yet denying that he desired it. The reader will want to decide for himself whether there was anything unusual—or characteristic—in Stinnes's view of his own role, his expectations from his own and from foreign governments, and his attitude toward German workers and consumers.

The last selection in this chapter is taken from a speech by Rudolf Havenstein (1857–1923), who was President of the Reichsbank from 1908 until his death on November 20, 1923. Havenstein certainly did not originate the fiscal policies that produced the inflation, or the reforms that eventually ended it. Insofar as any single individual was responsible for the deficit financing practiced during the First World War, that man was Karl Helfferich, a bank director, Secretary of the Treasury in 1915 and 1916, an aggressive leader of the right-wing Nationalist Party during the Weimar period, but also one of the chief theoretical sponsors of the currency reform of 1923. From August to October 1923 the socialist Rudolf Hilferding was Minister of Finance in the cabinet of Gustav Stresemann, which abandoned the struggle in the Ruhr and prepared the grounds for monetary stabilization. The currency reform was actually carried out under Hans Luther, who replaced Hilferding as Minister of Finance in October 1923. Luther retained the post until January 1925, when he became Chancellor in a cabinet of the moderate right. In need of help during the difficult period of stabilization, Luther appointed Hjalmar Schacht Commissioner of the Currency on November 15, 1923. Schacht was a banker and one of the founders of the German Democratic Party. Though a determined nationalist and later Minister of the Economy under Hitler, he was considered a reliable supporter of the Republic during the 1920's. He actually took over as President of the Reichsbank after Havenstein's death. But Schacht's extraordinary appointment as Commissioner of the Currency even during Havenstein's tenure at the Reichsbank suggests how thoroughly Luther, among others, lacked confidence in Havenstein.

As a matter of fact, Havenstein, like most German officials under the Empire, was trained in law. He began his career in the judicial branch of the Prussian bureaucracy, before moving into the Ministry of Finance in 1890. He then became President of the Prussian State Bank in 1900, and of the Reichsbank in 1908. He has been described as an honest but undistinguished official of the old regime.

He chose to "remain at his post" after the fall of the Empire; but
he had little sympathy or understanding for the new conditions. It
may be that he simply could not master the complexities of the
currency crisis; but it has also been suggested that he lacked the
determination and courage to resist pressures which were brought
to bear upon him.* The speech which is excerpted at the end of
this chapter was delivered before the Executive Committee of the
Reichsbank on August 25, 1923. It was a response to public
criticism of Reichsbank policies. The newspaper which reprinted
the address was owned by Hugo Stinnes.

GERMAN ECONOMIC ORGANIZATION AND
ECONOMIC CONDITIONS BEFORE 1914

GUSTAV STOLPER

The German Economy

Like the United States of America, the German Reich began as a confederation of sovereign states, and this status survived until the revolution of 1918. As far as foreign and even many domestic affairs were
concerned, Germany rapidly developed into a unified state; but financial
and administrative powers remained chiefly with the individual states
through all the decades up to the Weimar Constitution of 1919.

The Reich of 1871 had no administrative organs except the army,
the navy, the foreign service, the customs administration, the post office,
and, somewhat later, the colonial administration. The entire internal
administration—police, judiciary, public finance, and education—remained in the hands of the federal states. Accordingly, the Reich was
left with little freedom of action in the field of fiscal policy. It had
inherited from the Zollverein control over customs revenues and over
some excise taxes, which until the first world war were rather narrow in
scope. Older even than these customs revenues was another peculiar
Reich revenue, the so-called matricular contributions. Originally, these
were payments the member states of the German Confederation—the

* Kurt Singer, *Staat und Wirtschaft seit dem Waffenstillstand* (Jena: Gustav
Fischer, 1924), pp. 195–198.
From *The German Economy, 1870 to the Present* by Gustav Stolper, Kurt Häuser,
and Knut Borchart, translated by Toni Stolper, © 1967 by Harcourt, Brace &
World, Inc. and reprinted with their permission and with the permission of George
Weidenfeld & Nicolson, Ltd.

Bund, formed in 1815 after Napoleon's collapse—made to the central authority to keep up its somewhat shadowy existence. These contributions were continued into the North German Confederation and into Bismarck's Reich. With all this, the Reich was largely dependent on the federal states. After 1880, when the states were awarded a share in certain indirect Reich taxes, this was a mere matter of form. The matricular contributions of the states to the Reich and the payments of the Reich to the states approximately canceled each other out.

The only new source of revenue of the North German Confederation and Bismarck's Reich was the revenue from the post and telegraph administration, to which was added in 1871 income from the management of the Alsace-Lorraine railroads. It is hardly surprising that in 1913, on the eve of the first world war, the Prussian revenue of 4.2 billion marks exceeded the ordinary and extraordinary Reich revenue by 100 million marks. In addition, the other federal states had revenues of a total of 2.5 billion marks. As of October 1, 1913, the Reich debt, 4.9 billion marks, was considerably below the Prussian debt of 9.9 billion marks and of the aggregate debt of the other states, 6.3 billion marks (figures for most of the states as of April 1, 1913). It should however be noted that the states' debt included their railroad bond indebtedness.

Before the Weimar Constitution, the entire field of direct taxation was a prerogative of the states, which also received considerable revenues from their railroads. The municipalities derived most of their income from real-estate taxes, but they also put surtaxes on some of the state taxes.

Only in the last years preceding the first world war did the Reich succeed in entering the field of direct taxation to some extent. In 1906 the Reich was allotted a share in the inheritance taxes, which previously had been reserved to the states. The states continued to administer these taxes, however, and the Reich share remained inconsiderable. The first really significant inroads into the traditional tax system were made under the shadow of the impending war. In 1913 the Reich imposed a capital levy combined with a surtax on higher incomes for the purpose expressed in its name: defense contribution (*Wehrbeitrag*). The revenue from this levy that reached the Treasury in 1914 and 1915 amounted to approximately one billion marks. . . .

Unification of the Currency

When the Reich was founded, Germany was still divided into seven separate currency areas. There were thirty-three banks of issue, totally unconnected with each other and carrying on their issuing activities under widely differing rules and regulations.

With such a chaotic currency system no monetary policy consistent with the needs of an industrialized country could be devised. The one feature common to these currencies was that silver was the legal tender, with the exception of the Bremen currency, which was based on gold. The states entered certain agreements as to the relative values of their respective currencies. In addition to silver, gold coins also circulated in all German states; the ratios between these coins and the legal silver currencies fluctuated, except in Prussia, where the ratio between gold and silver money was fixed by law.

The unified currency of the new Reich was based on the gold standard. The immediate adoption of the gold standard was a step of extraordinary significance at a time when no great country besides Britain had yet introduced it. When Germany reached this momentous decision, the great crisis of silver was already in the offing, and it could be foreseen that before long France and the United States would join the gold-standard countries. By taking the lead the young German Reich served the world economy well. It cleared the path toward a unified international currency based on gold and thus strongly encouraged rapid expansion of world trade in the decades preceding the first world war. Credit for this move is primarily due to the liberal statesman and economist Ludwig Bamberger,* though some of the credit belongs to Bismarck himself and to his Secretary of State, Rudolf Delbrück, whose influence on German economic policy, up to his resignation in 1876, tended toward strengthening liberalism. For Germany herself the adoption of the gold standard expressed the ascendancy of the liberal "Western orientation" which in Bismarck's earlier years characterized his personal attitude.

The new currency system was set up in three stages. (1) In 1871 a law regulating the minting of gold coins was passed. The mark was adopted as the currency unit, its ratio to the values of the circulating silver coinage was defined, and the silver coins were withdrawn. (2) In 1873 the gold standard was established by law, and the use of silver

*[Ludwig Bamberger (1823–99) was an ardent economic and constitutional liberal, a participant in the Revolution of 1848, and one of the most prominent founders and leaders of the National Liberal party. He stood on the left wing of the party's parliamentary delegation. Alienated by the anti-socialist law and even more by Bismarck's turn to protectionism after 1878, Bamberger helped to lead the left-wing "secession" out of the National Liberal party in 1880. The "secession" became the Liberal Union (*Liberale Vereinigung*). Bamberger's parliamentary career, which had begun in 1871, ended in 1893 with his retirement. Ed.]

was reduced to small coins. (3) In 1875 one of the thirty-three banks of issue, the Prussian Bank, was reorganized as the Reichsbank. The other banks of issue were left in a precarious situation, both in relation to the Reichsbank and to the private commercial banks. The plan was to induce them to relinquish voluntarily to the Reichsbank the rights which still belonged to them by law to issue fixed contingents of banknotes. By 1910, in fact, twenty-seven of them had yielded to this pressure; the rights of issue of the remaining five banks were canceled only as late as 1935. The note circulation of these "private issuing banks," as they were called after the Reichsbank had been organized, was so small and so strictly regulated that it counted for little in the new monetary setup. . . .

Germany's Industrialization

On the eve of the founding of the Reich, Germany's economic character was predominantly agricultural, but the process of industrialization had begun. The very existence of the Reich was the source of powerful impulses toward further industrial development, and within a few years Germany had joined the ranks of the leading industrial nations. In contrast to Britain, however, Germany did not sacrifice her agriculture to her industrial expansion. As will be shown more extensively later, the German government came to the aid of agriculture by means of a tariff as soon as the threat of American competition began to be felt on the grain market, the broad basis of German agriculture. This protection was given at the price of raising the cost of living for the urban population, but it enabled German agriculture to take advantage of new agricultural methods to continue its spectacular expansion during the era of rapid industrialization. Between the founding of the Reich and the first world war, German grain and potato production approximately doubled, partly from increased acreage but mainly as a result of improved yields per unit under cultivation. For example, a comparison of the yields of 1878–79 with the average yields of the decade 1901–10 shows that the average yield per hectare (2.47 acres) rose for wheat from 1.35 to 1.86 metric tons, for rye from 1.06 to 1.63 metric tons, for potatoes from 7.11 to 13.51 metric tons.

Population Growth

Despite this favorable development, German agriculture was no longer able to satisfy the food requirements of the German population. Gradually the country was transformed from a grain exporter to an importer. The population increase was so dynamic and the standards of nutrition improved so drastically that even though grain production doubled it did not cover the demand. Along with industrial expansion the population grew steadily up to the first world war, in its turn furnishing the basis for further industrialization.

Actually, the natural increase in the population was even greater than shown in Table 1. Part of the increase was offset by emigration, which between the 1840's and the 1880's became a mighty stream. It was only

Table 1
Population Within the Territory of the Reich, 1816–1915

Year	Population (millions)	Increase during preceding decade (per cent)
1816	24.8	
1825	28.1	13.2
1835	30.8	9.6
1845	34.3	11.3
1855	36.1	5.4
1865	39.5	9.4
1875	42.5	7.5
1885	46.7	9.9
1895	52.0	11.3
1905	60.3	16.0
1915	67.9	12.5

Sources: *Statistisches Jahrbuch für die Bundesrepublik Deutschland 1965*, p. 31; *Statistisches Jahrbuch für das Deutsche Reich 1882*, p. 5.

Table 2
Overseas Emigration from Germany, 1821–1930

Years	Number of persons
1821–1830	8,500
1831–1840	167,700
1841–1850	469,300
1851–1860	1,075,000
1861–1870	832,700
1871–1880	626,000
1881–1890	1,342,400
1891–1900	529,900
1901–1910	279,600
1911–1920	91,000
1921–1930	567,300
TOTAL	5,989,400

Source: Friedrich Burgdörfer, "Die Wanderungen über die Deutschen Reichsgrenzen im letzten Jahrhundert," *Allgemeines Statistisches Archiv* (1930), vol. 20, pp. 161 ff., 383 ff., 537 ff.

at the end of the 1880's that German national wealth had increased sufficiently and German industry developed a large enough demand for labor to cause the economic motive for emigration practically to disappear. Between 1840 and the first world war five million Germans emigrated overseas, but most of this took place before 1890. After 1890 emigration petered out, as shown in Table 2.

From the beginning of the nineteenth century the country of destination of the emigrants was almost exclusively the United States. Of the roughly six million Germans who emigrated overseas from 1821 to 1930, 5.3 million went to America.

Overseas emigration was partly balanced by immigration from other European countries, chiefly from Austria-Hungary, Italy, and the western parts of Russia, especially Russian Poland. This immigration increased steadily until in the last two decades preceding the first world war emigration was more than balanced by immigration. According to the figures on population movements, Germany had become an underpopulated country.

Transition from an Agricultural to an Industrial Society

Despite the technical intensification of agriculture, the rural sector absorbed but a negligible part of the population increase. As happened in other industrial societies rural life lost its attractions. A flight from the land began, and the natural population increase was drawn into the cities by the greater demand for labor there, by rising wages, and by the promise of the amenities of urban life. This shift is shown by Table 3.

Table 3

Gainfully Employed; Selected Years, 1882–1964

	1882	1907	1925	1939	1950	1964
Total gainfully employed (in millions)	17.0	25.4	32.3	35.7	20.4	27.0
Distribution by sectors (as per cent of total)						
Agriculture and forestry	42.2	33.9	30.3	25.0	24.6	11.4
Industry and crafts	35.6	39.9	42.3	40.8	42.7	48.3
Commerce, communications, other services	22.2	26.2	27.4	34.2	32.7	40.3

Territories involved: 1882–1939, borders of 1937; 1950, Federal Republic without West Berlin and Saar; 1964, Federal Republic including West Berlin and Saar. Sources: Statistisches Bundesamt Wiesbaden, *Bevölkerung und Wirtschaft. Langfristige Reihen 1871 bis 1957 für das Deutsche Reich und die Bundesrepublik Deutschland*, vol. 199, p. 30; *Statistisches Jahrbuch für die Bundesrepublik Deutschland 1965*, p. 151.

The trend from country to town between 1871 and 1882, for which period no detailed census is available, was no different. Thus it can almost be said that after the founding of the Reich agriculture and industry exchanged their relative importance in Germany's economic life.

The broad foundation for Germany's economic expansion was provided by the development of heavy industry. The German steel industry grew rapidly, as much because of progress in coal mining as because of the ore mines of Lorraine. In coal mining, Germany never quite caught up with her rival, Britain, but even so German coal mining expanded at a rate with which only that of the United States can compare. Coal production rose from an annual average of 34.5 million tons in the period 1871–75 to 191.5 million tons in 1913. The rich lignite mines were increasingly developed, and the production of lignite rose from 9.7 million to 87.5 million tons during the same period. In iron mining, ore production increased from an annual average of 5.3 million tons in the period 1871–75 to 28.7 million tons in 1913. These developments in coal and iron mining led to the growth of the steel industry. In 1871 pig iron output amounted to only 1.6 million tons; in 1910, 14.8 million tons were produced (Luxembourg's production included in both figures).* As late as 1900 the British pig iron output of 9.1 million tons exceeded the German-Luxembourg production of 8.5 million tons, but in steel Germany had already outdistanced her British rival— 7.4 million as against 6.0 million tons. In 1910 German production of 13.1 million tons of pig iron and 13.0 million tons of crude steel led that of all other European countries by a wide margin; Britain with 10.2 million tons of pig iron and 7.6 million tons of crude steel had been left far behind.

Germany utilized her heavy industries (1) to build up her railroad system—the mileage of which increased from 18,887 kilometers in 1870 to 60,521 kilometers in 1912; (2) to construct one of the mightiest merchant fleets in the world—steam-powered ships in the merchant marine increased from 147 units with a total of 81,994 gross register tons in 1871 to 2,098 units with 4,380,348 gross register tons in 1913; (3) to expand her machinery industry at a remarkable pace, making machinery one of the largest exports—51,000 workers were employed in 1861, 356,000 in 1882, and 1,120,000 in 1907. Within

*[Luxembourg production figures were long counted with German figures because the grand duchy of Luxembourg was a member of the German Confederation from 1815 to 1866, and became a member of the North German Customs Union (*Zollverein*) in 1841. In 1867, the sovereignty and neutrality of Luxembourg was guaranteed by the great powers in the London Conference. Ed.]

the machinery group the importance attained by the armament industry deserves attention. In 1912 the firm of Krupp in Essen employed 68,300 workers. . . .

The Role of the Banks

No account of German industrialization would be complete without full consideration of the important function of the banks. The dynamics of economic development can be assessed only if due weight is given to the peculiar banking system, which, in contrast to what took place in Britain and America, gave a most powerful stimulus to industrialization. The difference between the German and Anglo-Saxon banking system becomes apparent in the respective connotations attached to the term "bank" in German and English. The German bank is a combination of commercial bank, investment bank, and investment trust—a combination which, as will be shown in detail, can function only with the backing of a central bank.

Before the first world war, only a minor part of the funds of a typical bank was invested in government securities—long-term bonds and treasury bills. Another part was invested in commercial bills, which could be rediscounted with the Reichsbank and were therefore regarded as a liquid reserve. But primarily bank funds were used for direct loans (mostly long term, partly secured and partly unsecured) to industrial and commercial enterprises, and for industrial promotion. Industrial promotions or capital issues were either made by one bank alone or, when large-scale enterprises were concerned, by a group of banks, the so-called consortiums or syndicates. The bank or group of banks would take over the stocks or bonds to be issued at a fixed price and then try to place them with the public. In consequence, the banks kept substantial holdings of stocks and bonds of commercial and industrial firms in their own portfolios. They also traded in stocks and bonds either to regulate the market or for speculation.

To shoulder the risks connected with such transactions, the banks needed a large capital of their own. As a rule, capital, reserves, and undistributed profits amounted to 25 per cent of their deposits and other liabilities. When later, as a result of the first world war and the subsequent inflation, the capital of the banks had melted away, this in itself inevitably led to a crisis of the entire banking system. The banks derived their deposits largely from the enterprises they financed, while the savings of the public at large went mainly into the savings banks, most of them municipal.

From their very inception, German banks were planned primarily as institutions for the financing of industry, not as sources of current business credits after the British and American pattern. According to Gerhart von Schulze-Gaevernitz (*The German Credit Banks*), the banks, after 1848, were founded in a revolutionary spirit as instruments of the industries for their financing needs in opposition to the private bankers, who represented *haute finance*. These bankers were at the time the almighty masters of the capital market, typified by the House of Rothschild, originally stemming from Frankfurt but now international in scope. It was not by mere chance that the first German banking company of the modern type, the *A. Schaaffhausensche Bankverein* in Cologne, was founded in a year of revolution, 1848. The first constitutional administration of Prussia granted this institution its charter, which included the privilege of issuing banknotes. . . .

The Interdependence of Banking Capital and Industrial Capital
Up to the second world war, the German banks remained essentially true to their original pattern. This should not, however, be taken to imply that all industries were founded and permanently controlled by the banks. Frequently, perhaps even in the majority of cases, the initiative lay not with the banks but with individual industrial promoters. The importance of the original contribution of the banks, and accordingly of their lasting influence, varied widely with different industries and enterprises. But in one way or another the banks had their hands in almost all developing and promoting activities and remained financially interested in the industries concerned.

The influence of the banks on the industries they promoted was made permanent by voting practice in stockholders' meetings. The banks' voting powers were derived not only from their own stock holdings in these industrial companies but also from those of their customers. Possessed of such voting power and relying on their influence as underwriters, the banks themselves were active in industrial management, delegating their own officers to the boards of directors of industrial corporations. Conversely, the large industrial concerns were represented on the boards of the banks with which they had business connections.

In the heavy industries the large enterprises, such as Krupp's and Thyssen's, were originally independent, but gradually their relations to the banks became closer, and the leading banks started a keen competition among themselves for establishing intimate contacts with the major industries. In the end, every one of the large banks had its connections with at least some of the foremost groups of heavy industry.

The interrelations between banks and industries fostered the process of concentration in both fields. In the course of its rapid growth, industry shifted its weight more and more from the smaller and medium-sized companies to those firms which by their nature required huge capital investments, such as the heavy industries, the electrical industries, and shipbuilding. It became increasingly necessary that large, efficient, and rich banks exist to shoulder the task of industrial financing. Thus industrial concentration became a powerful incentive to banking concentration. . . .

Government in Business

As in all other European countries, during the mercantilist era, government help and initiative in the development of industries were among the most potent driving forces in the history of German capitalism. Also as in other countries, state owned "factories" (*Manufakturen*) were established in Germany. Some of them remained state owned enterprises down to the second world war—for instance the Prussian and Saxon porcelain factories. The peculiar political conditions in Germany favored this kind of state ownership. The several dozens of princes reigning since feudal days owned domains, forests, and also some industrial enterprises that were in fact state property, although many were officially considered as the private property of the individual reigning houses.

Thus Germany entered the liberal era with a relatively large sector of the economy state controlled, and no purely ideological considerations could bring about the liquidation of such state properties. It was, however, of great significance for Germany's destiny that when she emerged from the liberal era there was an old mercantilist tradition to fall back upon and resume with growing impetus.

Public Ownership of the Railroads

The first and most important measure in this direction was the transfer of the railroads to public ownership. The first German railroad, connecting the neighboring towns of Nürnberg and Fürth, was built in 1835, and up to the first world war the tempo of development of the German railroad system must be considered as extraordinary when measured by European standards. As in other highly developed countries, the expansion of railroads stopped abruptly with the first world war. The pace of railroad construction is shown by Table 4.

In some of the German states—Baden, Braunschweig, Oldenburg, Württemberg—railroad construction was from the very beginning car-

Table 4
German Railroad Network, 1835–1915
(in kilometers)

Year	Track in operation	Increase during preceding decade
1835	6	
1845	2,300	2,300
1855	8,290	5,990
1865	14,690	6,400
1875	27,960	13,270
1885	37,650	9,690
1895	46,560	8,910
1905	56,980	10,420
1915	62,410	5,430

Sources: *Statistisches Jahrbuch für das Deutsche Reich,* 1880–1915; Hauptver-waltung der Deutschen Reichsbahn, *Hundert Jahre deutsche Eisenbahnen* (1935).

ried on by the states themselves. In others—Saxony, Bavaria—only part of the railroad system was state owned or subsequently taken over by the state. In Prussia, initially (1838) the state only organized an extensive system for supervising private railroads, reserving the right to acquire them after thirty years. Construction remained a matter of private enterprise, and not until 1874 did the Prussian state begin to build railroads on its own. Through the annexation of Hanover and several other territories in 1866, Prussia acquired additional state lines. The Reich itself up to the Weimar Constitution owned only one line, the Alsace-Lorraine system that had become Reich property in 1871. . . .

Prussia was the first to carry out nationalization. As provided for in the original charters, the private roads were purchased by the states. The governments raised the money by issuing bonds, which they ex-changed for the bonds of the private companies. In 1875, of a total system of 27,956 kilometers only 12,062 were state owned, another 3,253 were privately owned but under state management, and 12,641 were privately owned and operated. In 1912, of a total network of 60,521 kilometers, only 3,631 were privately owned, and of these only 277 involved main lines.

One of the advantages usually derived from nationalization, unifica-tion of management, could still not be completely realized in pre-Weimar Germany. Aside from the residual private roads, eight state owned systems remained in operation. The largest was jointly managed by Prussia and Hesse; six systems belonged to other federal states, and one belonged to the Reich. The constitution of the North German Confederation (founded in 1815) placed the federal government in supreme management control, and the same clause applied during Bismarck's Reich. After 1871, railroad services were unified as to many technical details. However, Bismarck's original plan of 1866 to unify all railroads under Reich ownership was defeated by opposing forces in the various states. As a result, the Reich's powers of control over the nationalized railroads were much weaker than those that the United States could exert through the Interstate Commerce Commission. The relationship among the eight public railroad systems was about what it would have been among private systems under loose state supervision.

The Weimar Constitution of 1919 at last achieved full unification by ordering all railroads to be transferred to the Reich. This was executed by contractual arrangements between the Reich and the railroad-owning states; the Reich thereby acquired a system (the *Reichsbahn*) of 53,000 kilometers.

Heavy Industries, Public Utilities, Banks

After the railroads had been nationalized, state entrepreneurial activities in many other fields of business grew apace. The federal states as well as the municipalities participated most actively in the development of industries, chiefly state owned mines and ironworks. Thus, at the beginning of the first world war, the Prussian state owned some forty mines and twelve blast furnaces. The slogan of "municipal socialism" began to be widely discussed in the Imperial era, not waiting for the Weimar Republic. The rapidly growing cities "socialized" more and more waterworks, gasworks, power plants, public transport systems, and slaughterhouses, or erected new, publicly owned plants.

Apart from those under full public ownership, companies of a new type, the so-called "mixed-ownership" companies (*gemischt-wirtschaftliche Gesellschaften*), originated in the twentieth century. These companies were under the joint control of private capital and public authorities. This kind of organization was tried out chiefly for public utilities, such as power plants, gas- and waterworks, and municipal transport. As a rule the companies were formed by private initiative, and the municipalities, in exchange for franchises, acquired part of the stock. The most important example of this type was the *Rheinisch-Westfälische Elektrizitätswerke,* located in Germany's main industrial region and providing several industrial cities with electric light and power. This company was formed in 1905 by private enterprise; later, the consumer municipalities participated in its management. Local distribution was as a rule in the hands of municipal companies, which bought power wholesale and derived substantial profits from these transactions. This process came to be one of the most important sources of municipal revenue.

The Republic thus inherited from the Monarchy a peculiar economic system of mixed ownership in which, in the aggregate, the sector of public ownership did not rank far behind the private. On the eve of the first world war the following services were entirely state owned: the postal, telephone, and telegraph system (with the exception of the overseas telegraph systems, which were in private hands), and the railroads. Almost fully under municipal or mixed ownership were the gasworks, waterworks, and transport systems. Power production was predominantly under state, municipal, or mixed ownership.

The state also played an important role in banking even apart from the central bank, which in the German economic system held a much stronger position than was true in this period of the central banks in the Anglo-Saxon countries. The Reichsbank stock was privately owned; however, its president and top officers were appointed by the Kaiser, and the stockholders had no say in management or policy. In addition to the Reichsbank there were several powerful state banks that together dominated the Berlin money market. The strongest among them was the Prussian State Bank (*Preussische Seehandlung*), founded in 1772. Practically the entire savings bank business was municipal, an important fact because the savings banks handled far greater funds than all the commercial banks taken together.

To round out the picture it should be noted that a very considerable proportion of the mines and other industries were state controlled, that state and municipal ownership was preponderant in forestry, and that even among the large-scale farms state owned units had some importance. Imperial Germany had gradually developed a system of partly private, partly public ownership. . . .

The Cartelization of Industry

In every country two conflicting trends have determined the development of modern industrialism. One trend has been the liberation of the individual from the shackles and codes inherited from medieval times and the mercantilist era; the other trend has been toward integration on a more or less monopolistic basis. The entire Western world experienced this conflict. With the marked exception of Germany, the various industrial countries defended pluralistic tendencies, while monopolies were broken up or at least placed under strict restraints. The Anti-Trust Laws of the United States, steadily improved upon since first introduced with the Sherman Act of 1890, were the conspicuous expression of this individualistic philosophy. Free competition was the only admissible economic policy; infringement of free competition was made a criminal offense. The western European countries did not go quite so far, but Britain, France, Austria-Hungary, and, in their wake, the smaller industrial countries declared agreements in restraint of trade void and therefore not enforceable in the courts. In Germany alone cartel agreements had legal status and were treated by law in the same way as any other private contract. Any contravention of contractual obligations by a member of the cartel could be brought into court or penalized by the forfeiture of bonds provided for the purpose of the cartel agreement. . . .

By the middle of the 1890's, aside from cartels in steel and coal, there were cartels in plate glass, cement, and certain chemicals. The era of almost total cartelization came only after the turn of the century. The attack on free individual competition was then launched both through comprehensive mergers—principally in the heavy industries—and through nationwide cartels. At the outbreak of the war in 1914 the structure of the German cartel system was virtually completed.

The term "cartel" actually covers a variety of trade combinations. The most stringent form provided for the sale of certain products by a centralized sales office, excluding any outside sales and purchases. Production was distributed by quotas among the member-producers, and the only entrepreneurial function left to individual firms was to ensure technical efficiency in order to reduce costs and raise the profit margin. In general such complete centralization was rather the exception; only in basic industries was it the rule. The thousands of cartels into which most German industry eventually became organized were much looser arrangements. Some of them fixed production quotas without centralizing sales; others assigned regional markets to the individual producers; still others only regulated business practices and terms of sale, for instance by listing conditions of credit or rules for the calculation of costs to prevent "cutthroat competition," and so forth. . . .

The Flowering of Trade Unions

As had been the case in Britain, the German workers were long hampered by anti-trade-union legislation in building up their unions. Only when the liberal era of the 1860's was well under way were most of the restrictions removed. First among the German federal states to repeal these antiorganization laws was highly industrialized Saxony, in 1861. In 1869 the new Trades Code of the North German Federation granted freedom of organization, at least to industrial workers. In 1871 this Code was adopted by the Reich.

Immediately after the legal barriers had fallen the first trade unions were formed: these were the national organizations of tobacco workers and of printers in 1865 and 1866.In marked contrast to the trade unions of Anglo-Saxon countries, the German unions were built up by central organizations decidedly political in character. As early as 1868 three separate attempts were made to organize a centralized union of unions. One of these experiments, at the time the most important of the three, was initiated by Johann von Schweitzer, leader of the group of unions originally formed by Ferdinand Lassalle. The second attempt, later to result in the dominant group, was made by August Bebel, leader of the Marxist International Workers' Association. The third effort came from two leaders of the Progressive party, Max Hirsch and Franz Duncker. All three attempts were at first surprisingly successful, but soon the Schweitzer unions began to disintegrate and, after the Lassalle and Marxist movements had merged, were taken over by the Marxist unions. The Hirsch-Duncker unions remained in existence to the end of the Weimar Republic, without ever gaining much importance. In 1899 a new group of unions became an active third factor, the Christian unions, a combination of scattered local unions formed in the 1890's by Roman Catholic workers' associations, later joined to a lesser degree by Protestant workers' groups.

Thus, from its beginnings to its dissolution in May, 1933, the German trade-union movement was politically oriented. The Free Unions, the name later adopted by the largest union body, were affiliated with the Social Democratic Party. The Christian unions, despite the denominational differences among their membership, were affiliated with the Catholic Center party, as were the Hirsch-Duncker unions with the liberal parties.

Later, especially in the period of the Anti-Socialist Laws, the contact between the Free Unions and the Social Democratic Party was temporarily somewhat loosened, since union as well as party activity had been declared illegal. Soon, however, organizations reappeared under the guise of nonpolitical professional associations, which in 1884 gained union status. Immediately after the end of the Anti-Socialist Laws in 1890, the Free Unions placed themselves under a General Commission, which they declared independent of the Social Democratic Party. This remained the central body of the Free Unions, changing only its name after the first world war to General German League of Unions (*Allgemeiner Deutscher Gewerkschaftsbund*, ADGB).

The lapse of the Anti-Social Laws opened the way to uninterrupted growth of the trade-union movement. In the period from 1890 to 1914 the Free Unions increased their membership from roughly 300,000 to 2,500,000, with the development of the other unions proportionate. Table 5 shows the total trade-union membership attained prior to the first world war.*

Table 5
Membership of German Trade Unions, 1913
(thousands of members)

Free unions	2,525
Christian unions	342
Hirsch-Duncker unions	107
Independent unions	319
TOTAL	3,293

Source: *Statistisches Jahrbuch für das Deutsche Reich 1915,* pp. 433ff.

The unionization of the workers was paralleled by activities among the employers, who also formed centralized organizations. In the entire pre-1914 era relations between employers and the employed remained an autonomous affair of these groups. Government kept aloof except for the protection that civil law accorded to industrial agreements just as to any other contract. However, the industrial courts (*Gewerbegerichte*) formed in 1891 may be regarded as the first step in the direction of government regulation of employer-employee relationships. Beyond this, the relations of the employers and their associations with the unions were free of government interference. The technique of collective bargaining developed very slowly, and the number of collective agreements remained small. The rapid expansion of industry and the comparative mildness of cyclical business booms or setbacks in this period helped to promote industrial peace and to keep labor struggles within moderate limits as to the number of strikes and workers involved.

Cooperative Societies
Parallel to the rise of cartels and trade unions, cooperative societies organized themselves in mighty associations, reviving a tradition dating in Germany from medieval times. Following the British example set by the Rochdale Pioneers in 1844, consumers' cooperatives were

*[The size of the Unions may be compared with Stolper's earlier figures on those gainfully employed in the various sectors of the economy, and with more detailed occupational statistics in Chapter Five. Ed.]

formed, which in membership and scope of activities—extending into the sphere of production—were second only to the British organizations of this type. For small tradesmen the ideas of Schulze-Delitzsch were decisive, for farmers those of Raiffeisen.* These two main groups of middle classes derived much economic support from the cooperative movement, primarily through cooperative credit organizations. Purchasing and marketing cooperatives were formed chiefly in the field of agriculture. . . .

ORIGINS OF THE INFLATION DURING WORLD WAR I
STOLPER (continued)

Germany's phenomenal rise to the rank of an industrial world power with a safe balance both at home and as a member of the economic world community ended in 1914 in sudden catastrophe. The first world war convulsed the entire globe; but in no other leading industrial country was the upheaval of the economic, social, and political structure as fundamental and as lasting as in Germany. To be sure, we see the actors who had dominated the public scene during the preceding forty years continue to perform throughout the four appalling war years. Indeed, as viewed from outside, these four years would even appear to carry the old system to its ultimate fulfillment and highest accomplishment. In reality, what was going on in Germany during the war constituted an entirely new departure, even though the threads that connected the present to the past seemed strong enough to make the change at least comprehensible.

Not only had Germany, and specifically the German economy, the tremendous task of providing alone, without outside economic or financial help, for all armament needs during the greatest war ever fought in history. Germany's fate was also decisively modified by the fact that, while the opposing industrial nations were able to call in the aid of the power with the greatest economic potential, the United States of America, Germany had to submit to a blockade of her shores. The blockade now imposed an involuntary but inexorable autarky. This

---

*[Friedrich Wilhelm Raiffeisen (1818–1888) became impressed with the peasants' need for cheap credit during the agricultural crisis of 1846–1847. He used his own limited fortune to start a system of rural credit cooperatives and banks, a system which developed into a nationwide agricultural credit federation by 1877. Hermann Schulze-Delitzsch (1808–1883) founded a number of cooperative banks, mercantile and consumer's cooperatives, all of which were designed to help the small shopkeepers and tradesmen. A general association of German cooperatives was formed in 1859, and a Prussian law of 1867 gave protection to the cooperatives. Ed.]

happened to a country that previously had taken a larger share in world trade than any other except Britain. This experience of forced autarky never faded from the memory of the German people. Without it the economic policy of the Hitler regime cannot be understood.

When the first world war broke out on August 4, 1914 (hostilities between Austria-Hungary and Serbia had begun a week earlier), Germany was utterly unprepared economically for a war that was to expose her for many years to the bitter endurance test of economic and financial isolation. German statesmanship had obviously envisaged only a lightning campaign. Nothing had been planned for the eventuality of a struggle over a long period of time with adversaries of equal strength, nothing for the possibility or the consequences of the blockade. The first Battle of the Marne in September, 1914, ended the German dream of quick military victory; it also gave the signal for starting a war economy in Germany.

Financial Mobilization

In one sphere of the economy alone had something in the way of a plan been prepared under which, in case of war, action was immediately possible: in the sphere of money and credit and of public finance. The authorities had not troubled their heads about the problem of how, should the dire necessity confront them, they would find bread for the German population and raw materials for army procurement. But they had taken well to heart the old and wise adage that to wage a modern war three things were indispensable: money, money, and again money. Soon it was to become apparent that this time the money that could be provided was not of much use.

On July 23, 1914, the Austro-Hungarian government had served a forty-eight-hour ultimatum on the Serbian government. In the following week, ending July 31, the Reichsbank lost more than 100 million marks in gold, the gold reserves decreasing from 1,357 to 1,253 million. Gold hoarding and the rush to change money from bank deposits into banknotes were clear evidence that the public had been gripped by the war scare. On that day of July 31, 1914, for the first time in its almost forty years of history, the Reichsbank discontinued redeeming banknotes in gold, in breach of its legal obligations. Note circulation was still 43 per cent covered by gold, banknotes plus demand deposits 30 per cent. (The statutory gold-coverage requirements of the Reichsbank, 33⅓ per cent, referred to banknotes alone, not to other demand liabilities. Therefore the public was not accustomed to regarding banknotes and other demand liabilities as essentially the same.)

In the memorable session for which the Reichstag assembled on August 4, 1914, it became evident that the suspension of gold payments was more than a precautionary measure to guard against the threat of a panic. It was, rather, the first step in the execution of a prepared plan. Several bills on public finance placed before the Reichstag that day were speedily enacted. One of them authorized the Reich government to borrow up to five billion marks for war expenditures. As is widely known, this was the formal act by which the Reichstag, including the Social Democratic deputies, sanctioned the war which had been decided upon over their heads on the monarch's prerogative.

The law on war credits was an enabling act such as is needed by any government in an emergency. The other financial laws enacted on August 4, 1914, were of greater immediate importance and more characteristic of the specifically German methods of war finance. They provided:

1. The obligation to redeem in gold the banknotes of the Reichsbank as well as of the private banks of issue was suspended, or rather the suspension ordered five days before was to be valid indefinitely.

2. The tax on all note circulation in excess of 550 million marks over and above the gold coverage was abolished.

3. Loan Banks (*Darlehenskossen*) were to be organized.

4. The Reichsbank was empowered to include in its note coverage the three-month treasury bills issued by the Reich, and in its "ready money coverage"(*Bardeckung*), the notes of the Loan Banks (*Darlehenskassenscheine*).

Of these four laws the first can be explained as a purely defensive measure against gold hoarding. In time of war a government is in such urgent need of keeping the centralized gold reserve intact that safeguards are imperative against its being scattered. By the three other laws the government was definitely, though at the time unconsciously, paving the way toward future inflation.

The Loan Banks were an emergency organization used for the first time during the Franco-Prussian war of 1870–71 to procure credits for business requirements. The Loan Banks of 1914 had the same tasks, for which they functioned up to the end of the inflation period in 1924. Apart from granting credit to business they served chiefly as supplementary agencies of the Reichsbank, in which function they profited from not being tied by various legal regulations that still hampered the Reichsbank itself. These banks were the first in a long line of auxiliary institutions of the Reichsbank, a feature that was to become characteristic of Germany's later monetary policy.

The Loan Banks were allowed to extend credit on collateral not qualifying for Reichsbank loans. They also gave credit to the federal states and municipalities and to the newly founded war corporations (*Kriegsgesellschaften*). Finally, it was their allotted task to advance money for the purpose of war bond subscriptions. The funds of the Loan Banks were simply provided by the printing presses. So-called Loan Bank notes (Darlehenskassenscheine) were issued to the full amount of the outstanding credits of the Loan Banks. These notes were regarded as legal tender and were in part taken up by the Reichsbank, in part put into immediate circulation.

The easiest opening for unrestrained inflation was created by the clause that allowed the Reichsbank to rediscount unlimited amounts of short-term Treasury bills against banknotes. The requirement of one-third gold coverage for note circulation might still have been a certain safeguard against inflation, had it not been rendered illusory by the fact that Loan Bank notes were included in the coverage; but later the gold-coverage requirement was formally repealed.

Thus, the government's financial war plans were as clear and simple as they were premeditated. The printing press had been chosen as the first and foremost resource both for the immediate war needs of the government and for the increased credit requirements of private business. It was planned that at some later time the credits for which the government had drawn on the Reichsbank would be refunded from the proceeds of war loans. But before 1916 it was not contemplated to finance war expenditures even in part by taxation.

The Costs of the First World War

War expenditures rapidly grew to a point where they could be expressed only in astronomical figures. In the last fiscal year preceding the war, 1913–14, Reich expenditures amounted to 3,848 million marks, to which must be added expenditures of the federal states of 8,507 million, forming a total of 12,355 million marks. Against this, the expenditures of the Reich "occasioned by the war" reached the figures given in Table 6, to which again substantial state and municipal expenditures must be added.

In assessing these figures it should be noted that in the course of the war years the purchasing power of the mark declined substantially. The simple summing up of war expenditures from year to year, based as it is on the fictitious rule of "mark equals mark," fails to convey a

Table 6

German War Expenditures, First World War

April 1 to March 31	Millions of marks
1914–15	6,936
1915–16	23,909
1916–17	24,739
1917–18	42,188
1918–19	33,928
ACCOUNTED AFTER 1918	32,599
TOTAL	164,300

Extraordinary expenditures of the General Finance Administration. Source: *Statistiches Jahrbuch für das Deutsche Reich,* 1918 to 1921–22.

true picture. The erratic rise of war expenditures from 1916 to 1917 and 1918 is due at least in some degree to the marked rise in prices. But even if a usable formula could be found to reflect the change in prices, war expenditures should probably be estimated at well above 100 billion prewar marks.

The public at large never was informed of the fact that at the beginning of the war Germany still hoped to receive some financial aid from aboard. A brief, inconspicuous report of the Reich Debt Commission indicates that on August 8, 1914, the Reich government printed Treasury certificates in the amount of 175 million dollars inscribed in English and sent them to the United States. The sum, after all, was almost 15 per cent of the first war-credit appropriations. In a later report the Reich Debt Commission drily remarks: "These Treasury certificates were never placed. They were cancelled in the Imperial Embassy in Washington and will be returned to the Control Bureau of State Securities (*Kontrolle der Staatspapiere*) as soon as traffic conditions permit sending them back from America."

Thus ended the first and most important attempt to raise war loans abroad. Similar efforts were later repeated on several occasions. Their success was never reported and can only have been paltry. The fate of these Treasury certificates sent to America in 1914 leaves no doubt on which side were the sympathies of the United States from the outset and how complete was Germany's isolation with respect to finance, as in every other way.

Thus Germany depended entirely on her own financial resources. Fortunately, the credit and currency systems of modern economies are sufficiently elastic to cope with even the most extreme strains to which they may be exposed, provided only that government authority remains intact. If the strain should eventually go beyond a nation's endurance, the final collapse need not unavoidably originate in the financial sphere. It may manifest itself as a purely physiological or psychological breakdown in the political or social sphere because of the utter exhaustion of the productive forces or of the human beings who must work with them.

War Loans and Bank Advances

As in all other belligerent countries, war loans were the most important means of war financing in Germany. Their success was great beyond expectations, though this resulted in considerable degree from heavy moral and political pressures on the public. Increasingly, and with little camouflage toward the end, the war loans assumed the character of forced loans.

The war loans were issued mostly in the form of 5 per cent perpetual bonds. Only a small part was issued in 4.5 or 5 per cent Treasury certificates with varying maturities. War loans were regularly issued in half-yearly intervals, nine times altogether. The proceeds kept growing from the first to the eighth loan. The first war loan netted 4,492 million marks, the eighth 15,126 million, and only the proceeds of the last loan, issued a short time before the collapse, showed a decline to 10,570 million marks. In sum total the Reich procured through these loans 96,929 million marks, the aggregate par value amounting to 99,265 million marks.

Although the sums these war loans poured into the Treasury were enormous, they did not cover more than 60 per cent of war expenditures. Only two orthodox methods were available to take care of the rest: the more orthodox method of increased taxation, and the less orthodox method of short-term credits extended by institutions other than banks of issue. Actually, the credit banks eagerly accepted the Treasury bills. The inflationary Reichsbank policy had greatly increased the liquidity of the banks and a short-term, rediscountable investment regarded as absolutely secure and bearing interest at 4 or 4.5 per cent seemed highly desirable. Hence the amount of Treasury bills held outside the Reichsbank had increased to 29,300 million marks by the end of the war.

War Inflation

Because most of the war loans had the character of compulsory loans, it should have been tempting to replace them by tax receipts and thereby save some of the rising expenditure for interest payments. Important psychological considerations should likewise have prompted a drastic increase in taxation, to make some concessions to the public's growing animosity against "war profiteers," the industrialists and tradesmen who as a result of the war boom enjoyed good business.

And yet, tax increases were resorted to only reluctantly and ineffectually. The Secretary of the Treasury, Karl Helfferich, before the war a director of the Deutsche Bank and the Anatolische Eisenbahngesellschaft, one of the most impressive figures among the civilian leaders of the war effort, and one of the few who continued to play an important role in postwar life (until his tragic death in a railroad accident in 1924), declared in open Reichstag session as late as March, 1915, that it was the intention of the Reich authorities to finance the war exclusively by borrowing.

Only slowly, under the combined pressure of public opinion and the political parties, were the methods of financing changed in some measure. Several tax laws were adopted, the first in June, 1916. Among the most important were a tax on war profits and a turnover tax, the latter at first at extremely low rates, one-tenth of 1 per cent on every subsequent turnover from producer to consumer. Both taxes were gradually increased, and others, primarily indirect taxes, were added, the most important of which were a coal tax and a transportation tax.

As a consequence of the new taxes, the revenues of the Reich did rise considerably. Net receipts (eliminating the budgets of Reich enterprises) increased from 2,357 million marks in 1914 to 7,830 million in 1917, followed by a slight decrease during the fiscal year 1918. However, this nominally large increase in revenues did not even suffice to balance the increase in ordinary expenditure that resulted from the depreciation of the currency and the inflated interest burden for the war debt. Reich expenditures, excluding direct war expenditures, amounted to a total of 26,449 million marks during the period 1914–18 as against only 20,740 million marks of revenue (excluding the proceeds of credits).

To explain the timidity of Germany's war fiscal policy it is usual to point primarily to constitutional difficulties. As noted in the preceding chapter, the Reich had very limited fiscal powers. However, the war had placed such concentrated powers in the hands of the Reich administration that with better judgment it could undoubtedly have wielded as much authority over fiscal matters as it did over industry and commerce.

If one includes as legal money coins in circulation, banknotes, Loan Bank notes, and the daily maturing Reichsbank liabilities, it is fair to say that the circulation of government money increased during the war from 7,400 million to 44,400 million marks, that is, to six times the original amount. Bank money, consisting of deposits with the credit banks, increased somewhat less, from 4,900 million to 19,100 million marks. The total result is an increase in government plus bank money circulation from 12,500 million to 63,500 million marks, five times the prewar amount.

The "German inflation" is usually thought of as a postwar phenomenon. The above figures indicate that in fact the inflation began with the war, and that by its end was already in excess of anything ever before experienced. However, when the war ended Germany found herself in such generally extraordinary and unprecedented circumstances that the economic consequences of the war did not clearly emerge at once and were partly disguised by other factors.

The German stock exchanges remained closed for the full duration of the war, and no quotations of foreign exchanges were published. Thus, people were kept ignorant of the effects of inflation on security values and foreign exchange rates. However, the mark was being traded and quoted on the exchange of neutral countries, and insiders were able to gauge by the continuously deteriorating mark values there what the effects of German inflation were. When the war was over, the mark had declined on neutral markets to about half its gold parity.

The effects of inflation on domestic prices were likewise obscured by the war economy measures. After the war the Reich Statistical Bureau computed that on the average the level of German wholesale prices had risen during the war years by 130 per cent. This only took account of the legal maximum and guideline prices, not of the prices actually paid by the public. As the importance of the black market (*Schleich-handel*) at far higher prices grew, the published indices became more and more fictitious. Only after the breakdown of the war economy with its framework of pervasive regulation did the full extent of economic dislocation and imbalance become discernible to all. . . .

ECONOMIC CRISIS OF
THE EARLY WEIMAR PERIOD

STOLPER (continued)

On entering the Weimar period, first of inflation and then of reconstruction, Germany as a territorial unit was far different from the powerful prewar Reich. She had been deprived of all her colonies, whose value, as we noted, had been questionable. But the main body of the Reich, too, had lost 13.1 per cent of its prewar territory and

10 per cent of its 1910 population (if the Saar region, which remained separated from Germany up to 1935, is included in the losses). The territories lost permanently (or until 1935) in consequence of the Versailles treaty and the partition of Upper Silesia (1921) were particularly rich in agricultural and mineral resources. They comprised 14.6 per cent of the arable land, 74.5 per cent of the iron ore, 68.1 per cent of the zinc ore, 26 per cent of the coal production. Added to this was the breakup of the German monopoly by the loss of the Alsatian potash mines and the conversion of the Alsatian textile industry from one of the most prosperous parts of German textile manufacturing to its most dangerous competitor. Finally, the loss of Alsace-Lorraine and, even more, the loss of half of Upper Silesia, disrupted some of the most important connecting links in the industrial and transportation systems.

In fact, Germany had become very much poorer by these territorial changes. This loss was greatly intensified when the armistice and the peace treaty imposed on Germany huge deliveries in kind to her former adversaries. First, Germany had to deliver all armament material and her entire navy. In addition the deliveries included:

all merchant ships of more than 1,600 gross tons;
half of the merchant ships of 1,000 to 1,600 gross tons;
one-quarter of the fishing fleet;
one-fifth of the river and lake fleet;
5,000 locomotives, 150,000 railroad cars, 5,000 motor trucks;
the entire Alsace-Lorraine railroad system with all rolling stock;
all material left behind in the combat zones;
all public property in the ceded territories and colonies.

Furthermore, the Allies reserved the right to confiscate all German private property in their own countries and in the ceded territories, the German owners to be compensated by the Reich government. This threat was subsequently carried out in the Allied countries, though not in the ceded territories. The United States alone provided a notable exception by later returning the seized German properties.

All these deliveries were to be credited to the reparations account at wholly arbitrary valuations, a purely fictitious procedure. In view of the astronomical reparations figures, recording these credits amounted to pouring wine into a bottomless barrel.

The territorial losses and the deliveries in kind resulted in a dangerous deterioration in the German balance of payments. More foodstuffs had to be imported; minerals heretofore mined in Germany now had to be purchased abroad; exports of other raw materials had to be curtailed. The loss of the merchant fleet deprived the country of the foreign exchange paid by other countries for the fleet's services. The loss of capital invested abroad cut down the influx of profit and interest payments. Even without reparations obligations it would have been hard for Germany to re-establish a sound balance in her external exchange accounts unless foreign aid were forthcoming.

Reparations

The reparations made the German situation hopeless in the years to come. When on October 3, 1918, Prince Max von Baden's government accepted Woodrow Wilson's Fourteen Points it thereby assumed the obligation to repair the devastated war zones. In his note of December 5 addressed to the German government, Secretary of State Robert Lansing defined the reparations obligation more precisely. Germany was to undertake reparation of all damage to private property of the Allies with the exception of Russia. "Compensation will be made by Germany for all damage done to the civilian population of the Allies and to their property by the aggression of Germany by land, sea, and from the air." Had there been any fair computation of these damages, the reparations debt would very probably have been balanced to a large extent by the deliveries in kind enumerated above. However, reparations as ultimately defined lost all relation to the original American definition.

The Versailles treaty obligated Germany to pay all costs of Allied occupation troops on German territory, this superimposed obligation not to be credited to the reparations account; the treaty also extended the definition of reparations to include all capitalized pension payments to Allied combatants. Thereby, reparations obligations were inflated beyond all bounds. However, the peace treaty stated no definite total for the reparations debt; it only stipulated that the German government was at once to issue and deliver bonds to the amount of 100 billion gold marks, of which 20 billion were to serve as security for the interim payments due prior to May 1, 1921. Interest on and amortization of the balance of 80 billion gold marks were to be paid over the following thirty years. This alone would have entailed reparations payments of one billion gold marks each year after 1921. The Reparations Commission povided for by the peace treaty was assigned the task of determining the definite amounts and modes of payments in a general reparations plan to be completed by May 1, 1921.

The Versailles treaty only came into force on January 10, 1920, but payments were to begin earlier and by May 1, 1921, were to amount to 20 billion gold marks. The value of the deliveries in kind was to be credited against this sum. Part of the balance of 80 billion marks was also to be paid in kind. On this account Germany was ordered to deliver annually during the following decade at least 38 million tons of coal and large quantities of chemicals and other goods. These deliveries actually began in August, 1919, that is, before the peace treaty was in force.

The following years, up to the time of the Dawes Plan of 1924, were filled with bitter and harmful wrangling over amounts and modes of reparations payment. At last, in January, 1921, the Paris Resolutions set up a payments plan which provided for payment of 2 billion gold marks in each of the next two years, 3 billion gold marks in each of the following three years, 4 billion for three years, 5 billion for three years, and finally 6 billion gold marks annually over the subsequent thirty-one years. In addition, 26 per cent of the proceeds of German exports were to be paid in each of these forty-two years. Since the reparations payments themselves forced Germany to increase her exports to a fantastic level, the 26 per cent export duty meant an additional burden that would rapidly rise to from 2 to 3 billion gold marks per year.

The Allies sought to force the German government to accept this preposterous play by imposing "sanctions," as provided by the peace treaty. In March, 1921, several towns on the Rhine and in the Ruhr region were occupied, and the customs receipts in the occupied territories were impounded.

The "final" payments plan, known as the London Ultimatum, which the Reparations Commission worked out and the Allied governments presented to the German authorities in the first days of May, 1921, was hardly closer to reality than the Paris Resolutions. First, Germany's reparations debt was fixed at 132 billion gold marks, an amount which, according to the most eminent economic expert on the Allied side, John Maynard Keynes, was three times the maximum that Germany was able to pay. Second, the reparations debt was to bear 6 per cent annually in interest and amortization. For the moment, the Reparations Commission was to issue only 50 billion in gold mark bonds to be serviced by the reparations annuities. The balance of 82 billion was not to be issued until the Commission was satisfied that Germany would be able to bear the added burden.

The first reparations annuities were set at 2 billion gold marks plus

the 26 per cent export duty, a sum virtually identical with that provided
by the Paris Resolutions for the first year. As a down payment Germany
was to deliver one billion gold marks over the next few months. The
full receipts from German export duties, plus the 26 per cent special
duty, plus several taxes were to serve as guarantees for this payment.
A guarantee committee sitting in Berlin was to watch over the execution of the plan. The Reparations Commission was empowered to demand payment in kind for any part of reparations. The German
government was obligated to let the British government cash in its share
of the 26 per cent export tax through its own agents (British Recovery
Act) while the German government had to compensate the German
exporters.

This reparations plan was presented to Germany in the form of an
ultimatum. Unless it were accepted within six days the Ruhr basin
would be occupied. In the Reichstag a bare majority acceded. In the
following months the plan was actually executed within the prescribed
time limits, and even the one billion marks cash payment was delivered
before the end of August, 1921. Only in December did the government
ask for a reduction. In January, 1922, it was agreed that payments
were to be reduced for that year to 2.17 billion marks, the additional
payments for the armies of occupation to be canceled. Of the total, not
more than 720 million marks were to be paid in cash, the rest in kind.
This agreement was implemented up to July, 1922.

Meanwhile, Germany's situation had deteriorated to such a degree
that the government begged for a moratorium on cash payments until
the end of 1924, declaring itself ready to continue payments in kind to
the agreed maximum of 1.45 billion marks. This request was turned
down, but in September, 1922, an agreement was reached that allowed
Germany to pay, in addition to the deliveries in kind, 270 million marks
in the form of six-month treasury certificates.

The Struggle for the Ruhr
Thus to a large extent reparations payments had been converted into
deliveries in kind, and it was in this field that the severe struggles of
1923 were carried on. The Poincaré government in France was convinced that Germany was evading her obligations in bad faith and
that the only way to retrieve reparations was to go and get them. Consequently, Poincaré decided to occupy the Ruhr basin, center of Germany's iron and coal production. A minor conflict between Germany
and France, or rather between Germany and the Reparations Commis-

sion, had arisen over the delivery of telegraph poles and a small deficiency in coal deliveries. This was used as a pretext by France and Belgium to order troops to march into the Ruhr region in January, 1923.

For the first time Germany went into open revolt against a measure taken by the victors. The moment the French and Belgian troops entered the Ruhr the German government stopped all reparations payments to these two countries and forbade all German officials, including Reichsbahn personnel, to take orders from the occupying authorities. These responded by evicting all German officials from the Ruhr district. They organized a civil and railroad administration of their own and cut off the Ruhr from economic communication with the rest of Germany. Funds of the banks and Reichsbank branches and inventories of mines and factories were seized. After passive resistance, which at first had been ordered for the civil servants only, had spread to the workers in mines and factories, the occupying authorities tried to keep up activities in the workshops partly by force, partly with their own men.

The Ruhr struggle plunged Germany into dire straits. She was now separated from her most essential raw material resources. Moreover, the government had to feed the workers and civil servants who had struck in the Ruhr territory or had been evicted from it, to maintain the families of thousands who had been jailed by the occupiers, and, on top of all this, to compensate industry heavily for the losses incurred in the conflict. And yet, reparations deliveries in kind to the Allies, except to France and Belgium, together with payments under the British Recovery Act, were kept up until August, 1923.

Add to this plight the mounting political chaos in consequence of the currency collapse, and it will be seen that ultimately resistance was bound to crumble. In August, 1923, the Cuno cabinet, which had carried through the Ruhr conflict, resigned. The new coalition government headed by Gustav Stresemann at once ordered passive resistance ended and payments to the resisting workers and officials stopped. In November, 1923, agreements were signed between the occupiers and representatives of industry, with the German government concurring, pursuant to which the companies were to pay taxes and deliver their products directly to the Allies. These agreements remained in force until the Dawes Plan was adopted in August, 1924.

Certainly not by mere chance, the end of the Ruhr conflict coincided with the end of the great inflation. The situation called for a thorough rehabilitation of German finances and currency on the one hand, and of the relations between Germany and the Allies on the other. Both had to be accomplished together or not at all.

Financial Reforms

Despite all these tribulations the German government had made serious attempts from time to time, even prior to the Dawes Plan, to rid itself of budget deficits. The Reich Treasury was overburdened by reparations, the service of the huge war debts, and the relief for war victims. Decisive financial reforms were undertaken in 1920 but even before that several taxes, chiefly the turnover tax, had been increased and export duties had been introduced. In December, 1919, the Reichstag voted a capital levy, the Reich Emergency Levy (*Reichsnotopfer*); it was to take up to 65 per cent from the largest properties while also reaching down to the smallest, and it was expected to net not less than 80 billion marks; at the time the bill was passed this represented a sum equal in purchasing power to more than eight billion prewar marks.

Only too soon the intrinsic weakness of a financial policy that defined taxes in terms of nominal money values at a time of progressive currency depreciation was to become apparent. Necessarily, there are considerable delays between the assessment and the payment of a tax, and meanwhile actual revenue will shrink to a fraction of expected returns. This weakness was especially marked for the Emergency Levy because long-drawn-out installment payments had to be granted. The purchasing power of the mark did not vary much during 1920, but began to decline in 1921 and continued at such a rate that soon it was no longer worthwhile to enforce payment. Accordingly, installment payments on the levy were suspended in 1922 and replaced by a property tax.

The most comprehensive and systematic attempt to solve the financial problems was undertaken in Erzberger's fiscal reforms. The importance of these reforms transcends the mere restoration of a balanced budget. The novel theoretical concepts of the Weimar Constitution were now made a vivid reality in the field of public finance: Germany was transformed from a federated group of states into a federal state. While Bismarck's Reich could use only the few sources of taxation not preempted by the federal states, now the Reich was made the supreme bearer of financial sovereignty and the states were limited to those taxes not claimed by the Reich.

Despite the confusion incident to the inflation period, the Erzberger reforms initiated a system of taxation which, with relatively few changes, remained the basis of German fiscal affairs into the second world war. At the same time, the Reich organized a well-planned fiscal administration. It was the first comprehensive nonmilitary executive organ of the Reich, which until now had depended on the cooperation and goodwill of the states.

Matthias Erzberger should be given credit for other achievements beside those of a minister of finance. As a leader of the Center party during the war, he had been the foremost backer of the Reichstag's peace resolution of July, 1917. Representative of the new Germany, he was one of the main targets of the Rightist opposition, particularly after he had courageously attempted to tax property heavily. A campaign of vilification forced him to resign his office as finance minister. In August, 1921, he fell victim to nationalist assassins. His end paralleled the fate of another great leader of the young Republic, Walter Rathenau. After rising to power Hitler personally honored the murderers of both men by dedicating public monuments in their names.

Well thought out and efficient as Erzberger's reforms proved to be after the inflation had been stopped, they were bound to fail, as had all previous experiments, under the overwhelming impact of currency depreciation. When, during 1922, the momentum of the mark's decline had mounted, there was a renewed political struggle for a large-scale capital levy. The Socialist parties demanded it in the belief that the levy could be protected against depreciation by tapping so-called real property values (Sachwerte). This rather nebulous term was at the time meant to designate all property titles not immediately affected by money valuations, such as factories, stocks of commodities, and real estate. The "bourgeois" parties were opposed since they sensed the danger of a partial socialization of business under the guise of fiscal measures, which would nevertheless fail to solve the financial problems. The eventual compromise provided for a compulsory loan to the government of one billion gold marks, in the first three years bearing no interest, later 4 to 5 per cent. As this loan was written in "gold marks," the fictitious notion of "mark equals mark" was officially abandoned for the first time. Once more, however, depreciation between assessment and payment was so rapid that again the scheme remained largely on paper.

Thus all financial efforts had mostly negative results as long as the inflation proceeded. Tax increases, the emergency levy, and the forced loan notwithstanding, fiscal receipts dropped off hopelessly when the devaluation of the currency had become catastrophic.

Defining the "purchasing-power mark" as the paper mark divided

by a cost-of-living index, the record of Reich income and expenditure
may be computed as set out in Table 7.

Table 7
Reich Finances, 1920–23
(in millions of "purchasing-power marks")

April 1–March 31	Income	Expenditure	Excess of expenditure over income
1920–21	4,091	11,266	7,175
1921–22	5,236	11,964	6,728
1922–23	3,529	9,665	6,136
1923–24	2,913	14,963	12,050

A "purchasing-power mark" is defined here as the actual "paper" mark divided
by the cost of living index. Source: *Statistisches Jahrbuch für das Deutsche Reich,*
1924–25, p. 348.

The deficits were covered by "floating debts," in other words, by the
printing press. As the table shows, the decisive turn for the worse
occurred in 1923. This was the price Germany had to pay for fighting
the Ruhr resistance.

Currency in Distress
From May, 1919, when the peace conditions became known, to February, 1920, the dollar quotation (parity 4.20 marks) moved from 13.5
to 99 marks. This period was characterized, on the one hand, by the
shock that followed the announcement of the terms of the peace treaty,
and on the other hand, by the domestic turmoil which culminated in
the Kapp putsch of March, 1920. After this putsch had been successfully put down in the same month, the dollar rate rapidly improved to
40 marks in June, 1920, and then oscillated between 60 and 70 marks
for an entire year. This was a time of domestic consolidation in which
the first deflationary effects of Erzberger's reforms and a breathing
spell in reparations made themselves felt. Two events that deeply depressed the German people, the London Ultimatum of May, 1921, and
the partition of Upper Silesia in October of the same year, sent the
dollar quotation up to 270 marks in November, 1921. A short interval
of receding foreign exchange rates followed when the German government was granted a partial moratorium on reparations payments. But in
June, 1922, following large disbursements on reparations account and
the assassination of Walter Rathenau amidst growing domestic tensions,
the dollar rate resumed its upward surge. In July, 1922, the mark sank
for the first time below 1 per cent of its original value; and when
Raymond Poincaré's reparations policy was seen to drive straight to-

ward conflict, the plunge became ruinous. By January, 1923, after the Ruhr adventure had begun, the dollar rate had reached 18,000 marks. Then, surprisingly, the exchange market quieted down somewhat. German strategy in the Ruhr conflict demanded that the currency be defended by all possible means. But after May, 1923, the economic consequences of the Ruhr resistance on finance and business became so catastrophic that support for the mark had to be discontinued. A new break followed, and now nothing could hold the downward race of the mark.

Disregarding intermediate fluctuations, Table 8 shows the dollar quotations on the Berlin exchange at regular intervals. They convey a graphic picture of a phenomenon not previously recorded in history. Reality was just as fantastic as the visual impression of the curving statistics. For several years the German people had to live through such chaos.

Table 8
Dollar Quotations for the Mark;
Selected Dates, 1914 and 1919–23
(monthly averages)

July, 1914	4.2
January, 1919	8.9
July, 1919	14.0
January, 1920	64.8
July, 1920	39.5
January, 1921	64.9
July, 1921	76.7
January, 1922	191.8
July, 1922	493.2
January, 1923	17,972.0
July, 1923	353,412.0
August, 1923	4,620,455.0
September, 1923	98,860,000.0
October, 1923	25,260,208,000.0
November 15, 1923	4,200,000,000,000.0

Jan. 1919 figure computed from Swiss quotations. Source: *Statistisches Jahrbuch für das Deutsche Reich,* 1921–22 to 1924–25.

The table shows the abrupt turn of events in July, 1921, following the London Ultimatum. The legendary inventor of the chess game, wishing to demonstrate to the Shah of Persia the meaning of a geometrical progression, is said to have asked as a favor to have his chessboard heaped with grains of corn in such a way that one was placed on the first field, two on the second, four on the third, and so on to the sixty-fourth field. The Shah soon realized that there were not enough grains in his realm to fill the last field alone. This legend became a bitter reality in the great German inflation.

Soaring Prices

In the first inflationary period there was actually a considerable time lag between the movement of external exchange values and the domestic purchasing power of the mark. Commodity prices rose much more slowly than the dollar quotation. After the devaluation had gone wild, prices adapted themselves with increasing speed. Finally, after 1922, when the entire nation had come to understand the connection between *Devisen* quotations and commodity prices, the adjustment became almost immediate.

Table 9
Indices of Depreciation of the Mark;
January, 1920–November, 1923
(1913 = 1)

Date	MEASURED BY	
	Foreign exchange	Wholesale prices
January, 1913	1.0	1.0
January, 1920	15.4	12.6
July, 1920	9.4	13.7
January, 1921	15.4	14.4
July, 1921	18.3	14.3
January, 1922	45.7	36.7
July, 1922	117.0	101.0
January, 1923	4,279.0	2,785.0
July, 1923	84,150.0	74,787.0
August, 1923	1,100,100.0	944,041.0
September, 1923	23,540,000.0	23,949,000.0
October, 1923	6,014,300,000.0	7,095,800,000.0
November 15, 1923	1,000,000,000,000.0	750,000,000,000.0

Source: *Statistisches Jahrbuch für das Deutsche Reich,* 1921–22 to 1924–25.

Accordingly, the dollar now became the yardstick of values and the determining factor for setting prices. The daily dollar quotation replaced the weather as a topic of conversation. Every guttersnipe was accurately informed about it, and of course every merchant had it at his fingertips, adjusting his prices automatically or even anticipating the forthcoming dollar rates. It became customary to close shop at lunch time and to reopen in the afternoon with new price tags after the dollar quotation of the day had been reported.

A comparison of the foreign-exchange index with the wholesale-price index reveals the growing speed of adjustment. The lag in adjusting retail prices was also diminishing.

In the headlong course of depreciation the volume of money in circulation began to lag behind the depreciation of the mark in terms of the dollar, particularly after the middle of 1921. Table 10 shows the banknote circulation computed in gold marks.

Table 10
German Banknote Circulation, 1913 and 1920–23
(in gold marks)

Average, 1913	6,070,000,000
January, 1920	3,311,000,000
July, 1920	7,428,000,000
January, 1921	5,096,000,000
July, 1921	4,745,000,000
January, 1922	2,723,000,000
July, 1922	1,730,000,000
January, 1923	173,000,000
July, 1923	168,000,000
August, 1923	282,000,000
September, 1923	752,000,000
October, 1923	300,000,000

Source: *Statistisches Jahrbuch für das Deutsche Reich*, 1921–22 to 1924–25.

The paradoxical situation indicated by these figures can be clarified as follows: the increase in note circulation, especially in the last phase of the inflation, was so explosive that the printing presses were literally unable to keep up with demand. In the last months before the collapse more than 30 paper mills worked at top speed and capacity to deliver notepaper to the Reichsbank, and 150 printing firms had 2,000 presses running day and night to print the Reichsbank notes. Even with this mass production, disturbances in the money supply to the public could not be prevented. As prices followed the exchange quotations in ever closer succession, the commodity turnover had to be handled with a relatively shrinking money supply, and the velocity of circulation was accelerated even more. Since cash in hand was exposed to daily, later to hourly, devaluation, everyone took the utmost care to hold as little of it as possible. Money in the till burnt like fire and had to be gotten rid of at the first opportunity, preferably the minute it was received. While people became poorer and poorer there was a general scramble for goods.

As has been shown, the inflation resulted not only from the Reichsbank financing of government deficits but also from inflationary credits to business granted by the Reichsbank and commercial banks. In themselves these credits would have been normal features of an inflationary situation, but in the context of this particular German inflation they acquired a special economic and social connotation. With the growing speed of depreciation, credits made out in paper marks became an abundant and riskless source of profits and led to the accumulation of huge new fortunes.

The trick was simple. The businessman procured short-term bank credit not only to keep his shop going but also for investment in other "physical values." Such investment entailed long-term immobilization of the funds in expanding the debtor's own plant or in acquiring additional facilities. When the time came to repay the debt, payments were made with devalued money. Thus the new plants or the materials to run them were acquired virtually without cost. German industry experienced a time of frantic activity of the kind described, limited only by the availability of materials and manpower.

Naturally the demand for these magic credits rose by leaps and bounds, and private interest rates scaled astonishing heights, a progressively greater devaluation factor being calculated into the interest terms. Yet this devaluation premium usually lagged far behind the actual depreciation, mainly because the Reichsbank as the ultimate source of credit held interest rates down by granting voluminous business credits on short-term, low-interest bills.

This Reichsbank policy of pumping inflationary credits into business—aside from the inflationary credits to the government—began in 1922. At the end of 1921 commercial bills and acceptances in the Reichsbank portfolio amounted to only 1.1 billion marks. By the end of 1922 the portfolio had increased to 422 billion compared with a holding of Reich treasury bills of 1,185 billion. Thus, to the inflationary effects of Reich deficit financing, the Reichsbank added as much as another third in credits to business. Approximately the same ratio between public and private Reichsbank credits prevailed in 1923, the year of the Ruhr conflict and of the highest inflation fever.

The most objectionable feature of these inflationary business credits was the interest rate at which they were granted. Up to July, 1922, the Reichsbank kept its discount rate at 5 per cent. In August, 1923, it was still only 30 per cent; in September, 1923, it was raised to 90 per cent, where it was held to the end of the inflation. Thus the Reichsbank calculated a devaluation premium of from 25 to 85 per cent per annum while the actual devaluation rate was more than 3,000 per cent in 1922 and several million and billion per cent in 1923.

Inflation Profiteers

Persons who were resourceful and had the necessary banking connections to procure a maximum of commercial credit had nothing to do but invest the money without delay in "physical values" in order to amass a gigantic fortune in no time at all. The most typical example of such practice and, in general, of the trend toward capital accumulation was the case of Hugo Stinnes.

Hugo Stinnes was not, as were so many other inflation figures, a newly rich man. He was heir to a large and reputable coal-mining and shipping firm and during the war had himself become a dominating force in the Rhenish-Westphalian heavy industry. When the first world war started he held the majority of shares of the *Deutsch-Luxemburgische Bergwerksgesellschaft,* one of the largest German steel and coal-mining companies, and of the Rhenish-Westphalian Electricity Company, the leading power producer in this foremost industrial area. Not until the postwar inflation did the Stinnes group become the voracious octopus of world fame.

The resources with which this group expanded came in one part from contributions paid by the Reich for properties ceded in Alsace-Lorraine, in another part from inflationary credits. Stinnes used these means to strengthen his position in heavy industry by forming a "joint venture" (*Interessengemeinschaft*) with another large group, the *Gelsenkirchener Bergwerksgesellschaft,* in 1920. In the same year he formed a further joint venture with the powerful electricity group of Siemens-Schuckert. In addition, he began to buy up at random and in large numbers the most varied businesses, including banks, hotels, paper mills, newspapers and other publishing concerns.

With Stinnes' economic power his political role grew apace. Stinnes was among the few German business men—Walter Rathenau occupying a comparable position at the opposite political pole—who had the courage to descend in person into the political arena in order to exercise in a straightforward manner the political influence inherent in his economic position. He did this both as one of the leaders in Gustav Stresemann's German People's Party (*Deutsche Volkspartei*) and through a daily newspaper which he had recently acquired, the *Deutsche Allgemeine Zeitung.*

Stinnes died in April, 1924, almost immediately after the mark was stabilized, just in time to save his reputation. For with the end of the inflation boom the inorganic giant business agglomerations were doomed.

As soon as inflation was replaced by stabilization, prices inevitably began to decline and as the nominal value of the excessive debts that had been incurred remained unchanged, the burden became overwhelming. With uncanny speed the entire structure Stinnes had built foundered. His heirs retained a comparatively insignificant remainder of the industrial grouping, and central concern disintegrated into its elements. Only the "community of interests" between the Deutsch-Luxemburgische Bergwerksgesellschaft and the Gelsenkirchener Bergwerksgesellschaft survived under different management, later to become the nucleus of the German steel trust, the *Vereinigte Stahlwerke*.

Inflation Victims

Thus, while immense fortunes were piled up, the broad strata of the middle classes sank into poverty. All property invested at fixed money values, such as government bonds, mortgages, mortgage bonds, savings bank deposits, and the like, became worthless. Hence the economic basis of a social class that had been so important in prewar German society and politics was destroyed.

After the end of inflation various efforts were made to repair, at least in part, the ravages to Germany's political and social life wrought by the pauperization of the rentier class. All long-term money debts were "revalued" by law at a certain percentage of their original gold value. Mortgages were revalued at 25 per cent, all other titles at lower rates. But these efforts did not suffice to reconcile the estranged rentiers to the young Republic, which they held responsible for the catastrophe. Naturally, the ones to fight with most energy for a policy of revaluation were the anti-Republican parties on the Right, while the Republican parties on the Left showed little understanding for the real social and political problems involved.

As the inflation progressed the number of victims kept growing while that of the profiteers dwindled. In the first phase of the inflation boom, industry and trade had profited much more by the opportunities opened to them in the consecutive waves of rising prices than they were harmed by the secondary effects of inflation. Since at that time the domestic price level lagged far behind prices on foreign markets the margin gave exporters a welcome incentive. This created the appearance of an industrial boom, at least as far as the volume of production and employment was concerned. Not even the world depression of 1921 interrupted this German boom.

Only slowly, frequently not before the end of inflation, did German businessmen realize that the prosperity of industry and trade during the inflation boom had been utterly imaginary. The great bargain turnover in the end stood revealed as a huge liquidation sale. No one experienced any difficulty in finding customers for his wares, which were on the contrary pulled out of the tradesmen's hands. But as costs of replacement continuously exceeded selling prices, stocks dwindled and plants were worn down. At the same time, in view of the prevailing "seller's market" at home and abroad, incentives for technical progress disappeared.

Gradually everyone came to realize that the industrial boom fed on a waste of substance. Now the workers and white-collar employees too began to notice that high employment was purchased at the price of decreasing real wages. Although the unions puzzled out ingenious devices to adapt wages to living costs, in this breathtaking chase prices outpaced wages by growing margins.

Finally the collapse of the monetary system was complete, and all and sundry were swept into the disaster. Money no longer fulfilled its essential functions for a modern economic system. Hence some people reverted to primitive methods such as barter. Domestic trade resorted to pricing in foreign money denominations. Business calculations and every sort of economic relationship became utterly confused. In the end, the disruption of every economic mechanism was so acute that unemployment increased despite a continued rise in prices.

Stabilization

By the Autumn of 1923 fundamental reform of the currency system had become a matter of life and death. How was the transition from an inflated to a stable currency to be brought about? Immense obstacles lay in the path, of which the following were the most thorny:

1. At no other time and in no other place had a currency and the faith in its functioning been undermined so thoroughly. Yet, without advance confidence it would be impossible to build up a new currency. Lacking such initial confidence the new currency was bound to be rushed into rapid circulation again, which would spell a new depreciation.

2. There was no hope of a foreign loan, which in other cases of exhausted reserves had been the main step toward stabilization.

3. The central problem was how to procure resources for the time of transition. The Reich Treasury's principal source of revenue had been the printing press. How could normal revenues be found to replace banknote creation? From what source could the Reich draw a fund

sufficient to carry the administration through the interval until taxes would once more begin to flow with regularity? During this time of suspense it would be just as impossible to float a domestic as a foreign loan.

4. Any plan of currency reform would be doomed unless there were at least an armistice in the reparations conflict and a breathing spell in reparations payments.

After the Ruhr struggle had been abandoned in September, 1923, and after negotiations between the occupying powers and the Ruhr industries had been initiated—which was tantamount to an armistice in the reparations struggle—with the aid of some imagination all other problems began to appear solvable. Even the particularly perplexing problem of how to stabilize the currency while continuing to resort to the printing press for the government's immediate financial needs was found to yield to simple theoretical reasoning.

As described above, the public's cash reserves in terms of gold had finally dwindled to almost nothing. Such cash reserves would presumably regain their normal proportions as soon as the public became convinced that no further devaluation was in the offing. A certain supply of newly printed currency would therefore not exert inflationary stimuli but only prevent deflationary pressures on prices from developing. Within these limits there would be little danger attached to the further temporary use of the printing press.

The "Miracle of the Rentenmark"
To implement this reasoning, all that seemed to be required was to convince the public of the soundness of the new currency and to keep the circulation within narrow bounds. This was achieved by a psychological device which has been written into history under the label of "the miracle of the *Rentenmark*."

Basically the idea of the Rentenmark had some resemblance to the assignats of the French revolution of 1789. In the case of the assignats the collateral for the money issued consisted of real estate. In the case of the Rentenmark collateral consisted of the "real-estate debts" of agriculture and of the analogous debts of industrial companies. In both cases the "backing" was fictitious since it could be used neither abroad to regulate foreign exchanges nor at home by being turned into cash. More significant than the similarities between the assignats and the Rentenmark, however, was one decisive difference: the fictitious backing of the assignats was devised to cover up inflationary designs, whereas for the Rentenmark it was a psychological device used in a determined effort at stabilization.

These scruples over how to "back" the Rentenmark were really beside the point and arose either from a misconception of the nature and function of a modern currency or from the notion that it was of the essence to "create confidence." All through the inflation period the Reichsbank had managed to preserve a certain gold holding which, to be sure, in the end amounted to only a few hundred million marks. As against the flood of paper issuing from the Reichsbank this gold fund was obviously without power to stem the inflationary tide; any amount used would have dissipated like a drop of water on a hot stone. When in 1924, by means of the Dawes Loan, a sizable gold fund was once more accumulated in the Reichsbank, the currency had already been stabilized. It remained stable not because of any "backing" but because the Reich budget had been balanced and the currency in circulation could be kept scarce.

As often happens when an idea is "in the air," the Rentenmark had many inventors. There was a Minoux Plan with the first germs of the mature idea. Then the former Secretary of the Treasury, Karl Helfferich, proposed a plan that closely resembled the ultimate policy; he suggested a "rye mark," a new currency unit to be defined in rye instead of gold, even though rye prices were especially unstable from year to year depending on the harvests. Rudolf Hilferding, Finance Minister in the first Stresemann cabinet, replaced rye with gold. Finally Hans Luther, at that time Food Minister, a few days later Finance Minister, afterwards—in the days of Locarno—Reich Chancellor, proposed the Rentenmark.

This stage was reached September 17, 1923. Nine days later the hopeless Ruhr struggle was abandoned. On October 15, the Rentenbank Decree was published, and on November 15 the mark could be stabilized at the rate of 1,000,000,000,000 paper marks for 1 gold mark, which at least gave Germany title to the uniqueness of her inflation.

The German currency was reconstructed in the following manner: the Reichsbank fully retained its function as a bank of issue, but it was prohibited from further discounting Reich or state Treasury bills. As in the prewar period, only genuine commercial paper was eligible for rediscount. Moreover, a second bank of issue was founded, under the name of Deutsche Rentenbank. It was nominally furnished with a capital of 3.2 billion Rentenmarks, not one cent of which, however, was actually paid in, the capital consisting exclusively of agricultural "soil debts" and analogous industrial debts. These obligations paid interest to the Rentenbank, constituting in essence a special tax on agriculture and industry; from this source the bank was in due time to accumulate a genuine capital. (It is a curious detail that this tax in the form of revenue from the Rentenbank real-estate obligations outlasted the Weimar Republic and Hitler's Third Reich, and continued to be levied on agriculture up to 1959.) The Rentenbank claims on agriculture and industry served as collateral for the Rentenbank notes which the bank was allowed to issue to a maximum of 2.4 billion Rentenmarks. These *Rentenbankscheine* were not legal tender but had to be accepted in payments to public agencies and thus circulated alongside the Reichsbank notes. Half of the maximum amount of Rentenbank notes, 1.2 billion Rentenmarks, was to be issued as credit to the Reich government, the balance in credits to business.

The basic question was not whether the collateral was fictitious or real; it was, rather, whether the public could be made to believe that the currency had a "stable value," an expression in fashion at that time. This was actually accomplished, primarily because it proved feasible to implement the plan from beginning to end exactly as scheduled. The Rentenmarks in strictly limited amounts flowed into the gap opened by the depleted cash holdings of the public. The Reich government received its credit of 1.2 billion Rentenmarks, and with this it managed to bridge over the time until tax revenues would once more begin to flow.

This favorable situation was temporarily interrupted when the government suggested to the board of directors of the Reichbank that the credit to the Treasury be increased to 1.6 billion Rentenmarks. Immediately the foreign exchanges resumed their upward movement. The Reichsbank directors turned the proposal down and this negative decision, undoubtedly justified at this juncture, contributed a great deal to strengthening confidence in the soundness of the new currency. Before long taxes, having at last been restored to a stable currency basis and slightly increased at the end of 1923, began to yield returns sufficient to re-establish a balanced budget. The situation was of course materially improved by the temporary breathing spell in reparations. When in March and April of 1924 the foreign exchanges again threatened to slip, the Reichsbank imposed a radical credit freeze, thereby demonstrating its steadfast determination to fend off all dangers to the new currency. The definitive settlement of international currency relations was reserved for international agreements to be drawn up within the framework of the Dawes Plan.

Plans for Reparations Payments: the Dawes Plan

In October, 1923, the President of the United States, Calvin Coolidge, took up a suggestion made by Secretary of State Charles Evans Hughes that the reparations problem be submitted to an inquiry by nonpolitical experts. On November 30, 1923, after the Ruhr struggle had been called off, the Reparations Commission nominated two committees of experts to study various aspects of the problem and to propose— though this was not officially required—a new payments plan. The more important of these committees worked under the chairmanship of General Charles C. Dawes, later Vice-President of the United States. After careful studies the Dawes Committee presented the Reparations Commission with a new payments plan on April 9, 1924. A few days later it became evident that peace in the reparations controversies had thereby been assured for a considerable time to come. The plan was at once accepted by the Reparations Commission, and immediately afterward by the German government. After the French general elections in May, 1924, the Poincaré government that had waged the Ruhr conflict was replaced by Edouard Herriot's cabinet of the Left, which was favorably inclined toward peaceful arrangements. In July a Reparations Conference assembled in London, in August the Dawes Plan was adopted by all governments concerned, and on September 1, 1924, the Plan went into force. On August 30, 1924, Germany passed a monetary law giving the new currency the name of *Reichsmark* (RM).

Although the Dawes Plan was meant to offer only a temporary solution—a fact emphasized by the plan's failure to determine a definite total for reparations payments—it had two decisive merits as compared with all previous arrangements. First, the fantastic annuities of former plans were replaced, at least for the first few years, by more manageable amounts, which promised a fair period of quiet relations between Germany and the Allies. Second, the plan contained the acknowledgment that Germany was in need of a period of recovery. The experts realized that the German economy, buffeted by the most harrowing experiences for almost a decade, had to be granted a respite if it were to produce surpluses for delivery abroad.

EXPLAINING THE NEED FOR INFLATION

HUGO STINNES

On His Interview with the American Ambassador, June 23, 1922

As I entered the Hotel Esplanade from the Reichstag, I was addressed by the Belgian representative on the Reparations Commission, Mr. Bemmelmans. He informed me that relations with the Entente had become very serious. In his opinion we had neglected to bring the sharp slump in Ruhr production punctually to the attention of the French, and the same was true of the decline in deliveries of coal from the part of Upper Silesia which has become Polish, so that the Guarantee Commission, which had no power to make decisions on its own, had no alternative but to file a report on the facts.

I replied to Mr. Bemmelmans that I too considered that the Entente had a right to be informed punctually of necessary drops in production and delivery, but that did not prevent such cases from suddenly arising, especially in view of the unrest which had spread among all classes of the German population because of the rising cost of living and the catastrophic fall of the mark. . . .

Mr. Bemmelmans also said that it would be wise to avoid all conflicts, because in 4 to 5 months the French would be ready, in his opinion, to accept the American, English and Belgian view that a final settlement of the reparations and loan problem had to be reached.

Just as Mr. Bemmelmans and I parted I was telephoned at 10:15 by Dr. Rathenau from the American Embassy and asked to come to the American Embassy as soon as possible for a thorough discussion of the coal problem with the American ambassador and the American representative on the Reparations Commission; for it was Dr. Rathenau's opinion that this would be more effective than for him to describe the situation. . . .

At the request of Dr. Rathenau and of the two other gentlemen, I analyzed the situation in all its details. . . .

The memoir, from the Stinnes papers is reproduced in Gert von Klass, *Hugo Stinnes* (Tübingen: Rainer Wunderlich Verlag, 1958), pp. 284–291. It is also reprinted almost completely in Herbert Michaelis and Ernst Schraepler, *Ursachen und Folgen: Vom deutschen Zusammenbruch 1918 and 1945 bis zur staatlichen Neuordnung Deutschlands in der Gegenwart* (Berlin, 1959 ff.), vol. V, pp. 514–517. The editor's translation of selections for this book was undertaken with the permission of Gert von Klass.

The greater part of the conversation dealt with the reparations problem, rather than with the coal situation. At Dr. Rathenau's request I expressed my views on the several aspects of the reparations problem. Usually, Dr. Rathenau then stated his own position on these things, and thus the whole problem was discussed.

First the reasons why Germany carried on the inflation policy which it did after the war were established. I pointed out that after the lost war it had been absolutely necessary for Germany to bring four million men then in the field, out of the habit of regular work, back into the regular routines of useful activity; and for that raw materials and employment were necessary. To get the raw materials and obtain the markets for production, it was necessary to sacrifice some capital for the purpose of sustaining the life of the nation, if it could not be avoided; for if the masses had remained unemployed, then doubtless Bolshevism would have seized Germany. And however dreadful the ravages of Bolshevism had already been in Russia, there is no doubt they would have been even worse in Germany, because in Germany it was a matter of a predominantly industrial country, where the effects of food shortages, caused notably by the maintenance of the blockade, would have brought a far worse manifestation of Bolshevism than in agrarian Russia.

I also informed the gentlemen that the weapon of inflation would have to be used in the future too, without regard to the resulting extraordinary capital losses, because only that made it possible to give the population orderly and regular activity, which was necessary to preserve the life of the nation.

It was further established in the discussion that the American gentlemen had been told not only by Germans but especially by the French that I deliberately aimed at growing inflation as something economically desirable, whereas in their view the growing inflation meant an extraordinary loss in national wealth.

I called the gentlemen who had expressed views like that to the American gentlemen fools; and Dr. Rathenau, who in all respects took the same positions I did, compared the situation of Germany to that of an army which is completely surrounded, and which to preserve its existence must break through, however great its losses, so as to get air and a chance at life for the whole.

Dr. Rathenau also pointed out that a people grown so poor as the Germans could not support wealth, unearned income or pensions for large groups of the population—a position the Americans did not believe they could follow, on the grounds that a population that could support large groups of rich profiteers could also support larger bodies of decent people. It was on this question that the single instance of differing views among the four persons present arose that evening.

Beyond that, the Americans did agree that lives were worth more than money, and that from this standpoint they understood why Germany followed a policy of inflation, if that was the only way the life of the nation could be sustained. . . .

The gentlemen were of the opinion, just as Mr. Bemmelmans was, that in a few months the "final decision" would come.

Dr. Rathenau and Mr. Logan spoke openly about the forthcoming cessation of payments to the Entente. To the best of my recollection the feeling was that only one more installment would be paid.

Dr. Rathenau affirmed that there were no longer any differences of opinion between himself and me on the management of things, for he too considered that the time had come to reach a final solution in the next months. . . .

In conjunction with that I declared that my first thought on the solution was that Germany, in return for a loan set not too high, should be freed completely of occupation, sanctions, and reparations; and that in addition the unilateral most-favored-nation conditions must absolutely and everywhere be changed to mutual most-favored-nation conditions, for it was utterly impossible to bring even the balance of payments in Germany into equilibrium unless outlets for German products throughout the whole world were reestablished.

The Americans agreed completely with this opinion. The ambassador declared that one reason for his coming to Berlin had been to establish mutual most-favored-nation conditions.

Dr. Rathenau made a most impressive analysis of the effects of mutual most-favored-nation conditions.

Further, Dr. Rathenau and I together sought the total removal of internal economic controls, whether on coal, grain, rents, demobilization, or whatever, and similarly the restoration of state enterprises and the complete release of import and export trade. In this matter too the American gentlemen agreed.

When asked whether Dr. Rathenau and I believed that such totally changed conditions of life and production would have enough effect on the workers' state of mind to make them work as much harder as was absolutely necessary, we both answered that we were convinced that if the workers were handled correctly, such an increase in labor was attainable, and this to a degree which would make possible an active balance of payments for Germany, including moderate reparations.

The ambassador doubted this, because in his experience, both in America and in England, only the bitter compulsion of hunger could bring the masses sufficiently to their senses to see that only more work and a productive economy could bring salvation. But he conceded that in Germany it was a question of a highly developed, intelligent and industrious laboring population, so that the optimism of Dr. Rathenau and myself was perhaps justified after all.

For the rest, we were also in agreement that simultaneously with the granting and accepting of a loan, the currency problem would have to be solved in such a way that debts would be converted into gold debts. The Americans were highly satisfied to hear that both Dr. Rathenau and I would rather undertake the stabilization of the mark today than tomorrow and tomorrow than the day after, and that we would also have the courage to convert paper debts into gold debts. Following the consideration of these problems, which lasted until about one o'clock, we left, after I had promised the American ambassador to discuss the Russian problem and other similar matters with him in the near future.

Dr. Rathenau brought me to the Hotel Esplanade, where we parted after one o'clock, about ten hours before he was murdered.

DEFENDING THE POLICY OF THE REICHSBANK

RUDOLF HAVENSTEIN

Address to the Executive Committee of the Reichsbank, August 25, 1923

It is said . . . that the Reichsbank bears . . . a large part of the blame for the disorganization of the currency and the still increasing inflation. We are unanimously of the opinion that all these reproaches are unjustified. . . .

The credit policy of the Reichsbank is supposed to be an essential cause of the inflation; attention is drawn to the Reichsbank's apparently great and rapidly growing holdings in commercial bills. These holdings have in fact climbed to 49 million marks, but about ¼ of this consists of checks and very short-term bills, for which the Reichsbank is certainly not a source of credit, figuring merely as a depository. The credits

The speech was reprinted in the *Deutsche Allgemeine Zeitung* of August 26, 1923, and partially reproduced in Michaelis and Schraepler, *Ursachen und Folgen*, vol. V, pp. 543–545.

covered by the remaining bills amount to little more than one hundred million peacetime marks, calculated at the time of the discounting, as against a peacetime portfolio of about one billion. That the extension of credit by a bank of issue increases the circulation of paper money is doubtless true; but insofar as the bank gives economically justified and necessary credit which serves the production and sale of goods, it creates no artificial purchasing power. What matters is that unjustified bills be kept out of the Reichsbank. The Reichsbank has hitherto made every effort to reach this goal through the most careful examination and restriction.

As a source of inflation, the Reichsbank credits are completely insignificant in comparison to the fundamental cause of our inflation. This fundamental cause, insofar as it does not rest on the balance of payments, is . . . the boundless growth of the floating debt and its transformation into the means of payment . . . through the discounting of the Reich Treasury bills and the Reichsbank. The root of this growth, the enormous burden of reparations on the one hand, the lack of sufficient sources in income for the ordinary budget of the Reich on the other, are known.

Here too the Reichsbank is alleged to be guilty, because it has not opposed the Reich government and fiscal administration by refusing to continue the discounting of Treasury bills. This reproach is also unjustified and completely misjudges the actual situation. The Reichsbank has done all it could do with any chance of success. For years . . . it has continually called attention to these conditions and demanded a remedy in the most serious and urgent way, but it was not in a position to stop the discounting of Treasury bills as long as the Reich had no other available means to cover its deficit, and as long as all groups in the legislature were not fully convinced that such means absolutely have to be found. For the Reich must live, and real renunciation of discounting in the face of the tasks set by the budget . . . would have led to chaos. The threat of a general refusal to discount Treasury bills would have been nothing but a futile gesture. Only very recently, under pressure of dire necessity, have all groups in the legislature been convinced . . . that fiscal policy absolutely must be based upon adequate sources of income. This has made it possible for the Reichsbank in principle to envision and actually to prepare the ground for a recovery of its position as purely a central bank of issue. But it is also clear to us even now that, given the enormous tasks which confront the Reich government and fiscal administration, this solution will take time, and that for the present we must anticipate a further extraordinary growth of the floating debt and of the paper flood. . . .

The deterioration of economic conditions and the devaluation of the mark have called forth an ever more passionate demand from the people for drastic measures in the banking and currency fields. Everyone believes that salvation lies in the concepts of "gold credits" and "gold accounts," although everyone must admit that a real improvement requires far more general, deeper and more inclusive measures. As a beginning, the Reichsbank has introduced the so-called "stable value credits" for its own operations and for those of the Loan Banks. The credits will be both given and repaid in paper marks; on both occasions, amounts must be calculated in a stable currency—at present the pound. In this way both the Reichsbank and the receiver of credit risk a loss, the latter if the mark deteriorates, the former if it improves. As long as the Reichsbank must make its payments in paper marks, it can grant stable value credits only if the debtor guarantees (to repay) the amount of paper marks received for the event that the pound should sink below the rate current at the time credit was extended. Although everyone who owes paper marks runs this risk, the ruling is considered somewhat one-sided in business circles, and not entirely without reason. The Reichsbank therefore believes that it must offer a certain quid pro quo, whereby the debtor in turn is not made responsible for the full amount of the depreciation, but only for $\frac{4}{5}$ of it, and interest is charged only on the sum originally advanced in paper marks, not also on the depreciation. Finally, the Reichsbank will begin as soon as possible to set a much lower rate of interest for these credits than for credits in paper marks. . . .

Until July 28, 1922, we maintained the discount rate of 5%, which prevailed since December 1914. We found this necessary because until that time the easy availability of currency caused cash payments to become customary, and the demands made upon us by industry and commerce were relatively small and had no significance in comparison to the Reich's demands for credits. In mid-1922, the conditions of the money market changed. The reliance of the business community upon the Reichsbank increased. The use of commercial bills became, though only gradually, common again, the purpose being to supplement operating capital which was reduced by the increasing currency depreciation. In the past months, the discount rate of the Reichsbank has followed the rates of private exchange . . . only gradually and at a still significant distance. We did this because, in view of the ever growing scarcity of credit, the central bank of issue, the economy's ultimate and most fertile source of credit, had to take the condition of the overall economy and of its several parts into account in the setting of its discount rate. It could set only *one* discount rate, and a way had not yet been found completely to exclude those borrowers who, despite all scrutinies and restrictions, were still able to derive unfair profits from the currency depreciation through the cheap paper mark credits of the Reichsbank. . . .

The wholly extraordinary depreciation of the mark has naturally created a rapidly increasing demand for additional currency, which the Reichsbank has not always been able fully to satisfy. A simplified production of notes of large denominations enabled us to bring ever greater amounts into circulation. But these enormous sums are barely adequate to cover the vastly increased demand for the means of payment, which has just recently attained an absolutely fantastic level, especially as a result of the extraordinary increases in wages and salaries.

The running of the Reichsbank's note-printing organization, which has become absolutely enormous, is making the most extreme demands on our personnel. The dispatching of cash sums must, for reasons of speed, be made by private transport. Numerous shipments leave Berlin every day for the provinces. The deliveries to several banks can be made . . . only by airplanes.

SOCIAL CONSEQUENCES OF
THE CURRENCY CRISIS

The four selections that make up this chapter deal with the sufferings of various German social groups during the inflation. In Chapter Two, Gustav Stolper distinguished between "inflation profiteers" and "inflation victims." The profiteers were those who could borrow money cheaply, invest in productive resources, and thus acquire fortunes. The victims were primarily middle-class investors and consumers, whose savings were destroyed. Stolper also mentioned salaried people and workers, whose fate depended upon their ability to enforce more or less rapid adjustments of wages and salaries to price levels. He had less to say explicitly about merchants and shopkeepers, many of whom were forced to give credit to buyers. Unless they managed to do their accounting and billing in terms of gold or some other stable standard, they inevitably lost ground during ordinary business transactions. Like Stolper's other inflation victims, they were in the position of creditors, and it is the essential contrast between the creditor and the debtor which dominates Stolper's analysis.

It is interesting that the force of Stolper's argument does not derive primarily from direct empirical evidence. Once we are convinced by the economist's explanation of inflationary dynamics in general, it strikes us as logically necessary that creditors lost and debtors gained in Germany around 1923. All the rest of the analysis seems to follow naturally from this axiom. A leading expert on our subject argues that mercantile and financial capital on the whole did not do as well as industrial capital during the German inflation.* He bases his case in part upon direct observation; for he cites the histories of a few important private banks and industrial concerns. The whole of his account also contains more, and highly complex, statistical material than we could handle in this introductory study. Once again, however, his argument is strengthened very much by the contrast between capital which was invested in factories and machines, and wealth which was partly in the form of currency, securities, outstanding loans, and other credits.

Readers who are uncomfortable about this state of affairs will be pleased to find a little less argument and a little more circumstantial reporting in the four selections that follow.

The first of these is from Moritz Julius Bonn's autobiography, *Wandering Scholar,* which was published in 1948. Bonn was a German academic economist, a one-time rector of the Munich and the Berlin Colleges of Commerce (*Handelshochschulen*), and a frequent economic adviser to German governments and to international commissions during the Weimar period. His testimony is that of a highly qualified eye-witness.

The second set of selections is taken from a little book by Georg Schreiber, another German professor and a Reichstag deputy for the Catholic Center Party during the 1920's. The title of his book, which was published in 1923, might be translated as "The Distress of German Learning and of the Intellectuals." Schreiber describes conditions at the German universities. He also shows intense resentment at the "proletarization" of German culture and learning, the decline of the "cultured middle class," and the "mechanical equalization" of incomes.

The third passage stems from the statistical appendix to an essay by Alfred Weber. Weber, not to be confused with his even more famous brother Max, was a very prominent German sociologist and economist. Politically active on the non-socialist left even before 1918, he became one of the founding fathers of the German

---

* Costantino Bresciani-Turroni, *The Economics of Inflation: A Study of Currency Depreciation in Post-War Germany, 1914–1923,* trans. M. E. Sayers (London: Allen & Unwin, 1937), pp. 296–298.

Democratic Party after the First World War. In September 1922 he lectured on "The Distress of the Intellectuals" at a meeting of the Social Policy Association (*Verein für Sozialpolitik*), the foremost association of German academic social scientists and social reformers. An expanded version of this speech was published in 1923, together with the appendix excerpted below.

The final selection in this chapter is part of a speech delivered by Franz Bumm (1861–1942), President of the German Reich Department of Health, before the Reichstag on February 20, 1923.

THE REPORT OF AN EXPERT EYEWITNESS

MORITZ JULIUS BONN

The Last Phase of Inflation

One morning I arrived in Munich on my way to the country. While strolling outside the station, I ran into an acquaintance, a charming woman, who almost embraced me in public. "Do give me something to eat," she said, "I am famished. I went to the country," she explained, "with a supply of five-dollar bills. Yesterday the mark broke so rapidly that nobody could change one for me. I had no dinner; I took the earliest train to town this morning; I am waiting for the banks to open, and hope that they have enough marks to change a five-dollar note. I would have had to go without breakfast, if I had not met you." During the late phases of the inflation such experiences were common. Anybody who had foreign exchange was rich, provided that his money was in sufficiently small denominations to make an exchange possible. Germany was invaded by hosts of profiteers, by no means all of them from countries with high standards of solvency. Czechoslovakian, Italian, and even Austrian currencies circulated freely; they possessed a fairly high purchasing power when converted into marks. Germany was a rapidly decomposing corpse, on which the birds of prey were swooping down from all directions.

We had rented a farmhouse in Bavaria, where my wife lived most of the year, and where I used to spend my vacations. We kept one or two cows and had a vegetable garden; fields and pastures were leased.

Moritz Julius Bonn, *Wandering Scholar* (copyright © 1948 by The John Day Company, Inc.), pp. 286–290. Reprinted with the permission of The John Day Company, Inc., publisher.

Our neighbors were farmers, owning isolated holdings on the top of hills similar to ours. They depended mainly on dairy farming and the sale of young livestock; they grew few crops. Each of them possessed a piece of timberland, and in the winter the young men went lumbering in the state forests. These farmers did not suffer badly; they had got rid of their surplus crops against cash, in order to make a few purchases, and to pay taxes, which were not very heavy. They had been accustomed to take in a few summer boarders, who helped them to eat up their surplus stuff. Now if they liked them, they let them come again, and even accepted their cash. But they would not sell anything against marks, though they did a lively trade by way of barter. For a pair of old flannel trousers or a few leather straps we could buy grain to feed our cows. Moreover we were in a privileged position. My wife had a small sterling income of her own, and at that time I was very much in request as a contributor to American papers. We always had a few legally acquired dollars or pounds to spare. My wife, living on the farm all the year round, was on friendly terms with the neighbors. They visited her and asked her to their family feasts, whereas I, being only a summer guest, remained a "city dweller," quite a low type of human being. They were more than eager to sell goods against foreign currency, the acceptance of which was forbidden—but nobody cared any longer for the law. In these faraway mountain villages, every well-to-do peasant followed eagerly the quotation of dollars, of Dutch florins and of Czech crowns. He was not so keen about sterling, for the conversion of a pound sterling, being equal to four dollars, into marks represented a larger transaction than he was willing to go in for. In these last stages inflation seemed to affect even the animals; cows no longer gave surplus milk, and chickens refused to lay eggs, as the peasants cut their output down to their home needs. Goods were becoming much more valuable than money.

Shopkeepers were never sure of covering the cost of replenishing their stocks, irrespective of the prices at which they sold the goods; many goods had completely disappeared. Factories were no longer interested in selling to the home market against money, the value of which was rapidly vanishing. Foreign goods were scarcely obtainable. Manufacturers were permitted to acquire foreign exchange in order to buy raw material abroad for keeping their plants and their workers employed; mere consumers were disregarded. Shopkeepers treated their customers almost as enemies—they deprived them of stock which could not be replaced. Buying, like kissing, went by favor. In the late summer of 1923 the mark had ceased to function even in these rural areas.

Artisans and tradespeople in our village were very much worse off than farmers, since they could not get sufficient food from their small plots of land. Raw materials were scarce, and they had few opportunities for making goods. One day the village authorities approached my wife. A truck of potatoes, the village winter supply, had arrived at the local station. Since ordering the load, prices had risen so rapidly in paper marks that the village had not enough cash to pay for it. Would she lend them a couple of pounds or so and ensure the potatoes' being unloaded? Naturally she gave them the desired amount, and the village hurriedly raked in its potato supply.

In the big industrial cities no one was self-supporting. Yet people were no longer willing to carry on their transactions in marks, especially as they frequently encountered technical difficulties in getting a sufficient amount of them. Big industrial concerns made their own money to pay wages with it; it was accepted by the local business community. Municipalities printed notes, which circulated freely within their confines but were not valid in neighboring areas. Emergency money to the amount of 200 billion paper marks was in circulation. In July 1923 the cost of living index had risen 39,000 times. An unskilled metal worker, whose weekly wages before the war (1912) had been 24.44 marks (6 dollars) was getting only 73 per cent of his former income's purchasing power: his weekly wage amounted to 531 million marks in September 1923.

Workers were not the chief sufferers. Thanks to strong trade unions, their wages were regularly revised upward, though generally with a lag. In the earlier stages, before the Ruhr invasion, unemployment was low, as it always is during the inflation upswing. For this reason labor had not strongly insisted upon stabilization. Accounting was becoming a nightmare. Before the war a weekly wage of ten dollars was written in two numerals; it now took seven or nine. An army of clerks had to be recruited, and as many of them were inexperienced, business became very involved—prices were being quoted in millions, a habit that continued in Austria long after inflation had stopped. Banking activities were feverish. Most banks added new floors to their buildings to house new employees. Yet they were no longer keen on getting customers. The handling of an account of 100,000 marks was expensive when its gold value had shrunk to 25 dollars, so they asked depositors, frequently in rather peremptory language, to take away their accounts. Wages were adjusted at least twice a week according to dollar quotations; so were salaries of civil servants. Most of them asked for cash and rushed immediately to the shops to buy such goods as were available. A few hours later the mark might have gone down another 100 per cent, and the purchasing power of their salaries might have been halved. Those who had spare cash or credit gambled in stocks. As shares were supposed to represent stable physical values of a tangible nature, such as factories or stock piles, their quotations followed, and sometimes even outran, prices. A good many members of the middle class made a precarious living by gambling on the exchange. One of my colleagues was regularly late for his eleven o'clock class. He had to telephone instructions to his brokers before the exchange opened, and he rushed back to the phone as the clock struck twelve to give new orders. Big industrialists like Stinnes were habitually borrowing money from the banks, with which they bought up shares, enterprises, properties of all sorts, and created huge combines, many of which, being without internal cohesion, were mere gigantic junk shops.

Universities and colleges were overcrowded. Tuition fees had been but slightly raised; the only actual expense was the cost of transportation; fares were frozen and raised only slowly. For the time being house property had little value. Rents had been "ceilinged" early in the war, and had not been moved; by and by they amounted to next to nothing. Notwithstanding a housing shortage, little new construction was under way. Rents of new houses were not controlled, and were by comparison exorbitant, for building costs had gone up with prices and wages. The shortage of private dwellings had led to severe rationing. In order to hire an apartment, one had to have a ration card issued by local authorities. When I was called to Berlin as adviser to the Chancellor, I had not looked into the housing question. I had assumed that, being appointed to a high office, I would have no difficulty in finding a suitable apartment; but the housing authorities were local and did not take the slightest notice of me. Yet I was very lucky; an elderly widowed banker, who owned a beautiful house in one of the best parts of Berlin, gave me a small apartment in which I lived comfortably for nearly three years. Thus he was spared compulsory tenants, who might have been less desirable, and I had the advantage of a private home at an almost nominal rent. But for the housing shortage, a large part of the smaller "idle rich" would have gone to the wall completely. The value of their investments, insurances, and life annuities had been wiped out; apartments and furniture were often enough the only wealth which remained to them. They generally lived by subletting, payment to house owners being purely nominal. House owners defended themselves as well as they could by making no repairs, or by insisting on the tenants' paying for them. As most apartment houses were heavily mortgaged, owners defrauded creditors while tenants defaulted on them. Owners of mortgage-free homes who had let them to tenants fared worse. They either had to pay for repairs or let their property go to rack and ruin, and they had no creditors whom they, in their turn, could defraud.

The so-called *rentiers* were almost wiped out—though they got a pitiful compensation later on. By 1925 their real income had fallen from over 2 billion dollars (in 1913) to 300 million. They were not the victims of socialism, for the working class, too, had lost heavily, since their savings and their social insurance contributions had vanished (the reserves of the social insurance institutions had been invested in government bonds and mortgages). Their destroyers were the producers, the active businessmen. They had successfully expropriated investors; they had secured additional "tangible values" (they called them values of substance), such as land, houses, stock piles, shares, by systematically making new debts, which they paid back in rapidly deteriorating marks. Many of the huge combinations they had assembled disintegrated rapidly when the Reichsbank, under its new leadership, refused them the credits with which they had been in the habit of exploiting their fellow capitalists.

When it was all over, the social structure of Germany had been profoundly altered. The steady middle class, closely connected, though not identical, with the professions, was proletarianized at a time when the rising working class ceased to consider itself proletarian and was ready for incorporation with the middle class. It was a genuine revolution, far more devastating than the political collapse in the autumn of 1918 had been.

THE COMPLAINTS OF SCHOLARS

GEORG SCHREIBER

The Distress of German Learning

When the devaluation of the mark started during the war and especially during the post-war period, only a few people thought of the consequences which resulted for the affairs of learning. And yet it was after all perfectly clear that the foundations of German scholarship rest

Georg Schreiber, *Die Not der deutschen Wissenschaft und der geistigen Arbeiter* (Leipzig [now Heidelberg]: Quelle & Meyer, 1923), pp. 6–7, 17–18, 19–20, 26–27, 34–35, 41–42, 45–48. Excerpts translated with the permission of Quelle & Meyer Verlag, Heidelberg.

not only upon the researchers' idealism, but just as much upon the solid rock of a gold currency and an active balance of payments. But what has been built with gold marks cannot be maintained or yet extended with paper marks. And a maintenance without simultaneous extension is unthinkable. For all learning and science requires progress to give it content and to enrich and stimulate it. Years of paper currency therefore mean no more and no less than the distress of learning and, if the sickness of the currency lasts a long time, the death of learning and science. Such meager years bring about the dismantling of our culture, which in turn leads to pseudo-culture.*

Our feelings actually rebel against recognizing these things as facts. Years of growing prosperity, which the nation experienced before the World War, have estranged us from such truths, certain and natural as they are. The fundaments of German learning seemed to stand unshakable. Today, however, one must importunately urge the German people to become aware that all flowering of learning and science is tied to certain economic pre-conditions. One is inclined to use the facts of history as warning demonstrations. The Age of Pericles and the golden age of ancient Roman literature, the heroic epics of the medieval Empire and the richly colored Venice of Titian, the creations of Rembrandt and of the Dutch School, but also the classical pathos of Bossuet and Bourdaloue are rooted in the political and economic efflorescence of their countries. But in the impoverishment of a people, in the cold night air of political decline and in the sultry atmosphere of economic fever crises, no truly great . . . culture can thrive.

Like any threatened life, learning went on the defensive about 1920 and asked for help. Primarily because of the decisive countermeasures which were triggered by the Emergency Society of German Learning (*Notgemeinschaft der deutschen Wissenschaft*), the distress of learning could be kept bearable until the beginning of 1922; but conditions became catastrophic when in 1922 the dollar climbed from 300 to a rate of 7000–8000 marks to the dollar and the purchasing power of the mark constantly declined at the same time.

Now we find ourselves in the middle of the worst economic crisis, the seriousness of which increases from month to month. Each further postponement of the reparations question, each inconclusive conference, above all each act of violence, such as the occupation of the Ruhr area, not only creates political, financial and economic difficulties, but also simultaneously weakens German learning. The disintegration of our research goes hand in hand with the ruination of our economy. In

*[The German original for "pseudo-culture" was *Halbkultur,* "half-culture." The term implies the sort of "little learning" which is said to be a dangerous thing. Ed.]

this way, the Dollar also becomes the fever-thermometer of our learning's declining health and vitality. . . .

The emergency also results in an unpleasant scarcity of materials of all kinds. It is caused, of course, by the high prices. As a matter of fact, the sums which are spent for apparatus, for chemicals, for materials and for the entire equipment of the researcher have climbed to a monstrous level. These prices are naturally quite comprehensible in terms of economic development and world trade; but on the level of the individual institute's budget, they are unbearable.

A microscope for medical investigations which cost 1000 or at most 1500 gold marks before the war could still be obtained in August and September of 1922 for 80,000 to 100,000 paper marks; in December 1922, it already cost 400,000 marks, while in April 1923, it involved an expenditure of 3.5 - 5 million. The German microscope had at one time begun an entry into all the culturally advanced parts of the world, an entry which was a veritable victory procession, in which German science and technology simultaneously took part. At present, this German product has become almost unobtainable for the purchasing power of German science. It is a painful feeling for us Germans that these instruments, which stemmed from our initiative, are today being drawn off into foreign countries which have stronger currencies. . . .

To be sure, all those price increases which have assumed extraordinary dimensions since the beginning of the year 1923 are only expressions of the falling mark. Unfortunately, however, . . . the situation of the research institutes is such that their budgets are not increased by a corresponding increment of income which would be necessary to enable them to adjust to the devaluation of money. One need only leaf through the volumes which list the expenditures of the state governments or to look through the budget of the Emperor William Research Institute (*Kaiser-Wilhelm-Forschungsinstitut*) in order to measure the tremendous gap between actually available and really required resources. A leading physicist told me in the fall of 1922 that his physics institute at the university used to have a budget of 6000 gold marks for the acquisition of instruments before the war and that this institute in 1922 would really need 2,400,000 marks for the same purpose. The sum actually granted by the ministry remained far below this estimate. Another example: in 1918, the institute for applied chemistry at Erlangen received a yearly stipend of 16,000 marks from the state. It was no improvement when this sum was raised to 80,000 marks in 1922. Such sums only characterize the decline in which we are already involved.

A further example from the area of the humanities and social sciences: in the budget year 1922, all of 2000 marks were stipulated for the library of the seminar on church law at the University of Munich. And this in a situation in which the price of the yearly volume of (a very important research journal in that field), which is absolutely essential, was already 10,000 marks. The seminar for church history of the Catholic Theological Faculty at the University of Muenster was not able to buy the successor volume of Pastor's *History of the Popes* because of its great expense. These are unbearable examples of decline. . . .

The more the prices climb, the more the purchasing power of the libraries decreases; for the public contributions do not grow at the same rate. According to a comparative statistic which was presented at the last conference of German librarians at Kassel . . . in 1922, of 16 large German libraries, eight do not have even one-fourth of their pre-war purchasing power. Thus the decline in potential services has become considerable.

Already in June, 1922, Director Leyh of the Tübingen Library was able to ascertain on the basis of reports received by the information office of the German libraries that even standard works of German learning were available only at one or two libraries, and these are works the availability of which must be regarded as an absolute necessity. . . . One need hardly describe in detail how the situation has deteriorated since then: on September 13, 1922, the book trade still had a multiplication number of 60; on December 27, it was 600; on February 19, 1923, it already amounted to 2000, and on June 4, 1923, it climbed to 4200. The multiplication number is applied to a basic price, which is fixed rather arbitrarily here and there. On the other hand, the budgets of the libraries have changed only a little. At most there are a few 100,000 marks more available for purchases. . . . Unfortunately, this is the situation: compared with peacetime conditions, all these efforts have to be regarded as insufficient. The devaluation of money and the long time-span which passed until the money reached the library in the form of a book have brought it about that the standard of the German libraries has declined terribly. . . .

The decline of libraries and the sale of German libraries abroad goes hand in hand with a serious decline in the production of books in all fields of learning. To be sure, the production of books as such, if it is compared with its peacetime stand, has been raised considerably again; but where scholarly literature specifically is concerned, one does notice more clearly from month to month how production is decreasing. Understandable enough. In mid-November, 1922, the prices for a printed sheet for a scholarly work amounted to 30,000–35,000 marks, and they were soon superseded. In early January, 1923, a cost of 60,000 marks had already been passed. In early May, it had climbed to 500,000 marks.

How drastically the prices have shot up in the market for scholarly books may be seen in the following example. A monograph with a retail price of 4 marks in peacetime could not be bought for under 3000 marks in early January, 1923. Even a simple textbook cost 4000–5000 marks at that time; a dictionary at least 15,000 marks, and an encyclopedia in several volumes, which came to about 100–200 marks in peacetime, cost at least 120,000 marks used in January. Such price revolutions suggest a dim future for the great undertakings the continuation and completion of which is an unconditional obligation for German research. . . .

A word yet about the manual labor of German instructors. Conditions are such today that we have not only working students at our universities, students who obtain their livelihood through manual labor, but already working faculty members too. We have a whole row of instructors who are already busy during vacations in digging canals, building railroad embankments, excavations and other laboring jobs. Or they try to take on the difficult battle for existence by tutoring children in order to obtain some meager support. . . .

As for the income and the standard of living, I have in front of me a series of questionnaires which were filled out in the fall of 1922 and which show the way in which unheard-of personal tragedies are today permeating our learned world. Thus I have here the questionnaire of an instructor who indicates exactly what sort of an income he had for 1922. It amounts to 150,000 marks for the whole year. "No outside income. If some does come in, then it is because he was occupied for a few weeks during the vacation in an excavation." "My salary," this instructor writes, "has not nearly approached the minimum necessary to exist. I am forced from time to time to sell personal belongings."

The questionnaire of another instructor. Number of children: "four." Yearly income: "190,000 marks." Outside sources of support: "Soil-moving in railroad building." This instructor also mentions his wife's serious tuberculosis.

The third questionnaire of a German instructor. Number and age of children: "two girls." Yearly income: "190,000 marks. Wartime activity: 1914–1919. Working for the railroad during vacations for day wages."

The rubric "Special difficulties of economic position" is filled out with this statement: "As a consequence of scarcity for years, both children undernourished according to school doctor. Repeated sicknesses in the family. After active service in the army, disabled for two years with serious rheumatism." . . .

The scholar of former times who could support and continue German research from his own means no longer exists. Instead we have today a proletarization which involves all bearers of German learning. Sven Hedin pointed out at the centennial of the German Natural Scientists' Conference at Leipzig (1922) that the learned middle class in Austria is nearly destroyed and that the German cultured middle class is about to disappear. An all too true assertion. The impoverishment has the consequence that the middle class finds itself unable to send its sons to the universities in as large numbers as formerly. The devaluation of money, the weight of taxes and the social restratification presses too heavily upon it. It is a dangerous cultural gap that other social groups, the children of workers and children of the newly rich, do not fill in as rapidly; the latter groups also still lack some valuable traditions.

The weakening of the learned middle class especially involves the position of the German university professors. Here a great deal has already been destroyed. Illustrative material is not lacking. Thus it is certainly a case of painful resignation if as early as 1921 a leading German professor of law had to sell a part of his valuable library in order to relieve the distress of his family, especially of his numerous children. A separation from a part of his self. . . . It would not be difficult to bring further details. Suffice it to point to the words of Harnack, who has characterized this sad section of German social life as follows: "Proven scholars have to struggle with serious cares of subsistence and often do not know from what to live in the coming week. They look for outside occupations and part-time earnings. They are too proud to complain. But bitter scarcity consumes their strength."

In fact the remuneration which is granted to the German university professor for his scholarly work is insufficient. . . . The income of the university professor must be measured out in such a way that he is in a position not only to support his existence but also to serve German research as he once did. A mechanical equalization with other levels of income means no more and no less than a tearing down of the mental and spiritual culture of our country. . . .

But the picture of the German university professor would be incompletely drawn, if no mention were made of the psychological pressure which noticeably weighs on him. Especially in the Germany of today, one should not overlook such psychological circumstances. . . . The scale of psychological bitternesses and disturbances is easy to read. It is really painful for the scholar to have to see that a part of his research work is for nothing, useless and fruitless, because it never gets into print. One knows that it becomes ever more difficult to bring out larger scholarly works. . . . But to work in manuscript alone . . . is as harmful for the scholar as for the work itself. For literary production receives its spiritual baptism only in the fire of intradisciplinary criticism. Add to this the lack of literature and other research aids. As was already suggested, it is becoming impossible for the scholar to keep his disciplinary library up to date; the German journals which he has come to regard highly are becoming more and more expensive, and he has long had to do without foreign periodicals. The budget of the university library or of whatever other library he has come to work in is becoming more and more tight on top of it all. In peacetime he was used to having his area of acquisitions paid attention to in some detail at this library. Now that is scarcely possible any more.

But this psychological pressure moves in another direction as well. Learning too strives for rejuvenation and reproduction, for a continuation in the younger generation. Thus, for the German scholar, his seminar stands by his side as a seedbed of mind renewing itself. . . . But for several reasons (scarcity of material, working students, reduction of the seminar library, impossibility of printing theses), it is possible only to a small extent for the scholar of today to form a circle of pupils to carry on the task of the master. After all, the printing of even a small doctoral dissertation is no longer manageable with a sum under a million marks. Thus a reduction of literary production and a dying out of the lines of scholarly inheritance results from these psychological frustrations as well.

Finally, one has to think of the private scholars too. They are a disappearing segment of the population. I mean those scholars who are not really connected with the German universities officially or as teachers. Nevertheless, they have often done valuable services for German scholarship as researchers and collectors. One may only remember the areas of history, literary studies and art analysis. The devaluation of the rents, but also that of royalties forces them to seek other opportunities for earning something somehow. . . . Count Klinckowstroem has recently remarked . . . sarcastically but quite correctly that the scholarly writer doesn't even earn as much with one printed line as a street sweeper earns with two sweeps of the broom. . . .

ALFRED WEBER

The Distress of the Intellectuals

1. The de facto income of higher officials:
According to the salary regulation effective April 1, 1922, the average yearly salary (after tax deductions) for a married official with two children is:

in group X.	Councilors of State	65,026 marks
in group XI.	Councilors of State	70,228 marks
in group XII.	Chief Councilors of State	81,085 marks
in group XIII.	Ministerial Councilors	96,745 marks
in group B3.	Ministerial Directors	131,780 marks

Given a thirty-fold increase of living costs (a rate of increase which has in reality been far superseded even now), this income in paper marks is equivalent to a real income (peace-time income):

in group X.	of	2,168 marks
in group XI.	of	2,341 marks
in group XII.	of	2,703 marks
in group XIII.	of	3,225 marks
in group B3.	of	4,393 marks

In 1913, the corresponding average yearly income was:

in group X.	6,108 marks
in group XI.	6,916 marks
in group XII.	7,736 marks
in group XIII.	10,960 marks
in group B3.	16,520 marks

Thus, the higher officials presently earn:

in group X, only 35% of their yearly income [of 1913]
in group XI, only 34%
in group XII, only 35%
in group XIII, only 29%
in group B3, only 27% of their [former *real* income].

For the unmarried official, even greater cuts are involved. His salary in group X is only 31% of his peace-time income, in B3 only 25% of his peace-time income.

Thus, higher officials presently have on the average only a third to a fourth of their pre-war income. In other words, they have had to

Alfred Weber, *Die Not der geistigen Arbeiter* (Munich and Leipzig: Duncker & Humblot, 1923), pp. 41–45. Excerpts translated with the permission of Duncker & Humblot Verlag.

reduce their living standards by up to 75%. Thus it happens that a Ministerial Councilor, for example, presently does not even earn the salary of an office-assistant or postal clerk before the war. This loss of 65 to 75% of the peace-time income is especially onerous, since, as is well-known, the higher officials were very poorly paid even before the war. Add to this the fact that the higher officials are less able today than formerly to rely upon income from their own capital. The officials had generally invested their money in government bonds with fixed interest rates or in other safe ways. These capital investments have shrunken to nothing as a result of the currency devaluation. . . .

2. The incomes of higher officials as compared with those of other officials and workers:

The income reduction for higher officials is not nearly matched by a similarly pronounced income reduction for other officials and workers in the administration and in government enterprises.

a.) The salary of officials in groups II to IX:

The real income (peace-time income) in:
 group II   is   1,347 marks or 82% of peace-time income
 group IV   is   1,495 marks or 78% of peace-time income
 group VII is   1,744 marks or 48% of peace-time income
 group XI   is   2,012 marks or 43% of peace-time income.

Thus, although the full peace-time income has not been maintained for these groups either, their salary increases do not lag nearly so far behind the increase in living costs as those of the higher officials. . . .

b.) The income of workers in government enterprises:

For workers (married, with two children, in Berlin in government enterprises), yearly wages (after taxes) presently are:
 for skilled workers, 40,608 paper marks—real income 1,354 marks
 for unskilled workers, 30,474 paper marks—real income 1,282 marks

The peace-time wage for skilled workers was 2,212 marks,
                  for unskilled workers was 1,349 marks.

Thus, compared with pre-war conditions, the skilled workers presently have 38.8% less, the unskilled workers in government enterprises have 4.9% less [income].

c.) The relative ranking of salaries and wages:

The different developments in the salaries and wages of the several groups of officials and workers have resulted in a leveling tendency which greatly exceeds the bearable and even the objectively permissible. . . . *The higher official, who earned 7 times as much as an unskilled worker in 1913, today earns only twice as much: after tax deductions, as little as 1.8 times as much.*

A REPORT ON THE NATION'S HEALTH

FRANZ BUMM

Speech before the Reichstag, February 20, 1923

In the session of the Prussian legislature for January 23, the Prussian Minister of Welfare, drawing upon the report submitted for Prussia, has already given us a picture of the most grievous want and deep misery in matters of health in that state.

Unfortunately, this picture of accelerating and shocking decline in health conditions applies to the whole Reich. In the rural areas, where many self-sufficient farmers are able to feed themselves and the difficulties resulting from a great density of population do not exist, conditions seem to be better. But in the towns and in the districts with an industrial mass population, there has been a decided deterioration. Especially hard-hit are the middle class, those living on small annuities, the widows and the pensioners, who with their modest incomes can no longer afford the most basic necessities at present-day prices. It is going just as badly for those who can not yet earn. I mention students only as an example. The expense of even the most essential foodstuffs— I need indicate only fats, meat and bread—and the want of coal, linen, clothing and soap prevent any improvement in living conditions. The height to which prices have climbed may be shown by the fact that as of February 15, wholesale prices have risen on the average to 5967 times the peacetime level, those of foodstuffs to 4902 times, and those for industrial products to 7958 times. Meat consumption has fallen from 52 kilograms per person in 1912 to 26 kilograms per person in 1922. In the occupied zone, moreover, this small amount has presumably to be shared with many foreign mouths as well. For many people, meat has become altogether a rarity. A million and a half German families are inadequately provided with fuel. Thousands upon thousands of people spend their lives jammed together in the most primitive dwellings and must wait for years before they can be assigned quarters which satisfy even the most elementary hygienic requirements. The provision of linen and clothing becomes daily more difficult. The

Verhandlungen des Reichstags: Stenographische Berichte, vol. 358, pp. 9779–9784: 303. Session, Tuesday, February 20, 1923. Excerpts from the speech by Franz Bumm, the president of the Reich Department of Health, are reprinted in Herbert Michaelis and Ernst Schraepler, *Ursachen und Folgen: Vom deutschen Zusammenbruch 1918 und 1945 bis zur staatlichen Neuordnung Deutschlands in der Gegenwart* (Berlin, 1959 ff.), vol. V, pp. 523–530.

old pieces are worn out, and there is no money for replacements. The new materials are not at all durable. Because of its high price, laundry soap has again become unobtainable for many people.

It is understandable that under such unhygienic circumstances, health levels are deteriorating ever more seriously. While the figures for the Reich as a whole are not yet available, we do have a preliminary mortality rate for towns with 100,000 or more inhabitants. After having fallen in 1920/21, it has climbed again for the year 1921–1922, rising from 12.6 to 13.4 per 1000 inhabitants. In 1922, those familiar diseases appeared again in increasing numbers which attack a people when it is suffering from insufficient nutrition, when it also can no longer obtain the other necessities of life. Thus edema is reappearing, the so-called war dropsy, which is a consequence of a bad and overly watery diet. There are increases in stomach disorders and food poisoning, which are the result of eating spoiled foods. There are complaints of the appearance of scurvy, which is a consequence of an unbalanced and improper diet. From various parts of the Reich, reports are coming in about an increase in suicides, as Representative Dr. Moses has already told us here recently: suicides out of desperation and misery. More and more often one finds "old age" and "weakness" listed in the official records on the causes of death; these are equivalent to death through hunger. Just recently the painful news appeared in the daily press that a well-known German scholar, Professor Hayn of Dresden, has died of hunger. The frequent appearance of typhus epidemics and of skin diseases must be attributed to the increasingly unsanitary handling of goods and to insufficient personal hygiene. The increase in pneumonia and rheumatism points to chills resulting from inadequate heating of living quarters and from insufficient clothing. The medical determination that nervous disorders and heart troubles are increasing shows that people are suffering from serious anxieties over problems of nutrition and survival. And the fact that people are unusually vulnerable to sickness and that they take much longer than usual to recover from sicknesses shows that resistance to illness has declined as a clear result of poor living conditions and that the body only barely finds the nourishment necessary for full recovery.

Among the German people there is a special concern for their favorites, the babies and small children. It is well known that during the war, infants suffered relatively the least of all segments of the population, because the mothers shifted more to nursing their children themselves, and because private and public assistance was especially active in behalf of the infants. But now their situation seems to be growing worse again. Although in the years 1921/22 births in the large cities fell from 302,000 to 285,000, a decline of 17,000, the death rate rose from 12.1 to 12.8. Even though this increase in mortality is not very large, it is disturbing, because normally every decrease in the birth rate is accompanied by a decrease in infant mortality, whereas in the present case there has been a rise in mortality among infants despite the decline in births. In medical circles, there have been complaints about specially sharp increases in infant mortality particularly for the time since August 1922—that is, since the especially steep rise in the price curve. There are also frequent reports of an increase in sicknesses among infants, of rickets and digestive disorders. The deterioration must be comprehensible even to the layman: for when the milk supply available for infants not nursed at their mothers' breasts becomes much scarcer and at the same time more expensive—a liter of milk in Berlin today costs, I believe, 720 marks—, when a single diaper for a child costs 1000 to 3000 marks, when the many other things urgently needed for the cleanliness of infants cost a thousand times their peacetime price, when one infants' home after another must close its doors, it is understandable that the health of the little ones suffers and infant mortality increases. Indicative of the distress of infants is what Dr. Moses also recently pointed out here: that babies are brought to charitable institutions wrapped not in diapers but in paper.

Children in the age group from 1 to 14 years suffered a great deal during the war. The mortality figure climbed by 50%. After the conclusion of peace, from the spring of 1921 to the spring of 1922, an improvement set in. But this lasted only a very short time. From all parts of the Reich it is reported that since last spring, the condition of the children is causing more concern every day; the nourishment of the little ones becomes every day more insufficient.—I will return to this point!—Above all, there is a lack of milk, of protein-rich foods. The children are being fed an excess of carbohydrates, at the expense of proteins and fats. Most of the children's homes, nurseries and similar institutions have been forced to close for want of the necessary means. Nearly 40% of the former nurseries, admittedly including the emergency nurseries which were only established during the war, no longer exist. In Berlin, a sixth of the infants' homes and half the nurseries are closed already.

The children, who under these circumstances must increasingly do without systematic care and sufficient nourishment, are physically in a regrettably poor condition. One can discern this in the sad fact that in some places up to 20% of the children who register to begin school must be turned back, because they can be regarded as not yet ready for enrollment in view of their bodily weakness. From everywhere in the Reich, the doctors report that the children are anemic, listless, weak and subject to illness. [The state of] Hessen reports an extraordinary mortality since August 1922 among the children from one to five years old. The teachers lament a noticeable decrease in the intellectual receptivity of their pupils, and lack of physical endurance in gymnastics.

In the selection of children for supplementary meals at school last year, it was found that on the average no less than 50% of the children were undernourished. Where the findings were still relatively good, 20% undernourished children were found. There were places with up to 80% undernourished children.

The children were retarded in height and weight too. Thus the municipal doctor in Annaberg ascertained for the years 1913 and 1922, for the age group of 13 years, that there was a difference in height of 7.3 centimeters among boys and 5.3 centimeters among girls, and a weight difference of 4.3 [kilograms] among boys and 3.2 among girls.

The insufficient equipment of children with linen and clothing too has at present again become frightening. The pieces of linen and of clothing which were still available from pre-war times and have been mended again and again are used up and can no longer be mended. Therefore one can again see many poor shivering children in the streets and observe their unclean appearance. A municipal school inspector from Leipzig reports that during an unannounced visit to a school class of 27 girls, only three had proper shirts, only two had stockings without holes in them and only four were nourished in a moderately satisfactory way. . . .

The suffering of the children is again increasing in a deeply disheartening manner. Every friend of humanity must deeply lament the dreadful misery which the children have to face. The doctors can not yet explain why such diseases as diphtheria, scarlet fever and measles, which used to be frequent and which often took a heavy toll, have decreased in a remarkable way in the last few years. But this circumstance, while gratifying in itself, cannot reduce the anxiety over the children's future; for the fearful disease of tuberculosis, that great angel of death who pursues children particularly frequently, is now again to an increased degree at its destructive work. During the world war, the number of victims of tuberculosis was especially great, as was shown last year in a memorandum by the Reich Ministry of Health. Between 1914 and 1916, over 100,000 more people died of tuberculosis than was expected on the basis of the mortality figures for 1913. After a gratifying, by no means insignificant reduction of this mortality in the post-war years, there is now again an ominous growth. Tuberculosis is on the increase. In the large German towns with more than 100,000 inhabitants, 22,438 people died of tuberculosis in 1921; in 1922, 26,125, that is an increase of 3687. In Prussia, more people died of tuberculosis in the first three quarters of the year 1922 than in the whole preceding year. Among towns which, exceptionally, have had a small progressive reduction in tuberculosis, I can name only: Halle, Potsdam, Dresden, Stuttgart, Bremen, Braunschweig and Ludwigshafen. Even though the increment of tuberculosis mortality is not very great, it must yet be a cause of grave concern, for tuberculosis, like hunger, is known to be a slow murderer, which does not kill its victims immediately. If now, after the death of so many tuberculars during the war, the curve of tuberculosis mortality is climbing again, then it has to be assumed that a great number of new infections took place during and after the war, of which we are now seeing the consequences. Unfortunately, it has not been possible to produce statistical material on the increase in cases of tuberculosis for the whole area of the Reich, because there is no uniform requirement that all such cases be reported. But it may be concluded from the unanimous judgment of the doctors that new cases of tuberculosis are steadily and strongly increasing in Germany. Particularly children and young people are again being increasingly attacked by the disease. Thus one is shaken, for example, by the report of the director of the university clinic in Freiburg, which indicates that this children's clinic is again becoming essentially nothing but a tuberculosis hospital for children, just as it was during the war. The district doctor for Waldeck reports that he has never treated as many tuberculars as in the year 1922. From the state of Saxony we hear that an increase of tuberculosis is there observed especially among men and women between 18 and 25 years of age. A municipal welfare office from western Germany reports that the spread of tuberculosis and scrofula is especially great among the children. During an examination of children in a public school, which was undertaken by a municipal welfare office, every tenth boy and every tenth girl were found to be tubercular.

The fact is that tuberculosis is again encountering little resistance, because the misery in every area of life and especially in the field of nutrition is increasing. After all, a hearty diet is the best means of protecting people against tuberculosis or of making the tuberculars well again. Tuberculosis infection is also being favored by the way in which people are tightly jammed together in overcrowded houses and by the fact that the costs make it daily more difficult to admit and to keep tuberculars in the hospitals and sanatoriums. . . .

Ladies and Gentlemen! The various developments in the field of health which I have described to you demonstrate that there is an ominous decline in the year 1922. Among the causes of this decline, there is the bitter want which has affected the care of the sick too. The rising fees charged by doctors for their help—of course it is only fair that the doctors too, like all other employees, be granted an increased remuneration in this time of inflation—make it impossible for many sick people to call a doctor or at least to call him in time. But if the doctor comes to the sickbed too late, then he is generally helpless and powerless and can no longer help the patient.

The hospitals, to which we used to be able to bring the sick, are becoming more and more helpless every day. They can no longer fulfill their tasks. The daily costs of food, care, heat, water, light, personnel in these institutions run into the hundreds of thousands. I recently heard that a local hospital spends 1 million marks per day for coal alone. In the case of public, state and communal institutions, the deficit can at least be covered from public means. But in the case of the many charitable institutions, such recourse to a great purse is not possible. Some time ago, to be sure, the sum of one billion was released from Reich funds in order to support these charitable and general welfare institutions. But this sum is naturally insufficient for the many hundreds and thousands of institutions in the long run. Because of the high rates, people nowadays wait until the last moment before bringing the sick to the hospitals. It is a characteristic fact that, as a consequence, those who arrive at the hospitals are now very often already dying. The Reich Institute for the Prevention of Infant and Child Mortality in Charlottenburg reports that of the infants who died in the year 1922 after having been admitted to the hospital, 30% died during the first day and 40% within the first three days after admission. Hundreds and thousands of people who once used to find shelter in these institutions, in pregnancy homes, in hospitals, in children's and cripple's homes, in rest homes for the aged and infirm are today no longer able, given the rates of 3000 to 4000 marks per day, to avail themselves of the care of these institutions. The most passable lot is still that of those who enjoy the good fortune of social insurance and who are sheltered in these institutions at the cost of those who pay the insurance.

Now to a consideration of the difficulties associated with the supply of medicines nowadays. From week to week, the table of medicine rates lists higher prices for medicines. 100 grams of surgical cotton in 1914 cost 45 pfennigs, today 2552 marks; a bandage in 1914, 20 pfennigs, today 1270 marks; 100 grams of ether in 1914, 1.45 marks, today 1147 marks. This clearly indicates that many thousands of sick people must at present either do entirely without medicine or be only very marginally supplied with them.—The apothecaries must ask high prices—they are rigidly bound by the officially fixed medicine rates—, because the goods which they receive from the wholesalers are already delivered at high prices, so that no overly great profit is left over for them. Most apothecaries are heartily yearning for the times when they had a much greater turnover at lower prices and when they did not have to go through the sad experiences, which nowadays repeat themselves only too often, that people come with prescriptions, ask what the prescribed medicine costs and then turn around and don't have the prescriptions filled because they don't have the money. But the apothecaries' prices nowadays—if you want, I can prove it—have not gone up as much as other retail goods.

If the sick person is released from his suffering by death, the misery is not yet at an end, for then the cares of burial are added on for many people, because the unreachably high costs of burial make it impossible for them to fulfill even the duties of the most basic piety toward the dead.

Now all this misery is doubled and cruelly sharpened in those parts of the fatherland which have already been subjected to foreign occupation for four years, but more particularly for the inhabitants of the Ruhr region, which has recently been invaded by French and Belgian troops in violation of the peace treaty of Versailles. In its session of January 31, the Reichstag has already concerned itself with the abominable cruelties and atrocities which are following continually and in growing numbers upon the dastardly occupation of the Ruhr region, and the Reichstag has unanimously protested against the confiscation of the schools, hospitals and many other welfare institutions.

IV

THE INFLATION IN THE EXPERIENCE OF A GERMAN FAMILY

The selections in this chapter are from Pearl S. Buck's *How It Happens*. This book reproduces an extended interview between Miss Buck and Erna von Pustau, who reminisces about her family's experiences in Hamburg during the 1920's and 1930's. The passages reprinted here deal with the inflation. Erna von Pustau is the main speaker; only the short questions and interjections are Pearl Buck's.

Obviously, this type of report must be read with caution. Personal recollections are easily colored by hindsight and by borrowed interpretations of remembered incidents. Erna von Pustau was not a trained observer of social and political affairs. Her story is therefore especially likely to reflect the biases of her own rather limited circle of acquaintances.

Yet personal recollections, even those of ordinary people, are often more vivid, more charged with emotion—and therefore more fascinating—than other historical sources. A single example cannot sustain a generalization; but careful study of an individual case can be extremely valuable as a source of hypotheses and hunches about a period. Erna von Pustau's family may have been unique; but we tend to suspect that it was not. We feel justified in regarding much of what they experienced and felt as typical of other people in a similar situation. Thus we can certainly learn from the father's problems as a small businessman during the inflation, from the mother's difficulties with her inherited property, and from Erna's own visit to the rural "paradise of inflation."

119

At the same time, we are especially interested in what Erna tells about her own and others' *reactions* to the events of the early 1920's. She reports how poorly many of her contemporaries understood the causes of the currency crisis, and how easily they came to believe in the guilt of a few presumably all-powerful manipulators: financiers, politicians, foreigners, or Jews. Such popular sentiments were certainly of much consequence. It must have made a difference that middle-class businessmen came to hate the "bourgeois capitalists" and "capitalism" itself, without meaning to opt for proletarian socialism.

In Erna von Pustau's world, people used important words in ways which seem to us unusual. Particularly their social concepts differed from ours. But we cannot hope to understand the impact of the inflation, unless we can discover how Erna's friends defined the "bourgeoisie," "bolshevism," the "average middle class," the "ruling class," the "good families," or the "liberals." Erna herself associated the inflation with a much broader social and cultural trend, in which everything from modern art to sexual mores played a role. It is the attitudes she thus reflects or reports, more than the events she relates, which make the account an interesting and valuable source.

MONETARY CONFUSION AND MORAL DECAY

PEARL BUCK

How It Happens

"It sounds strange to me now to hear the word 'normalcy.' It seems stranger to me, looking back on all that has happened, to remember that we Germans really believed after the First World War that normalcy would come back. Yet the people believed it. After each new

Pearl S. Buck, *How It Happens: Talk about the German People, 1914–1933, with Erna von Pustau* (New York: The John Day Company, 1947), pp. 104–105, 107, 121–130, 132–133, 134–141, 142–145, 147, 151, 155, 179–180, 182, 188–191, 193–195, 201–203. Reprinted with the permission of Harold Ober Associates, Inc. Copyright © 1947 by Pearl S. Buck. Subtitles within the chapter are the editor's.

event that uprooted them, they settled down again until the next event came.

"People said, 'Well, after the war there is still unrest, but then normalcy will come.' They settled down, they made their plans for their lives. Then came political unrest to throw them off. Then came a short time of quiet and they had their hopes and their plans once more. Then came inflation. Then came again the time of stabilization. They settled down and had their hopes again, and began a new life. Then came the crisis. And then they were desperate. Then they really hoped that by voting for another form of government they could come back to normal life again.

"You can put it in this short sentence—people are always hoping to get back to their normal life, to their normal hopes, but this time their hopes failed.

"Then came Hitler, and then came the war, and now comes this hopeless situation of Europe. Do you see now that it was not one shock, but how it happened time and again?"

"These shocks, however, don't come as thunderstorms come, out of the heaven," I observed. "They are the result of causes in the people themselves."

"Yes, they are," she agreed. "And we have to speak of the causes. But I wanted to show you only the great line, the background of the mass of the people, who are at heart always unpolitical. All they want is to live, and only if they cannot find how to live do they become political. The masses of people do not care for politics normally, they are not educated for politics, thus they did not see through the forces that finally turned against them, too.

"At this time while people were trying to settle down, prices were going up and money values therefore were going down. We called it 'inflation,' just as you do here, and we thought it was only the aftermath of the war and that soon money and prices would be 'normal' again. When a thing cost double what it had before the war, we said, 'Life is really getting expensive.' When the same thing cost ten times what it had, we said, 'It can't go on longer. It must stop.'

"Sometimes it did stop for a few days or even for a week, and then it went on again until at last the mark of the good old times, which had been based on gold values, was worth a billion marks of these new times. By that time we had long ceased thinking. Life was no longer merely becoming expensive—life had become sheer madness. . . .

"Well, I must make it clear, since I have to come back to it time and again. We Germans looked, for years, at the dollar exchange in the newspaper. We used to say, 'The dollar goes up, again,' while in reality the dollar remained stable but our mark was falling. It seems a funny way of expressing it. But, you see, we could hardly say that our mark was falling, since, in figures, it was constantly going up and up and up, and so did the prices, and this was much more visible than the realization that the value of our money was going down. It sounds confusing, doesn't it? But this confusion belongs to inflation, is inseparably connected with it, and was one of the reasons why the people gave up thinking things out. It all seemed just madness and it made the people mad. . . .

"Before I tell you how I, personally, first experienced inflation with all its confusion, I want to explain the background. It is very difficult for America to understand, because the language deceives us and leads us astray. The same word 'inflation' is used here for two different things. You say, even now, 'This is inflation.' You mean only that life becomes more expensive. You see, it is different whether the price of butter is fifty cents or two dollars and whether it is fifty cents and later on one billion dollars. This latter is what happened to us, not for one year, not for two years, but until fall 1923, or five years after the end of the war.

"We were deceived, too. We used to say, 'All of Germany is suffering from inflation.' It was not true. There is no game in the whole world in which everyone loses. Someone has to be the winner. The winners in our inflation were big-business men in the cities and the 'Green Front'; from peasants to the Junkers, in the country. The great losers were the working class and above all the middle class, who had most to lose.

"How did big business win? Well, from the very beginning they figured their prices in gold value, selling their goods at gold value prices and paying their workers in inflated marks. Professor Emil Lederer, who later came to the United States, estimated that workers' wages and employees' salaries provided twenty-four to twenty-eight gold billions of extra profit for big business."

"Did the people know nothing of this?" I asked.

"They learned to know it," she replied. "In fact, the inflation stopped at the moment when the workers, through many strikes, succeeded in getting their wages paid daily in gold value. And then inflation had lost its value for big business. Yes, we found that inflation, which according to the bourgeois newspapers seemed to be a 'catastrophe of nature' or 'a thing which has slipped out of control of everyone,' could be stopped.

"The same devaluation happened to savings. It is estimated that approximately fifty gold billions of savings were lost, mostly by the middle class, through the devaluation of the war bonds, through the devaluation of the mortgages which were paid off in devaluated money, and so on. The average middle-class people learned far later than big business to figure in gold. They would buy goods, sell them with a small margin of profit as they used to do, only to find out that the new supply they had to buy had increased so much in prices that they could buy less for the same money. The middle class was far less organized than the workers were, and they were hard pressed from both sides, from the workers who demanded higher wages and from big business who increased the prices more quickly than they could follow.

"You see the great winner in inflation—big business! When inflation ended big business had not only reconverted its industry but had modernized it tremendously. The bourgeois press called it 'the miracle of German industry,' which had, despite war and inflation, recovered and reorganized completely, thus enabling Germany to face competition on the world markets. Sounds beautiful, doesn't it! The opposite however, was true, for German industry did not recover despite inflation but by means of inflation.

"You know, I, too, learned all this only many years after inflation. Sternberg explained it to me when I first met him. Yet, I was so used to the slogans of the 'miracle of German industry' that I must have seemed stupid. He enlightened me for the first time. I have seen him explain it to many other people of the middle class. Some of them wanted to beat him, others got so angry at big business that they wanted to start a revolution immediately.

"I must mention another thing. Many Americans have the idea that German industrial recovery was due to American loans. This is not quite true, either. We could say that they brought the already modernized industry into full gear. The American loans were given after the Dawes Plan, which came in 1924. Germany paid eight gold billions of reparations to the former Allies. Germany took, however, as loans from abroad, twenty-five gold billions—about seventeen gold billions more than she paid reparations, as you can see. And yet it was far less than the money which big business extracted from workers, employees, and the middle class during inflation, and from which they really modernized German industry.

"By the way, this is one thing I learned, too, many years later, and which at first I wouldn't believe, namely, that Germany never really paid reparations, because they took more in loans than they paid in reparations. They only paid in kind for the first year after the war, but later on, as you can see from the figures I just gave, they paid less than they got in loans. Mother always insisted that inflation came because of the reparations.

"Another thing that was rather confusing was the exchange course of the mark at the international stock exchange. I told you how we constantly looked at the dollar exchange in our newspapers, saying, 'The dollar goes up once again.' The Dutch, the Swiss, the Scandinavian, the British, the American money was stable money. But, as I want to stress again, for us they went up and our mark went down. Foreigners came to Germany, buying houses and estates from impoverished good families for a handful of dollars, crowns, or sterling. They were spending money at liberty. Those our people saw with their own eyes, while they did not see the new, the modern machines being installed in factories of big business. How easy for them to distract the people, to tell them, 'The foreigners take advantage of our misery!'

"And by the way, I saw this same thing happening in France when I first went there in 1927. France had inflation then, too, not such a big one as we had in Germany, but the franc was devaluating. But there were Americans with their dollars in the best hotels, buying the most expensive things, and I saw the French people demonstrate in the streets, crying, 'Down with the Americans!' I recognized then the same feelings that we had had.

"But let us go back to the German people and the way they were deceived and deceived themselves. Let's get back to the money exchange. You know, the foreign valuta jumped up quicker than the prices of consumer goods. Thus there was a widespread belief that prices rose because the foreign valuta went up. And why did the foreign valuta go up and the mark down? 'Because of the speculation on the stock exchange.' This explanation was the opposite of the truth, but millions believed it. It was just what the Nazis wanted. 'Who speculates? The Jews,' so they cried. Do you remember how Mother suddenly made such a clear distinction between the Jews, who know how to do business, and the Germans, who were not so clever at it? Well, this was the first reflection in our family of this anti-Semitic, National Socialist propaganda. It hammered into the heads of millions of people the combination of words: 'Money—exchange—inflation—and the Jews.'

Big business, in the meantime, could go on making business—undisturbed.

"Inflation finished the process of moral decay which the war had started. It was a slow process over a decade and more; so slow that really it smelled of a slow death. It gives the whole picture of Germany in all its ugliness, and it undermined the Republic of Weimar. When inflation was over, the psychological preparation for fascism was complete, the minds of the people were prepared for the Nazis.

"I have for my purpose divided the time of inflation into the first period, which I call the 'disintegration,' and the second, which I call 'the formation of the fronts.'

"For me, personally, the inflation began when Hilde had gone to the country, Lotte had gone to her school, and Father gave to his only daughter at home a double allowance, saying, 'I give you more and yet you get less.'

"I looked at him and said, 'What do you mean?' He said, 'Well, it is because of the inflation.' I shrugged my shoulders. I thought, 'Well, inflation is madness, anyhow. Anything can happen.' He said, 'Now, listen to me. I am explaining it to you. I figure in Swiss valuta. Now, formerly eighty pfennigs were one Swiss franc; now one Swiss franc is eight marks. Had I formerly given you two marks, I would have had to pay to you two and a half Swiss francs. Now, however, I have only to give you thirty Swiss cents for your two marks. So although I double your allowance, you get less than before.' I thought that over, and said, 'Well, then, couldn't you give me still more, because even if you give me double, you still pay me less than before?' Father laughed. Then he got quite serious and said, 'You are just like the workers in the factory.' And he wouldn't hear anything more. I didn't know quite whether I should be grateful or whether I should feel myself cheated.

"Yet another very confusing picture of inflation was that part of life wasn't affected by it at all. There were ceiling prices, for instance. What was important for me, although I couldn't buy a cup of coffee with this money, a bit of candy or chocolate, the theater prices had not gone up and the streetcar fares had a ceiling price and, really, the things that I had to pay from my allowance did not go up. So, in this complexity, although I got less, I had, in fact, more than before. All these technical questions made it very difficult for anybody to understand for a long time what was happening.

"When the mark really was falling, everybody began to ask, 'Who is guilty?' This question was confusing, too, because the ruling class, who wanted to mask the business they did, could give you a long list of guilty ones. For instance, take the question of reparations. The vanquished had to pay for the war. It had always been so. But wars had become more and more expensive, with industrialized warfare, and the reparations which all the former enemies now listed as covering the costs of their war were sums quite beyond our understanding. Moreover, the Allies did not make a bill that was definite. More could still be added. It was a Damocles' sword hanging over us, and a very good excuse to say, 'You see why we have the inflation; we have to pay so much to the Allies!' Thus I came to believe that foreigners are the guilty ones and would have gone on doing so, I think, if I had not met my Armenian friend, Lulu.

"She was in my high-school class and very soon we were friends. She was an only child of an Armenian father and a German mother; a well-to-do family, and of an atmosphere so different from ours that in our extremes we were attracted to each other. For instance, we went to her home and Lulu had a sitting room of her own! She showed to me her Negro sculptures and Negro pictures. That was a revelation for me. You must understand this, because, you see, there were Negro troops in Germany in the French occupation army, and all Germany cried out because these Negro troops were here, and what they were doing to German women! This being the first time that we had been confronted with the Negro problem, it seemed to us that they were primitive animals. And now I had a friend who showed me Negro culture! I didn't dare to tell Mother. I think she might have taken me out of school because I got to know such a girl. I asked Lotte about it. I said, 'Do you think Negroes have culture?' Lotte said, 'Why not? Why shouldn't they?' Then Lotte said, 'During the war we lived cut off from the world, and we grew up with the idea that our culture was best and our civilization was the only one. But now we have to see that we are in competition with the other world.' "

"Was Lotte so broad-minded?" I asked, somewhat astonished.

"Through a friend of hers," Erna answered. "But, you see, more and more families began to be liberals, and more and more the younger generation came into contact with these liberals."

"Was Lotte's friend also a foreigner?" I asked.

"No, no, she was a daughter of a Hamburg surgeon. This Hamburg surgeon had married the sister of a German painter, who became bolshevik after the war. He made a so-called bolshevik settlement near Bremen where Lotte went sometimes with her friend. It was very interesting. I visited there once, too. Christian communism, he called it. It was really a wild place. There were paintings of very strong colors and you couldn't see so much what the figures were. You know this kind."

"Modernistic painting," I said, recognizing it.

"It was all considered bolshevik," Erna said with decision. "But then anything that was new was red or bolshevik. There was naturally the sex question at that place. Everybody slept with everybody else."

"So it was not quite Christian!" I said, laughing a little at her grave look.

"No, but they called it Christian, because they had a common life, and a very primitive one and shared everything. They had made everything themselves, the houses and the paintings in the houses."

"Did your mother know that Lotte was there?" I ask.

"My mother knew," Erna replied, "but since Lotte's friend was from one of the best Hamburg families, she didn't dare object. But with me it was different, because my friend was only an Armenian. There she could say something. You know, my mother's values were society values. An Armenian family was different. That was not the best Hamburg society. So my mother's judgment was never a real judgment. Indeed, in her whole life I never found a judgment that came from the things themselves, but a judgment that came from social position. Which is, by the way, rather usual!

"This so-called decline of morals—although I always refused to say 'decline of morals'—I say, this gradual process of decay of the old and the search for new values was widespread in our younger generation. It was a sign that the old pattern of life had broken down, and, as my sister Lotte used to put it, 'The terrible thing is, we have to believe in something. When we do not know in what to believe, we believe every day in a new thing, and we have every day a new prophet. But better to have every day a new thing than to believe in nothing.'

"My friend Lulu also had a boy friend. It was amazing. I had a friend who had a boy friend!

"I was at that time an admirer of Wagner, and having now a double weekly allowance, I was able to go to *The Twilight of the Gods,* if I bought only a standing ticket. Lulu said, 'Oh, I would like to go with you.' I said, 'There are only twenty tickets for standing room and you have to be there at four o'clock!' Now Lulu shrugged her shoulders and said, 'Well, if you say so, I will come.'

"It was, however, very tiresome to stand. I had found out a trick. You had to have a stand leg and a leg on which you relaxed." Erna jumped up and showed me how to stand for hours, on one leg and then the other. "You had to stand on one leg, and then you changed it. So I taught Lulu this trick, and by and by, as time went on, everybody was tired and everybody got in bad humor.

"I tell you this, although it seems unimportant. Yet, standing with Lulu there and for the first time seeing it as a new thing, and looking back to the past, I saw really what had happened. Here was this standing for a few tickets for a few real music lovers who had no money. They regarded the tickets as their privilege. Most of those who were there with their scores were hostile to all the others who took their places. So it seemed to me that I saw in this a real symptom of what was going to happen. The pie was growing smaller and more people wanted to have pieces of the pie, and so there was nothing left from the 'good neighbor' atmosphere of former days. Even here, in the place of high culture, everybody saw an enemy in everybody else.

"Well, we got our tickets, we got in to hear *The Twilight of the Gods*. I shed tears, as I used to do, and was very ashamed, but Lulu didn't. After the opera, I said good-by to her and I went home, and on the way home, at night, I understood what I call the disintegration. There were the heroic gods. They set fire to the whole world, yet they did it for great things, for heroic deeds, for love—for this beautiful thing, love! And how is it with us? We fight for tickets, we fight for pennies. It is these ugly little small things that break us down. And I went there along the Alster with its big mansions and villas. A few were beautifully painted and well cared for, but most of them were ugly looking. And you could just see those beautiful ones were the homes of those who profiteered from inflation, and the others were the losers. There you had two Germanys, the *nouveau riche,* the profiteers, and the old good society that was going down.

"It was all so mixed up with money. We used to consider money as nothing, and we said, 'Money is dirty,' and 'One doesn't speak about money.' And now here everything was mixed up with money and with small sums only and small things, and everybody was going against everybody else.

"So the conception of a German mission, that I once had, went to pieces before my very eyes.

"Oh, yes, I forgot to tell you about the foreigners. Standing there in line for the opera tickets Lulu told me, 'By the way, we are moving next month.' I said, 'You are moving? From your beautiful house? But why?' Lulu said, 'My father has had great losses.' Her father had imported all kinds of fancy things from the Balkan States—gadgets, you would call them. He had now, however, to pay for them in valuta and could only sell them in paper marks in Germany, so he had lost so much money that he had to sell their house and they had to move into a small apartment.

"I saw then that there were foreigners, too, who lost money. As Lulu put it to me, 'Now, I am really part of you because I have the same fate that you have.'

"At this time of our great disintegration, the news came that Grandmother was going to die, and Mother went to the Rhineland to stay with her for the last days. While she was away I had summer vacation, and I was much in the garden. And, as was natural in those days, I was more thoughtful than ever before. Thinking of Grandmother and being quite aware of my always longing to go back there, I had a feeling that all my opposition was not a longing, actually, for new things, but a longing to go back to the safe old way which was no more. The new things I wanted to happen were really a longing for old things to come back. Yet, with Grandmother dying, they couldn't come back. Even the house, to which Grandmother had said I could always come back, wasn't Grandmother's house any more—it belonged now to a Dutchman. . . .

"Well, after four weeks Mother came back. She told us what was happening in Cologne. She had visited one of Grandmother's sisters who owned a big textile factory there. This factory was taken over by the occupation army. Mother had always said when mentioning her, 'The poor dear! How she must suffer!' Yet, now we learned that this family got so much compensation that they were soon starting to build a new, modern factory.

"Father immediately said, 'Well, now I know where our money is going.' Mother said, 'But that has nothing to do with our money.' Father said, 'Who do you think pays them? Do you think the Allies? No, our own government has to pay for it. And from what do you think they pay? From our money—from our taxes and from our inflated war bonds!'

"You see, the war had been paid mostly not by taxes, but by war loans. Almost all the savings of the small and middle-class people had got into war bonds during the war. Who pays for a war? Internationally, the vanquished nation is supposed to pay; actually it is the people with their war bonds—and in Germany these war bonds were being devaluated until we could paper our walls with the bills. . . ."

FAMILY CRISES AND THE REALITIES OF LIFE

BUCK (continued)

"Mother's own financial affairs looked bad too. Most of her inheritance was gone when Grandmother's houses were lost. Now the factory was to be sold. Her brother, my uncle Richard, had tried hard to bring the factory back to normal but, as Father said, 'Even if he had been a trained businessman he could not have saved the factory.' Why? Because he had not enough money to overhaul the old machines and to buy new and better ones. Oh, the son of Mother's friends, who had bought Uncle Richard's farm, did finally arrive in South America and found everything in order; and his parents did pay the sum that was due to Uncle Richard—in devaluated paper marks. Only, the prices for machines were now four times higher than at the time when Uncle Richard signed the contract for the sale of his farm. The money he got was therefore in reality but one-fourth of the money he had expected to get. Thus he could not buy the machines he wanted and he could not compete with the new machines which were on their way to big factories like those of our Cologne relatives. So the factory was sold at a terrible loss compared with the value it once had. Mother had even to renounce her share in the factory so that her brother, who had married in the meantime, could buy tickets to South America—which had to be paid for in dollars! In return for her share in the factory Mother was to get the remainder of Grandmother's fortune: money which had been invested in England, and had been confiscated during the war. This she would get if and when the British were ready to free these accounts, or if and when our government would decide to compensate its citizens for their losses. Mother was certain that some day she would get her money.

"Well, to end the story of my uncle Richard, I have to say that he returned to his former ranch but as the employee of the new owner. It seemed very unjust.

"Hitler later on said that the Treaty of Versailles was but 'a piece of paper.' Well, those words that were so shocking to the whole world were not so shocking for those millions who had seen their money, their savings, their contracts become but pieces of paper. And Hitler knew with his instinct for the emotional reactions that his words would remind the people of what had happened to them during inflation and would fill them with rage. That is why Hitler used exactly the words 'a piece of paper.'

"Now, Mother had still the two houses which she had taken over as part of Father's business. These houses, however, were troublesome. If, for instance, a window broke, the replacement of the window now would cost more than all the rent she got in, because rents had ceiling prices while windows had not. One year later, by the way, the price of a new window would be higher than the price of the whole house. Mother wanted to sell these houses.

"But Father was very much against selling Mother's houses. He said, 'Let the houses go to pieces; later you can sell them, after the inflation is over, and you can still get some good money out of it. And the rent you get from the houses is just the rent you have to pay here.' Naturally our rent couldn't be raised either.

"But there was Hilde. She wanted to marry, she wanted to have her trousseau. Mother had some things from Grandmother, good linen and table silver, but Hilde wanted more. You see, her mother-in-law didn't like the marriage. She thought that her son could have married a richer girl. She was a very funny woman—so small and childlike—and you could see that she had been used to be a doll rather than somebody—"

"Who was she?" I asked.

"Robert's mother? She was a Danish woman who had married a rich German merchant. Well, she was very upset about her son's marriage, and so Hilde said, 'I can't come before her unless I have a good trousseau.' Mother agreed to this. Father said, 'Well, if Robert can't get along with his mother, he should marry a girl whom his mother loves, or else be master.'

"But Mother thought Hilde was right and she decided to sell the houses, anyhow, and to buy the trousseau.

"While all this inflation went on through many years, in between were times when the mark seemed to stop devaluating, and each time we people got a bit hopeful. People would say, 'The worst seems over now.' In such a time Mother sold the houses. It looked as if she had made a good business deal, for she got twice as much cash as she had paid. But the furniture she bought for Hilde had gone up five times in price and the little money that was left Mother put in a savings account. The worst was not over. Soon inflation started again with new vigor and swallowed bit by bit the savings accounts of Mother and of millions of others.

"Mother had, however, still another reason why she insisted on selling the houses. Something terrible had happened in one of them. An old couple lived in one of them whose two sons had been killed during the war. In their good days they had saved for their old age. Now their savings were devaluated and they had no sons to care for them. So one night they gassed themselves. Their bodies were found the next morning. Mother had previously threatened to put them on the street because they could not pay the rent. Although she hadn't done it, now she felt terrible pangs of guilt.

"And then Mother, who had never dreamed in her whole life, had her first nightmare. She dreamed that she was drowning in the sea, only the sea was not of water but of stones. Next morning she was still so upset that she told me her dream. It was amazing, indeed, because she never had had a dream before and had always insisted that to be upset about a dream is quite silly.

"Lotte came home in the fall, full of courage and energy. If Mother had hoped she would be ready to conform to her wishes, she was quite wrong. Lotte was more set than ever on her dancing lessons. She did not go back to our father's office. She found a job in another office and again took her evening lessons in dancing.

"That went on for a month. Then one night Lotte came and said, 'Tomorrow we will have a visitor here.' I said, 'What visitor?' Lotte said, 'Juergen.' I said, 'Who is Juergen?' Lotte said, 'He is my friend.' 'Does Mother know anything of it?' I asked. 'No, you silly girl,' Lotte said. So here was quite a mess. What were we going to do about it? I said, 'Why haven't you prepared Mother?' She said, 'I just hadn't the courage. He is a painter—an artist.' I said, 'Oh, well, that looks bad! Does he have money?' 'No, he hasn't.' 'Is he of a good family?' 'His father was a peasant.' I said, 'Well, you will never get Mother to receive him into our house.' Lotte said, 'But I have to—I just have to!' Then I said, 'How do you know that he comes tomorrow?' Lotte said, 'He wrote me that he was coming to Hamburg, and I wrote him that my mother invited him to come to our house.' I said, 'Where did you get that letter?' 'Poste restante,' she replied. Now, that was for us a decline in morals—terrible! And I said, 'Couldn't you meet him even once secretly, and tell him how difficult Mother is?' Lotte said, 'You may be afraid of Mother—but Mother is nothing. What I am afraid of is myself.'

"Then she told me she had met Juergen in the little town where she was in school. It had happened in a little café when she had sat reading a book of poems and he had been interested in her book and so they talked and then they had walked together, and he had asked whether she would pose for him. And she had gone to his studio and he had painted her, and she had always wanted him to kiss her. But when he really tried to kiss her, she had slapped his face and run away. Then she regretted it. She wanted to see him. She had met him several times after that but she had not dared to go to his studio any more.

"Lotte had a very cynical way of expressing things. She said, 'Well, you know, that is what men are. They begin with poems and beautiful speeches and at the bottom it is every time the same. What do you think he said to me—that I am made to have a dozen children! So that is what it comes to—'

"I said, 'Don't you want children?' Lotte said, 'Naturally I want children, but only after I have finished my dancing lessons and I have done something.'

"So next day at the breakfast table she said, 'Mother, I am having a visitor this afternoon—a man called Mr. Sachs. I met him near the school and I have told him that you want to see him.' And then she was in a hurry to go to her office. Mother, knowing that Lotte and I were good friends, wanted to know more about it from me. Lotte left the whole mess to me. I told her only that Lotte had met him and wanted Mother to know him. Mother saw that she could do nothing against this visit.

"So Juergen came late in the afternoon. He was very tall, with water-blue eyes, reddish hair, very strong bone structure. He walked like a peasant with a very heavy step. He didn't fit anywhere in our family. But he came into the salon and Mother offered him a chair, and he just sat there with a folder with drawings on his knees and looking very uncomfortable. Lotte looked at me mockingly, and Mother was embarrassed, and Father asked him about his family. He answered questions shortly and never helped a bit in getting a conversation going. So at last Mother asked to see the drawings and he showed them to her. I was terribly interested in them because they were drawings from an old German saga, Wotan and Siegfried. I remember very well a picture of Seigfried, and this Siegfried looked just like Juergen—so strong.

"And then Juergen pulled out his last drawing. It was an illustration of Dante's *Inferno*. You know—'He who enters here has no hope to leave.' He had painted the earth as if it had been brutally cut to pieces and split all over; and there was but one tree left, bare and forlorn; its two branches stretched out toward the sky as if in endless mourning. It was so terribly desperate. Even Mother became silent.

"And then Juergen said, 'Yes, that is war. Only city people can do this to nature.' So he had been in the war and he made city people responsible for everything that had happened! He felt as a peasant and was convinced that peasants could never have done that to the earth and to the trees and to nature.

"Lotte said, in her cynical way, 'You know, Juergen is quite an amazing person. He says he can only paint if he feels the creative soil under his naked feet.' She wanted to help him—but he was hurt too, and he felt subdued by her.

"Mother was impressed by his drawings but she did not like him. 'He doesn't know how to behave,' she said after he had left and she did not want him to come to her house again. But Mother could only forbid him her house. She could not forbid her daughter to go out and meet him. Father warned her, 'Better receive him here or else Lotte will meet him elsewhere.' But Mother was, as always, certain that she knew her daughters better than anyone else. She said, 'Lotte is not really interested in him.'

"Well, Father did know his daughter better. Lotte and Juergen met elsewhere until he left Hamburg and went to Berlin.

"And then came Christmas! Hilde had come home to prepare for her wedding, which was to be in a few weeks. And then Robert came. And Hilde made a terrible fuss about Robert and her trousseau and her wedding. Lotte called her 'the Queen,' and was angry at Juergen, who did not write letters to her; she called him 'that idiot.' On Christmas Eve she went to a party at her dancing school and didn't come home all the night. She came home the next morning at nine o'clock.

"Now, I haven't to tell you what a tragedy that was in our home! I am still sure that nothing happened to Lotte but a nice dancing party with drinking and a few kisses maybe. Father believed so, too. But Mother was absolutely convinced that a girl who stayed out all night had done more than innocent things. 'Lotte has to leave my house immediately,' she said—to Father.

"While Father and Mother thus argued, Lotte slept. She slept through the morning, slept through noon, slept through the afternoon. Father and I went out for a walk. When we came home Lotte was gone."

"Gone?" I exclaimed.

"Gone," Erna repeated gravely. "Two days later a wire came from Berlin—'Juergen and I engaged.'

"Well, Lotte might have married her Juergen anyhow, but there is one thing I am sure of. When I urged her to postpone her marriage at least until she had got her diploma, so that she could give lessons, earn money, and be independent if she wanted to, she replied scornfully, 'Earn money! Ridiculous! Our money isn't worth earning!'

"Yes, life is a hard fight; we women have all too often the easy escape into marriage. I think this is one of the reasons why so few women are ever in higher positions. Men haven't this easy escape; they have to fight it out."

"As I told you," Erna began the next morning, "I have always divided the years of inflation in Germany into the time of disintegration, and the time of formation of the fronts. Naturally, this division is a bit forced, since they merge with one another. But, on the whole, at first the disintegration was more in the foreground, and then the building of the fronts came more in the foreground.

"One sign of the disintegration of the good families was Mother's consent to Lotte's engagement to Juergen. When her wire arrived, Mother said, 'Better to have her married even to Juergen than to come home some day with a bastard.' She said this in the presence of all of us.

"It seems incredible, yet it is true. You know, at that time, many a daughter of good families ran away with a man, and more than one natural child was born in the circle around our family. This was not only the aftermath of the war; it was due even more to inflation. The daughters of the good families could no longer get dowries; yet the young men who came home from war were not on a solid footing and they were more than ever dependent on dowries if they wanted to marry. The parents had still the old idea that a marriage had to be economically secure from the beginning. And, as Lotte and her girl friends used to say, 'If we wait until there is security in this world we must wait until we have no teeth and no hair!' The strongest impetus for many girls was to get away from their mothers, no matter how or with whom. The first man who offered a chance was the one with whom they went away, either marrying him or not." . . .

"I had written a little play when Grandmother died but I no longer believed in the ideas I had put into it. I wanted to write a new play, one that was to be more realistic!

"I spoke about it with Lulu. I said, 'I have a new idea for a play about a woman who seems beautiful and good, but behind her mask, she is evil.' Lulu said, 'That is a wonderful idea—a devil fights inside every one of us.'

"I looked at her. 'Once I would have thought your conception wonderful. But now I am not thinking of the good and evil within us. It is not even a question of guilt. It is the ordinary conditions of our life that make a woman evil.' So I replied.

"I was, in a half-conscious way, thinking of Mother. Yes, the values she had which we had accepted for such a long time made her, in this world of ours, the destructive power. I have told you the story of the house. Why, for instance, did she press this old couple that committed suicide to pay the rent or move out? It was only because she wanted to give her daughter a dowry, believing still in the old notions of how a daughter should be married. All my life now I am pursued by this idea, this conflict of the so-called good things. If we stick to them at the wrong time they can destroy other things, even human lives.

"I tried to write that play but I felt more and more convinced that I could only write realistically if and when I learned the 'realities of life.' This phrase was hammered into my head daily when Father came home, telling his womenfolks that he had to face the realities of life while we could enjoy it.

"He was, as you know, one of the very privileged people who earned in Swiss francs and had started his fish business in order to become 'independent from the fate of the German mark.' This independence, however, applied only to his business with Swiss customers, who made up but a small part of it, the much larger part dealing with German customers. Had business been as usual, his profits from his German business would have been far greater than that from Switzerland. Business, however, was not at all as usual and his small profits in Swiss francs amounted to a considerable sum, counted in German marks, while the profits from his business with German customers often enough amounted to nothing. Why? Father had explained it to Mother at the dinner table while Mother tried to listen patiently. He said he was 'surrounded by enemies.' There were, for instance, the big wholesalers, mostly shipowners, who brought the fish in and sold it only for payment in cash. Father, however, and all his fellow fish dealers gave credits of eight to ten weeks to the small fish dealers all over the country, as had been usual for generations.

"Father would come home and tell Mother, 'Today the customer from Frankfurt has paid his bill.' 'Good,' said Mother. 'There is nothing good about it,' said Father. 'When I sent him the fish, I had to pay five hundred marks for a hundred pounds; today I have to pay five hundred and seventy-five marks for the same amount of fish. And where is my profit? Gone with the wind! It is about time that I drop the whole German business and concentrate on the Swiss market.' Mother said, 'But why don't you stop giving credit?'

" 'Because,' Father replied with impatience, 'we live in a system of free competition and if I stopped giving credit while others go on I would only lose my customers. I tell you, free competition is a sound basis for business; the only trouble is that we have to pay cash to the wholesalers.' Mother said, 'Why don't you stop paying cash?' To that Father had but one answer: 'Because we of the middle class are not organized against the wholesalers while the workers are organized against us.'

"From there on he would go on complaining about the workers who constantly asked for 'the adjustment of their wages to the price increases,' who were, moreover, constantly demonstrating and every other week striking so that 'law and order' were far from being restored at the Hamburg port.

"The Holzmans came to visit us. 'What Germany needs,' Father said to Mr. Holzman, 'is a sound and healthy middle class, and what the middle class needs is a strong middle-class party.' Mr. Holzman, a member of the Social Democratic party, said, 'It would be wiser for you to side with the workers against the monopolies.' Father replied, 'Good, if only the workers would side with us instead of striking against us.'

"The Von Bülows, Mother's friends from the German Far East Asia Club,* also came to visit us, and Father repeated, 'What Germany needs is a sound and healthy middle class and what the middle class needs is a strong middle-class party.' To this, Mr. von Bülow, member of the German National party, the party of the old reactionary group, replied, 'We have already more than enough parties as it is. Why don't you side with us? We shall see that the law and order are restored at the port.' Father said, 'But who guarantees us that you won't swallow us after we have checked the workers?'

"Well, I must say that the argument became so heated after that remark that Mother thought it wise to suggest a game of cards. But that was, and is, the position of the middle class—squeezed between the two big classes of big business and the workers. As long as the pie of national wealth and income is big enough to provide everyone with a decent piece, this is no problem. But in Germany the pie was no longer big enough; it was much too small and the struggle for every piece of it was hard and bitter.

"Still, Father was not ready to side with the reactionaries against the workers; he hated the old ruling class too deeply and too bitterly for that, *and he saw, clearly enough, that once you side with them against the workers you may be the one who will be swallowed at the end.* So he said the republic should restore law and order—by force, if necessary. He had no objection to the use of the police force against the striking workers. . . ."

*[It was something of a tradition in German conservative and nationalist circles to form private clubs to discuss and to popularize German foreign policy objectives, generally in an unashamedly imperialistic spirit. Apparently, the German Far East Asia Club belonged to this category of associations. Ed.]

ECONOMIC CONTRASTS AND POLITICAL CHOICES

BUCK (continued)

"A few days after Lotte's marriage I went to the peasants. My mother had found an advertisement in one of her home family magazines about a peasant woman looking for company for her daughter, who was about my age. As this advertisement was in one of her home family magazines she thought that it must be a good family and she decided to write. Well, we'll call this family Meyer. She wrote to Mrs. Meyer. Mrs. Meyer lived near Mecklenburg. She wrote back that she would be delighted to have me. She had a daughter only half a year older than I, and it was settled that I was to go there. . . .

"I did not come closer to Kathe for about two weeks. Although we many times went up on our hill, she was reserved. But one day she had time in the afternoon and her mother said we should go and see the country. So we took a walk. As I told you, it was very flat country. You could see the horizon far away. While looking at it, I remembered Father, who had called the country the 'paradise of inflation,' and I wondered what the peasants were doing with all their money which we, in the cities, paid them for food. I asked Kathe, 'What do you do with all the money you get?'

" 'We are paying off our mortgages,' she replied.

" 'And do you buy more land?' I asked.

"Kathe shook her head. 'As long as I have lived here no land has been sold. The peasants who sell their land must really be of very low character. No sound peasant would ever sell land.' . . .

"I received letters from Mother and Father. In each of his letters Father asked, 'How do you like the paradise of inflation?' Well, I liked it, yet it was very strange for me, who came from the city where all was going down, to see how good times came back to the peasants. They really started life again. True, they did it at the expense of the cities; they did it by paying off their mortgages in devaluated marks; they did it by price increases for which we had to pay. But I thought of the city mostly when I received Father's letter, and I forgot all about it when Kathe showed me the new barn or when she spoke about her cows. They had had twenty-two cows before the war; during the war they had come down to eight because they could not get enough fodder and had to slaughter them. Now they were up to sixteen cows again and they hoped, in two more years, to be up to twenty-two. . . .

"I went back to the city. Well, coming from the country, the very sight of the city brought me down. It was not only that in a city you have no air and no wide view. It was that the houses showed the decline. Nobody could think of painting a house, of renewing anything but the most urgent for safety's sake. The people in the city looked gloomy and worried. There was no gaiety in the city. The talk in the family was about prices going up, about the credits which had to be reduced, about the middle-class party, about big business and the workers who always asked for more. It was really like coming back to another world. The contrast between country and city was so enormous that it cannot be understood by people who have not lived through it. . . .

"Robert wanted to enjoy life; it was so much more sensible to spend the money than to save it. Time and again, he invited Hilde to go with him to Berlin and have fun. Hilde always refused. Finally he gave up—not his trips to Berlin but asking Hilde to accompany him. While I was there, he went to Berlin for two days. When he came home, he brought a new hit song with him. It ran: 'We are drinking up our grandma's little hut and the first and the second mortgage, too.' Well, mortgages of two thousand, three thousand marks you could drink up easily. I could not help laughing about it, while Hilde cried and ran out of the room. Robert first looked puzzled, then he said to me, 'You know, Hilde is just how women ought to be. But it's madness to save, nowadays.' Saving is the very source of wealth and health of a sound nation. But, we were no longer a sound nation. We were on our way to become a crazy, a neurotic, a mad nation. . . .

"I want you for a moment to see the fish market. I had seen the fish, the people, and all the very picturesque and romantic life going on there. But now, having been a pupil of the Lichtwark School,* I saw it with other eyes.

"It was after the hour of the main market; the bosses were gone, the employees were busy packing things away. I saw an old couple, buying

*[A reform movement in German education, which began in the 1890's, acquired public prominence, along with some official support, during the Weimar period. Most of the reformers were interested in a socially less stratified school system. They also hoped to make education less passive and authoritarian, less routinized and esoteric, and more relevant to contemporary realities. Some of the reformers were extreme cultural nationalists, perhaps even racists; others held more liberal views. Many of them meant to give students a more active role in classroom discussions, so that they might acquire the spirit of a voluntary "working community." Experimental schools which were founded with such objectives naturally seemed vaguely progressive, modern, and democratic, when compared with the traditional school system. Erna von Pustau's Lichtwark School probably belonged to this group of progressive institutions. It was named after the reformer Alfred Lichtwark (1852–1914), who had been particularly interested in popular art education. Ed.]

some bones, and I saw the woman look at a bone on which a bit of meat was still hanging, not losing sight of it for a moment while it was wrapped. Such an intense and stern look I had never seen. I saw some children, with happy faces, putting a little money on the table and getting onions and a few potatoes. I saw three dirty boys buying some meat and putting a little money on the table and then running away and from a safe distance sticking their tongues out. And then I understood what was going on. I remembered Eddie's grudge against capitalists and capitalism. But I saw too that everyone was a prisoner of the system. The employee, being paid a salary which was by no means adjusted to the price increases, sold more than the reasonable amount of his bosses' goods. He didn't bargain much. You could see that he felt very benevolently toward those who were in greater need than he and from whom he extracted the deficit amount of his unadjusted salary.

"It was a sad world, a world in which none was better than the other; and all was a matter of chance and degree. A sad world, and a sad conception for a girl who still remembered the good old times of Grandmother! Our times made us cynical. . . .

"Inflation, however, was going now at such a rate that one day one dollar was worth a thousand marks, next month two thousand marks, and next month four thousand marks.

"The end of the year came. I had set a price for my private lessons, which the mother of the pupil increased a bit only after bitter struggles, and not at all according to the increase in prices. By the end of the year my allowance and all the money I earned were not worth one cup of coffee. You could go to the baker in the morning and buy two rolls for twenty marks; but go there in the afternoon, and the same two rolls were twenty-five marks. The baker didn't know how it happened that the rolls were more expensive in the afternoon. His customers didn't know how it happened. It had somehow to do with the dollar, somehow to do with the stock exchange—and somehow, maybe, to do with the Jews. Anti-Semitism was growing tremendously. 'Stock exchange' and 'Jews' were very much connected in the minds of the people, and when the anti-Semitic propaganda said, 'It is the Jews,' people were ready to believe it. Looking around for the guilty ones, in a situation which nobody really understood, made those who lost their fortune, especially the middle class, ready prey for anti-Semitic propaganda.

"I gave up my private lessons, convinced that I could not earn money by honest means. Father began to speak against the Jews more and more.

"He used to say, 'There are two kinds of capital; one is creative capital, the other is parasitical. Creative capital is where a man works; parasitical capital is the capital on which a man gets interest. Creative capital is the capital we Germans have, parasitical capital is the capital of the Jews.'

"I thought this very silly and I said, 'Now, Father, where did you pick up that theory?' He said, 'I bought a pamphlet on the fish market.' It was a well-known pamphlet by Feder, one of the Nazis.

" 'Well,' I said to Father with utter contempt in my voice, 'since when do you pick up your ideas on the fish market?' Father replied, 'Since I have to work in the fish market to earn a living for you.'

"He spoke more and more at mealtimes about these things. Mother sometimes said something about Shakespeare and Shylock, and 'maybe there is something in it.' Then Father came with a new slogan—'We are the serfs of the Jews.' The more he repeated it the more I worried, because until now I had not heard the conception of Jews as parasites. So I decided to face Father. I said, 'Your theory is really silly—give me one proof of it.'

"Father said, 'I can give you the proof. Where did I get the money for my business—from the Jew Holzman!' 'Father,' I said, 'it was pure friendship, and you were so happy and so thankful about it.' He said, 'But now I have to pay interest to him on the gold value of the mark, while I lose money. If I have to pay him his interest at the beginning of next year, as I have to do, I will have nothing left.' 'But, Father,' I said, 'I remember that you said it was the usual way of business to make a gold clause in the contract.'

"Father was getting impatient. 'But I looked at it then in a different way,' he said. 'Now I work hard, get up at six o'clock in the morning and come home late and where does the money go? To the Jews!'

"I said, 'But Mother gave you capital, too, and don't you pay her interest?' Father said, 'That has nothing to do with the Holzmans.'

"I thought it was just the same but there was no arguing with him.

"Then I said to Mother, 'Mother, you know the Holzmans are in a very difficult situation. Mr. Holzman is going to lose his sight and Mrs. Holzman is the best friend you ever had, the only one who stood by you when we had difficult times.'

"And then Mother said to Father, 'Well, Paul, I think in this case you have gone too far. Maybe there is something right in what you say about the Jews, but don't mention my friends Holzman in this connection any more.'

"I spoke with Wolfgang about it. I met him in a café. I still did not see Wolfgang the way he really was. I still saw him as one of the pupils of this Lichtwark School, and I thought that he was naturally as upset as I was. I said, 'Wolfgang, I am very, very worried about the anti-Semitism.' He said, 'Why are you worried?' I said, 'Because it is going on even in my family, and how can I look Heinz Schaefer in the eyes, who is one of the best friends I have? Besides, it is terribly silly.'

"Said Wolfgang, 'Well, why is it silly? For instance, Mother just recently told that the Jewish women wear silk stockings.' 'My own sister Lotte loves to wear silk stockings, and she is not a Jew,' I cried.

"Wolfgang said, 'There are so many "antis"—anti-left, anti-Jew, anti-right, anti-bolshevism, and anti-reactionary, so that this is only one "anti" of many "antis"!'

"I said, 'This is different, and I'll tell you why it is different. I can argue about political things, but here I cannot argue any more. You should have known my father as he used to be. The political education I had before I came to this school I got from him, and I learned so many things from him. He explained to me things against the Kaiser, and our parliament. But now he has stopped thinking and reasoning, and this will do more damage to us than it will ever damage the Jews.'

"I could say this with good conscience because at that time nobody could have foreseen the bloody anti-Semitism that was to come. It was still only a way of talking.

"Wolfgang said, 'I am sure it will get better. The little man must have something to cling to, you know, and anti-Semitism gives him a kind of superior feeling which he no longer has in any other way.'

"To end this I want to say that when the time to pay the interest came, Holzman made a very fair compromise with Father, before Father even mentioned it. Father acknowledged the fairness. Excluding the Holzmans, however, he went on with his anti-Semitic talk.

"We have now to come back to the most difficult national questions. In the beginning of 1923 came the Ruhr occupation. The formal reason given was that we had been short of some telegraph poles in our reparations payments. The Allies marched into the Ruhr in the midst of 'peace,' and united Germany, from the communists to the fascists, into one united front. The big Ruhr industrialists were imprisoned together with the workers. Some of the big-business men even made a big gesture and said, 'We want to be in the same jail with our workers, we do not want to have any special jail.'

"Our only weapon against the invasion of the Ruhr was peaceful resistance, striking. Yet all the slogans of the war came back. When I told you that in 1914, we spoke more in verses than in prose, now this was true again—our language became very poetic, and all the old patriotic songs were sung. That was seemingly a small thing, but it was symbolic.

"Great campaigns for money to help the Ruhr were going on. Even Father gave money. Our tenant had to give, too, since Mother insisted on it. Clothes were collected. The coal shortage began. We had cold houses again, but we were willing to suffer cold for our fatherland.

"At home, Mother was now really coming out. 'There—you see what happens if we don't have weapons—we have to have weapons again, we have to rearm, we have to be as strong as others or else we are at the mercy of our enemies, who want nothing else but to enslave us as soon as they can.' Father, who had not been interested in foreign policy for a long time, now went with my mother to a meeting of the Committee for Germans Abroad and came back very impressed, and said, 'Well, it would be good to have an army.' . . .

"With the Ruhr occupation, the mark went down even more. Father had tried to organize the fish market. Organize against whom? Against big business which asked for cash payment? That had once been his idea. But big business was much too strong. Father now 'united the fish market' to 'stand up as one man'—against the small store keepers all over the country. No more credits were given to them—they would have to pay first and then get their fish.

"Anticapitalist feeling was strong everywhere, and in this fish market episode Father saw himself as a true socialist, one who 'acted instead of talking.' What he had done was merely to return to the medieval guild system, when each guild made protective laws for itself and against everybody else. But Father benefited, at least, and for the first time since he had become 'a free and independent' man, he could go for a vacation. He took Mother along, and I was left at home—with millions of marks at my disposal, and permission to go to the movies if I wanted to!

"Actually, I didn't want to take Father's money even to go to a movie. We were growing more and more out of sympathy by that time. So I got money by another means. I sold some stamps he had once given me. From one set especially I made a lot—the stamps of our lost colonies. I took Wolfgang to the theater and had a wonderful evening—there were still times when we thought ourselves in love—and with what was left of the money I bought a pair of shoes, which I badly needed. But it was wrong of me, for although the stamps were a gift, certainly Father would not have thought me free to sell them. I suppose my callousness about this was just part of the general moral decay.

"When Father came back from vacation, he saw that the workers had discovered the 'trick of inflation,' which was to figure the value of money in gold. Time and again the workers struck for the 'adjustment of their wages.' After their strikes, their wages had been adjusted—to the actual price increases. But the price increases went on and so the workers had to strike again for new adjustments. What they asked for now was wages paid daily in exact accordance with the daily mark devaluation. Strikes followed strikes; the port, the workers' districts were seething with unrest. The closer the workers came to their goal, the quicker the mark raced down. June, 1923: one dollar equaled a hundred thousand marks; July, 1923: one dollar equaled two million marks; August, 1923: one dollar equaled one hundred million. What a time! What a race!

"The printing presses of the government could no longer keep pace. They were still printing ten-thousand-mark bills when one dollar had gone into the millions of marks. You could see mail carriers on the streets with sacks on their backs or pushing baby carriages before them, loaded with paper money that would be devaluated the next day. Life was madness, nightmare, desperation, chaos.

"The government struggled hard to restore the gold standard. But— the Minister of Finance was the socialist Hilferding! Big business was ready, now, to restore the gold standard; but the whole reactionary clique, including the 'Green Front' of agriculture, peasants, and Junkers, wanted to be given the credit for restoring sound and solid money. So they made an offer and a threat: either Hilferding must resign and one of their men take over the Ministry of Finance, or else they would not stop inflation. 'We'll see who can hold out longer— you or we,' they said.

"While this struggle went on, chaos increased. The Middle Ages came back. Communities printed their own money, based on goods, on a certain amount of potatoes, of rye, for instance. Shoe factories paid their workers in bonds for shoes which they could exchange at the bakery for bread or the meat market for meat.

"At this stage, the Communists believed that their time had come. They attempted an uprising. It began in Saxony, on October twenty-third. It was plain the very next day that it could not succeed, for the people had only one longing, for order, and only one dread, of further chaos. The Communist party sent couriers into all parts of Germany to call off the uprising which they had planned to spread all over the Reich. For some reason, however, the courier to Hamburg arrived too late, and so we in Hamburg had a Communist uprising.

"We did not notice it until the morning, when the streetcars stopped running. But we had our bicycles, and so Father rode to business and I rode to school. School was closed, and I rode right back home through streets which were crowded with people walking to work in silence, sometimes stopping, as if undecided whether to go on or to return home. I was almost disappointed. I had had a very different idea of strikes and disorders—with a great deal of noise and speeches at every street corner. But there was nothing like that to be seen. . . .

"Well, the uprising in Hamburg was over in a few days, and all over the country the leaders of the Communist party were arrested. Yet, at the coming election, in the spring of 1924, the Communist party increased from half a million votes to three and a half million votes. But I will tell you of the Communists later, when I tell you of the depression and the fateful division within the working class. At the end of inflation, I did not know much about the Communists. It was sometimes whispered at our school that two of our teachers were siding with them but at home we considered Communists dangerous criminals and knowing none, I had the idea that they must look quite different from any other human being, somehow wild and furious. Why, they wanted civil war! No, I didn't want to have anything to do with war, be it international or civil war.

"Shortly after this uprising in Hamburg Hilferding had to resign. The new Finance Minister was Dr. Hjalmar Schacht, who later became Hitler's finance expert, providing him with the financial means for rearmament and war. But at that time, when the 'honor' of restoring a sound and solid mark was given to him, he called himself a democrat!

"While the gold standard was being restored, we had another uprising, this time in Munich, where Hitler and his gang 'putsched.' Munich was far away from Hamburg. The Putsch made headlines in the newspapers for a few days, then it was all over. It was called the 'Beer Cellar Putsch,' because Hitler had his 'headquarters' in a beer cellar. He marched with his followers through the streets of Munich, Ludendorff at his side—our General Ludendorff who had so cowardly fled Germany in the days of the defeat! When the shooting began, Hitler was the first to run away.

"Mother, reading the headlines about the Putsch, said, 'That can only happen in Bavaria where the Catholics are.' We of the Lichtwark School laughed at the 'beer cellar hero.' He and many of his leaders were soon jailed and we thought all would be over. I should have known better because I heard Father say of Hitler and his gang, 'They are the young generation, the front soldiers generation, and we will hear more of them. They are still young and act foolishly, but they will grow up. If they will only drop Ludendorff and his kind, maybe some day I'll even give them a chance.'

"You see how the minds of the middle-class people were prepared during inflation? Father was not an exception. At the spring elections in 1924 when the National Socialist party put up its own candidates for the first time it got two million votes!

"So little is known here in America of this preparation of the minds of the people for fascism, during inflation, that I have told you as much about it as I can. Inflation is the source of fascism, and not only in Germany. And the preparation of the minds is the beginning. Let us not forget the French saying, 'It is the first step that counts.'

"Before I tell you, however, of the 'happy time of solid money and prosperity' that lay before us, let us once more look back at the battle-field of inflation and the Republic. For a battle it was, this inflation, fought out with financial means. The cities were still there, the houses not yet bombed and in ruins, but the victims were millions of people. They had lost their fortunes, their savings; they were dazed and inflation-shocked and did not understnd how it had happened to them and who the foe was who had defeated them. Yet they had lost their self-assurance, their feeling that they themselves could be the masters of their own lives if only they worked hard enough; and lost, too, were the old values of morals, of ethics, of decency. Would prosperity last long enough to restore them?"

V
CENSUS DATA AND ELECTION RETURNS

Precise information about the aggregate social consequences of the inflation is not available to us. We have encountered generalizations about the disadvantages suffered by creditors, small shopkeepers, various salaried occupations, and other economic groups. Many of these generalizations have been based upon logical inferences rather than upon direct empirical information. We have also read various eye-witness accounts, reports which are valuable especially for the light they throw upon men's feelings and rationalizations during the crisis. On the other hand, some of these accounts have been purely impressionistic.

If we were to increase considerably the scope of our investigation, we could certainly improve the quality of our evidence to some extent. We could comb statistical sources for further clues to the fate of the various segments of German society. We could look for records on actual bank deposits, on the buying and selling of stocks, on the number and size of retail stores, on bankruptcies, and so forth. We would be interested in everything from meat consumption and the proliferation of used furniture stores to the hoarding of foreign currencies. Scholars who have undertaken studies of this kind have been able to supply valuable details, particularly about the hardships of professional groups and the decline of the "old" burgher class of artisans and shopkeepers.* Yet all

---

* For example: Costantino Bresciani-Turroni, *The Economics of Inflation: A Study of Currency Depreciation in Post-War Germany, 1914–1923*, trans. M. E. Sayers (London: Allen & Unwin, 1937), esp. pp. 286–333; Rudolf Meerwarth, Adolf Günther, W. Zimmermann, *Die Einwirkungen des Krieges auf Bevölkerungsbe-*

such work necessarily depends upon elaborate arguments designed
to relate isolated but measurable phenomena to the general conditions that are to be described.

What we really need to answer all our questions is a series of
census reports for the years 1914–24 which list occupations, as well
as types and sizes of incomes, for all Germans. But here again we
encounter what might be called the principle of statistical pes-
simism. According to this principle, you can never find out exactly
what you want to know; available sources are never more than
indirectly relevant. Failure to understand this principle is the chief
cause of two common, apparently antithetical fallacies about the
use of statistics in history. One is an ignorant excess of reverence
for what "statistics prove." The other is an equally uninformed
sneering about the supposed simple-mindedness of statistical work.
Statistics, like other forms of historical evidence, must be interpreted; they do not speak for themselves. They limit the range of
possible interpretations: they must be "taken into account," and
that is no small matter. But they cannot eliminate the need for
qualitative models of human behavior, which is why fulminant
defenses of qualitative against quantitative methods in history so
often seem irrelevant.

We do not have the information we would like to have for the
years 1914–24; but we do have occupational census reports for
the years 1907 and 1925. These reports have three serious shortcomings from our point of view. They enclose a time period which
is much too long for us. They deal in rather crude occupational
categories, neglecting many of the distinctions we should like to
make. Finally, they tell us nothing about the types and sizes of incomes of Germans during our period.

The most serious of these deficiencies is the problem of the
time period. The inflation really began in 1914; but it did not
achieve the proportions of a social revolution until after 1920. The

---

wegung, Einkommen und Lebenshaltung in Deutschland [Wirtschafts- und Sozial-
geschichte des Weltkrieges, Deutsche Serie, general editor James T. Shotwell]
(Stuttgart, 1932), see esp. Adolf Günther, "Die Folgen des Krieges für Einkommen und Lebenshaltung der mittleren Volksschichten Deutschlands."

years 1907–14 witnessed a vigorous industrial expansion, which persisted in some respects until 1918. Moreover, the stabilization came in November 1923, so that the census for 1925 is actually more than a year too late for us. Thus only a part of the changes which occurred between 1907 and 1925 were consequences of the inflation itself. Some of them were undoubtedly due to continuing industrialization before 1914, while others may well have occurred during the months after the introduction of the *Rentenmark*. We are confronted with very serious problems of interpretation.

In dealing with these problems, we might begin by considering what census changes we would ordinarily anticipate during a period of rapid industrialization, and what shifts we would expect during a runaway inflation. Stolper has already given us some summary data pertaining to German industrialization before 1907. In principle—if we had the time, the expertise, and more complete census figures for the nineteenth century—we ought to be able to project roughly what occupational changes would have occurred by 1925, if there had been no inflation. In practice, such a task is beyond us. But we can make some educated guesses about the main trends in agriculture, industry, and commerce, and in the figures for self-employed, white-collar personnel, and workers. Stolper has shown that in some respects, the effects of the inflation resembled the changes attendant upon ordinary industrial concentration, though in an exaggerated and irrational form. He has also taught us to anticipate certain peculiarities of the inflationary process. Can we apply these ideas to our tables?

Quite apart from its long-term effects upon the occupational structure, the inflation caused a variety of short-term hardships which would have been visible in a 1923 census. Among the possible indicators of such distress, one might consider the proportion of the population in the labor force, the number of students living away from home, the count of family members helping on the parental farm, and the number of people drawing some sort of relief. (It might be noted here that even before 1925, many of the men listed under "rents" in the German census were not "rentiers" in the traditional sense; that is, they did not live comfortably and by choice on the income from their investments.) The question is should we expect to find such signs of acute economic hardship as late as 1925?

One has to remember that the social and psychological trauma of the stabilization was perhaps as great as the shock of the successive devaluations themselves. For many people, it was the stabilization which ended all hope, as it put the seal of permanence upon their losses. Besides, certain real costs in fact rose very suddenly at the currency reform. Tuition fees at the universities, for example, had never kept pace with the inflation itself. The cost of study therefore became almost negligible—until the stabilization simultaneously revealed the poverty of parents and made fees seem very high. Thus student enrollments at German universities did not decline until after the currency reform. Here was one case in which distress due to the inflation revealed itself after 1923. Different relationships may hold for other indicators. But it is hard to imagine that a year or two would suffice completely to erase even the short-term effects of so serious an economic dislocation.

The two other problems in the interpretation of the census stem from the crudeness of the categories and the lack of information about incomes. Obviously we would like to be able to distinguish the owner of a provincial blacksmith shop from one of the directors of a large industrial concern. However, our figures list both as being self-employed in industry. Such circumstances should cause us habitually to identify every census category with the most numerous among those it includes. We must be absolutely clear in our minds that there were many little artisans and shopkeepers for every Stinnes, and many petty clerks for every salaried junior executive. This seems obvious, and yet it is easily forgotten.

Beyond that, little can be done to increase the relevance of the census categories to the questions which really concern us. We could, again in principle, go back to the sources for more information. Ignoring the summary categories used by the German statisticians, we could try to work our way more deeply into the raw materials from which general results were computed. Several social historians have made such efforts and achieved some successes. But even the experts soon encounter the obstacles set by the limited availability of raw tabulations, and by the format of the original questionnaires.

Thus the imperfections of our data are nearly inescapable. We must use the reports with great caution. Still, it can be amusing as well as instructive to approach the census with some of the labels we have encountered in other sources. Where in these tables should we look for the "green front," the "producers," the lower middle class, the proleteriat, the "old" and the "new" middle classes, or the "steady middle class"? How about the groups whose fate was lamented by Schreiber, or the "good" Hamburg families regretted by Erna von Pustau's mother? Can we establish any consistent system of categories which would retain important distinctions and yet allow us to work with the census figures? These questions would be worth asking, even if they could not be answered with perfect clarity and precision. So perhaps we ought to transform the absolute number in the table into useful percentage ratios, and just see what we can make of the results.

In addition to the census for all Germany, the table describes occupational distributions for several regions, namely Hamburg, Rhenish Westphalia, East Prussia, Baden, and Southern Bavaria. This should enable us to infer the distinctive economic characteristics of these districts.

The northern city of Hamburg was one of the oldest and most important seaports and commercial centers in Germany. To the extent that the inflation harmed old, commercial, and financial capital more than industrial capital, we should expect Hamburg, Erna von Pustau's home, to have done rather badly during the 1920's. Rhenish Westphalia, by contrast, was and is a foremost center of heavy industry. The plains of East Prussia were the homeland of the junkers and of large agrarian estates, which were devoted to relatively capital-intensive cereal production. After the Treaty of Versailles, East Prussia was separated from the rest of Germany by

the so-called Polish Corridor. It was therefore in the position of a
border territory, and it probably harbored a good many paramilitary formations in 1925. Baden was a medium-sized southwestern
state, known for small agricultural holdings, some of them devoted
to the growing of vegetables, grapes, and other fruits. The lush hill
country of Baden was also dotted with handsome provincial towns,
in which one would expect to encounter a certain amount of light
industry. Southern Bavaria, which included Munich, encompassed
the south German subalpine region. There was much dairy farming
in that area, although the predominantly small agricultural holdings
were typically quite unspecialized and sometimes rather backward.
Of course, these characterizations are based upon vague impressions only. They can be made more precise through the statistics
themselves.

Having studied the census reports for all Germany and for some
of the regions, we can try to relate these occupational patterns to
the relevant voting returns. The first of our electoral tabulations
lists the number of Reichstag seats obtained by the major parties
during the entire Weimar period. We already have a historical impression of the parties, which we can now check against our
figures. We can try to assign various social and occupational groups
to the several parties. This is a perilous venture, but it should increase our insight into the politics of that time. It helps to know,
for example, that the constituency of the working class parties was
considerably larger than the segment of the population listed as
"workers" in industry and commerce. Of course, vocational and
social categories do not suffice to account for the voting pattern.
Confessional allegiances played a role in Germany, and so, undoubtedly, did other traditional and cultural commitments.

If we follow the fate of the several parties through the 1920's
and into the early 1930's, we can begin to distinguish individual
parties, or groups of parties, which maintained nearly their full
strength not only during the crisis of the early 1920's but also
during the difficult years of depression and political turmoil after
1929 which were to boost Hitler to the chancellorship by January

30, 1933. Some other parties, we notice, lost ground in early 1924, recovered partially for a few years, and then fell into rapid decline. It is probably safe to assume that the electoral shift visible in early 1924 was partly occasioned by the traumas of inflation and stabilization. If so, it is certainly interesting to compare the political crisis of 1924 with the fatal trend of the early 1930's. It is also worth noting that this trend had actually begun to reverse itself before Hitler came to power.

When a party loses votes in an election, we ask ourselves what groups might have deserted it, and what rival parties might have benefited from the change in allegiances. Here again, we relate occupational to electoral statistics, while simultaneously drawing upon our impressions of political attitudes among various social groups. This procedure becomes particularly intricate when we move from the national to the regional election figures for the critical interval between 1920 and the end of 1924. We are now dealing with percentages of the popular vote, and the five electoral districts tabulated are fairly well matched with the regions described in the census (as indicated in the notes to the occupation table).

Our interpretation of voting results in the districts must take into account such special factors as the presence of many Catholics in southern and western Germany, the importance of an indigenous liberal tradition in the southwest, and the high concentration of right-wing extremists in and around Munich in 1925. A long-standing tradition of Bavarian particularism was converted into right-wing separatist and monarchist sentiments during the Weimar period. After the overthrow of a short-lived soviet republic in Munich in May 1919, the Bavarian capital became the chosen home of various counter-revolutionary groups, among them the National Socialists.

But apart from such special circumstances, it is the correlation between social structures and voting patterns which interests us in our study of the regions. We expect that a high proportion of industrial workers in a certain district will be reflected in a correspondingly prominent socialist or Communist vote. Similarly, we antici-

pate a parallel between the presence of certain middle-class groups
in the census of an area, and the occurrence of characteristic
changes in the electoral returns for that area. We expect to find
such correlations, and we quickly alter our hypothetical view of a
given party, occupational category, or region if it leads us to anticipate correlations which cannot be found in our data. This is how
our interpretations are ultimately shaped and refined by our statistical evidence.

In France our procedure in this chapter is generally described as
"electoral geography." Elsewhere, it has been considered a part of
electoral sociology, or, more broadly, of political sociology. In one
sense, the word "sociology" seems more appropriate, since this type
of analysis is meant to reveal the social grounds of political behavior. From another point of view, however, the French label is
very well chosen, since it points up the geographical framework
in which the method must be applied. From motives which are
deeply rooted in the political and cultural history of France, French
scholars have always been particularly conscious of regional traditions in politics—and in other fields. They have been fascinated
with historical phenomena of the type represented by the liberal
tradition in southwestern Germany. Their preoccupation with such
persistent regional characteristics has probably caused them to
stress the geographical dimension of electoral analysis. On the other
hand, they have done this with some justification. If we were to
expand our study greatly, we could look into areas much smaller
than the five districts we have considered. We could try to penetrate into the original voting records for individual towns, or even
streets within towns, depending on the records still available to us.
Such a procedure would much increase our knowledge, since it
would replace a few vague correlations with many more specific
ones. Nonetheless, there would be no fundamental change in the
logic of our method. We would still be testing—and adjusting—
heuristic models of socio-political relationships in a geographical
framework.

OCCUPATIONS OF GERMANS IN 1907 AND IN 1925

Occupations of Germans in 1907 and in 1925

		All Germany	Hamburg	Rhen. Westphalia
Total population	1907	54,991,083	903,319	9,970,108
	1925	62,410,619	1,152,523	12,231,845
Fully employed	1907	25,156,017	416,891	4,142,198
	1925	32,009,300	586,407	5,726,313
Agriculture, Forestry	1907	8,556,219	11,710	989,830
	1925	9,762,426	14,385	1,127,475
Among these:				
Self-employed	1907	2,171,835	3,405	296,350
	1925	2,202,861	3,330	283,535
Workers	1907	2,878,661	5,729	223,852
	1925	2,607,282	6,007	184,188
Industry Crafts	1907	9,830,540	153,764	2,127,452
	1925	13,239,223	202,259	2,963,672
Among these:				
Self-employed	1907	1,531,271	28,367	244,047
	1925	1,510,868	26,985	257,096
Home-industry	1907	237,157	4,042	30,737
	1925	274,245	2,035	37,133
White coll. employees	1907	618,510	12,169	135,953
	1925	1,452,293	30,057	320,719
Workers	1907	7,324,894	108,797	1,705,197
	1925	9,781,396	141,188	2,313,863
Commerce, Transport	1907	3,496,055	169,048	543,724
	1925	5,273,502	266,540	962,074
Among these:				
Self-employed	1907	927,803	39,687	148,252
	1925	1,198,202	52,261	211,901
White coll. employees	1907	1,281,530	70,410	223,355
	1925	2,220,818	116,058	406,467
Workers	1907	1,054,858	56,779	136,107
	1925	1,440,376	88,200	268,308
Professions, Officials	1907	1,327,627	24,503	177,336
	1925	1,502,379	37,373	243,487
Health and Welfare	1907	323,724	10,185	51,717
	1925	588,788	22,599	112,338
Not employed	1907	3,077,947	48,790	445,384
	1925	3,844,430	76,816	560,529
Among these:				
Rents, supported	1907	2,241,906	37,465	314,869
	1925	3,152,279	63,633	440,517
Institutns., jails	1907	176,949	5,013	28,696
	1925	241,032	7,375	46,794
Students lvg. out	1907	558,058	5,677	84,399
	1925	330,032	4,777	52,555

Occupations of Germans in 1907 and in 1925

		East Prussia	Baden	South Bavaria
Total population	1907	2,096,255	2,057,561	2,903,542
	1925	2,256,349	2,312,462	3,299,932
Fully employed	1907	916,842	1,054,954	1,541,354
	1925	1,066,689	1,271,355	1,781,392
Agriculture, Forestry	1907	522,837	425,996	780,819
	1925	593,558	468,606	805,098
Among these:				
Self-employed	1907	100,361	132,112	190,480
	1925	106,108	129,033	196,495
Workers	1907	272,745	60,911	214,708
	1925	251,447	44,773	202,187
Industry, Crafts	1907	176,080	380,083	378,633
	1925	204,914	494,139	523,780
Among these:				
Self-employed	1907	43,374	65,774	83,628
	1925	39,170	65,051	88,429
Home-industry	1907	1,555	2,309	4,563
	1925	2,329	2,485	4,856
White coll. employees	1907	8,902	23,138	20,550
	1925	18,786	56,623	53,419
Workers	1907	119,843	281,259	253,589
	1925	140,230	365,025	366,797
Commerce, Transport	1907	87,139	135,531	190,921
	1925	129,829	179,568	245,132
Among these:				
Self-employed	1907	19,794	30,627	46,814
	1925	26,790	37,515	57,401
White coll. employees	1907	33,262	43,279	57,347
	1925	55,978	80,692	102,976
Workers	1907	30,516	43,743	58,309
	1925	39,642	46,251	62,446
Professions, Officials	1907	60,146	50,539	83,413
	1925	61,100	51,426	91,380
Health and Welfare	1907	7,868	14,624	18,037
	1925	14,788	26,000	31,713
Not employed	1907	136,464	119,002	224,499
	1925	175,019	115,294	274,477
Among these:				
Rents, supported	1907	106,243	80,223	142,894
	1925	149,936	90,608	184,530
Institutions, jails	1907	8,284	8,046	6,678
	1925	10,404	9,677	13,594
Students, lvg. out	1907	19,889	30,514	51,931
	1925	8,465	14,823	48,809

Notes to the Tables of Occupations

The tables are compiled from *Statistik des Deutschen Reichs,* vol. 408. In order to make a comparison between 1907 and 1925, the German statisticians had to adjust their original figures for 1907 in accordance with the territorial changes which followed the First World War. Not only the territory but also the occupational categories on which all figures are based are those for 1925. Thus, all 1907 figures involve re-tabulations and re-calculations.

The following is a fairly complete list of occupations tabulated under the various *major categories:*

Agriculture, Forestry includes all types of farming, gardening, raising vegetables or flowers for the market, raising non-agricultural animals, forestry, and fishing.

Industry, Crafts includes mining coal, ores, and salt; digging and preparing peat; mining and working stone; gathering and preparing gravel, sand, lime, chalk, cement, and brick; the ceramics and glass industries; the production, refining and preparation of all metals; locksmiths and plumbers; installing gas and water lines; building machines, automobiles, ships, planes, and railroad equipment; the electrical, chemical, and optical industries; all branches of the textile industry, including the tailoring of clothes, knitting, hat-making, and cleaning; all industries and crafts working in leather, wood, or basket materials; the processing of linoleum, asbestos, rubber, cork, ivory, and amber; making brushes, toys, and musical instruments; the whole food processing and canning industry, including milling grain, baking, refining sugar and coffee, brewing, making wine, and processing tobacco; the whole building industry on every scale; and the production, purification, or refining of gas, water, and electricity.

Commerce, Transport includes the entire retail trade, including street or door-to-door sales; publishing; libraries; art sales or rentals; banking and insurance; financial consultation and exchange services; the managing of public markets, exhibitions, or auctions; moving and storage; all shipping; postal and telegraph services;

railroads, buses, and other transit lines; air transport; travel agencies; and inns, restaurants, and hotels.

Professions, Officials includes all municipal, state, and national officials, including elected ones; law enforcement and interpretation, public and private; the army and navy; churches and missions; all aspects of education; lobbying and representing interests; artists, private scholars, and writers; and the entire entertainment industry, including professional sports.

Health and Welfare includes all hospitals, nursing homes, and quarantine institutions; doctors and nurses; swimming pools and commercial gyms; barbers and apothecaries; firemen, emergency, and rescue services; veterinarians and food inspectors; disinfection and insect-control; street cleaning, canal maintenance and garbage disposal; fureral services; and social work.

Not employed (and therefore not counted among the "fully employed") does *not* include the temporarily unemployed; nor does it include dependents living with an employed person who supports them. Rather, it includes those (often older people, women, or disabled persons) living on private capital, pensions, or state support; inmates of mental and quarantine institutions and of prisons; students living away from home (who were not counted in quite the same manner in 1907 and 1925); and those without any stated occupation.

In addition to the major categories which appear on the above tables, the statistical sources listed a major category of *Personal Services, etc.* among the "fully employed." This category comprised (for all Germany) about 1.6 million people in 1925 and about the same number in 1907. Included in this category were servants of all kinds, cleaning ladies, chauffeurs, and house-tutors. Also in this category in 1925 were 248,996 people (in all Germany) who had no single specifiable occupation at the time of the count, often because they worked at odd jobs or as general handymen, or because they were out of work just then. Note that there was no special category of the unemployed. The label "fully employed" as used in the tables is a translation of *"hauptberuflich Erwerbstaetige,"* which really means "those in full-time (rather than part-time) occupations." In other words, some temporarily unemployed persons were certainly counted as "fully employed" in the major category *Personal Services, etc.* and in other categories as well. There were 594,000 unemployed in Germany in 1923, and 542,000 in 1924.

Under the totals of those employed in the major categories *Agriculture, Forestry, Industry, Crafts* and *Commerce, Transport,* the statistical sources also listed (in each case) a sub-category of "members of the family who help in the business." Note that this sub-category is not specifically tabulated above under any of the three major categories involved. However, in each of the three cases, one can arrive at the number of family helpers by subtracting all the other (specifically listed) sub-categories from the respective major category.

Similarly, in the major category *Not employed,* a sub-category of "those without any stated occupation" is not separately tabulated. Once again, one can arrive at the number of such people by subtracting all the other (specifically listed) sub-categories from the major category.

The tables above make no distinction between men and women in the labor force. There were 8,501,005 women among the "fully employed" in 1907; 11,478,012 in 1925. Women were especially strongly represented in such sub-categories as "home-industry," "helping family members," "rents, supported," and "those without any stated occupation."

Included in the major category *Professions, Officials,* there were 14,805 people listed for the army and navy in 1925. It is estimated that this represented a decrease of about 483,000 over the comparable figure for 1907.

Note that the areas of Germany for which occupations appear in the tables coincide roughly with the electoral districts treated in the table of voting results which appears later in this section. However, the electoral district *Duesseldorf-East* is only a part of Rhenish Westphalia, and the electoral district *Upper Bavaria-Swabia* is only a part of South Bavaria.

GERMAN ELECTIONS, 1919-1932

Date of Elections	Jan. '19	Jun. '20	May '24	Dec. '24	May '28	Sep. '30	Jul. '32	Nov. '32
Seats to Communists	—	4	62	45	54	77	89	100
Seats to Independents	22	84	—	—	—	—	—	—
Seats to Social Democrats	163	102	100	131	153	143	133	121
Seats to Center	91	64 (21)	65 (16)	69 (19)	62 (16)	68 (19)	75 (22)	70 (20)
Seats to Democrats	75	39	28	32	25	20	4	2
Seats to People's Party	19	65	45	51	45	30	7	11
Seats to Nationalists	44	71	95	103	73	41	37	52
Seats to Natl. Socialists	—	—	32	14	12	107	230	196
Seats to Smaller parties	7	9	29	29	51	72	11	12
Seats out Total	421	459	472	493	491	577	608	584

Source: *Statistik des Deutschen Reichs*. Numbers appearing in parentheses under some of the figures for the Center Party refer to the Bavarian People's Party, a close ally of the Center, although more rigorously conservative than the Center and interested in Bavarian separatism for a time.

THE ELECTIONS OF JUNE 1920, MAY 1924 AND DECEMBER 1924

Party	All Germany 1920	May '24	Dec. '24	Baden 1920	May '24	Dec. '24
Communists	2.1	12.6	9.0	1.5	10.1	6.5
Ind. Socialists	17.9	0.8	0.3	10.9	0.7	0.7
Social Democrats	21.7	20.5	26.0	20.1	15.2	19.9
Center	13.6	13.4	13.6	36.4	34.6	34.5
Democrats	8.3	5.7	6.3	12.3	7.8	9.3
People's Party	13.9	9.2	13.4	6.8	7.9	11.5
Nationalists	15.1	19.5	20.5	12.0	8.0	8.9
Natnl. Socialists	—	(6.5)	3.0	—	(4.8)	1.9

Party	Hamburg 1920	May '24	Dec. '24	Düsseldorf-East 1920	May '24	Dec. '24
Communists	0.5	18.3	14.3	1.3	24.9	20.9
Ind. Socialists	15.1	0.5	0.3	32.8	1.0	0.5
Social Democrats	38.4	27.7	32.2	10.0	11.4	15.4
Center	1.0	1.5	1.7	24.2	22.5	24.5
Democrats	17.4	13.0	12.5	5.1	4.3	4.6
People's Party	15.0	12.2	13.2	13.2	12.0	14.7
Nationalists	12.4	19.5	21.6	12.5	15.0	15.3
Natnl. Socialists	—	(6.0)	2.3	—	(3.9)	1.6

Party	East Prussia 1920	May '24	Dec. '24	Upper Bavaria-Swabia 1920	May '24	Dec. '24
Communists	7.2	11.7	8.1	3.2	8.6	6.0
Ind. Socialists	5.5	0.6	0.2	11.9	—	0.2
Social Democrats	23.9	15.3	20.8	15.8	13.2	17.8
Center	9.5	8.3	8.0	44.0*	38.9*	38.8*
Democrats	5.6	3.5	4.0	5.6	2.1	2.9
People's Party	15.1	8.3	11.3	19.5*	11.4*	16.2*
Nationalists	30.9	38.9	39.2	—	7.5	12.4
Natnl. Socialists	—	(8.6)	6.2	—	(17.0)	4.8

Numbers are percentages of all votes (in Germany or in the respective district) which were obtained by the major parties. Source: *Statistik des Deutschen Reichs,* vol. 315. Figures listed for National Socialists, May, 1924, are actually votes for an electoral alliance of anti-Semitic groups under the name of *Deutsche völkische Freiheitspartei.* For December, 1924, votes for the middle-class "Economics Party" were tabulated together with those of the People's Party. In the case of Upper Bavaria-Swabia, votes for the "Bavarian People's Party" were tabulated as votes for the Center. The Center itself ran in this district only in May, 1924, at which time it received 1.1% of the vote. Also in Upper Bavaria-Swabia, votes for the "Bavarian Farmers' League" (which obtained 12.9% of the vote there in 1920 and 10.2% in May, 1924) were tabulated with the votes of the People's Party.

VI
THE INFLATION AND HITLER'S PUTSCH OF 1923

Electoral statistics can give us at least a general impression of political behavior among various German social groups. We know that the inflation and the accompanying disorders turned important segments of the population against the Republic and the liberal parties. We can try to interpret this reaction in terms of the materials in Chapters Three and Four. It is clear that the collapse of the mark was a shattering emotional experience for many people. It provoked a mood of profound helplessness and despair. To some, the death of money seemed the end of all order and of morality itself. A sense of universal chaos was accompanied by intense resentments. Many of the dispossessed gave way to all sorts of primitive hostilities. In an atmosphere of heightened political suggestibility, the agitators of the extreme right found their opportunities. Supported by an army of unemployed former soldiers, paramilitary groups, professional rowdies, and opportunists, the demagogues also profited from the hostility of the old ruling classes to the new regime.

The abortive Beer Hall Putsch of November 1923 was Adolf Hitler's first open attempt at right-wing "revolution." Although he failed, the adventure and his subsequent trial gave him a national reputation. During the years of relative stability after 1924, the National Socialists remained a numerically insignificant group. But when economic chaos again led to political turmoil between 1929 and 1933, Hitler was able to make his way to the chancellorship.

The passages that follow are from Konrad Heiden's *Der Fuehrer*. As Heiden explains in his preface, he was a contemporary observer

of the conditions he describes. This makes his work especially interesting. There is actually a good deal of similarity between his
account and Erna von Pustau's. Both place much emphasis upon
the psychological impact of the inflation. On the other hand,
Heiden, unlike Erna von Pustau, has supplemented his personal
impressions and recollections with archival research. He also dis-
plays the critical and narrative skills of the trained historian. It is
interesting to observe how his chapters blend general observations
upon the social psychology of that time with an account of selected
events. His story of the Beer Hall Putsch may serve as a fitting conclusion for this study. In a way, it tends to bring us back toward
the narrative approach which, rightly or not, is often considered the
historian's true vocation.

THE PARTICIPANT AS HISTORIAN

KONRAD HEIDEN

Der Fuehrer

Preface

It is twenty-three years now since I first attended a National Socialist
meeting, saw (without particular enjoyment) Herr Hitler at close
range, and listened to the flood of nonsense—or so it then seemed to
me—that he was spouting. It was only gradually that the effects of
these speeches made me realize that behind all the nonsense there was
unrivaled political cunning.

In 1923, as the leader of a small democratic organization in the
University of Munich, I tried, with all the earnestness of youth, and
with complete lack of success, to annihilate Hitler by means of protest
parades, mass meetings, and giant posters. And so I am entitled to call
myself the oldest—or one of the oldest—anti-Nazis now in the United
States, for there cannot be many in this country who came into conflict
with Adolf Hitler and his handful of followers at so early a date.

Those who experience history and have a share in its making rarely
see the enduring threads but only the whirl of exciting and quickly forgotten details. In 1920, and the years following, my friends and I

Konrad Heiden, *Der Fuehrer: Hitler's Rise to Power,* trans. Ralph Manheim
(Boston: Houghton Mifflin, 1944), pp. 125–140, 161–208. Reprinted with the permission of Houghton Mifflin and H. Pordes, London.

certainly did not view our modest fist-fights and other encounters with the National Socialists as an attempt to put a premature end to the career of the modern Genghis Khan, and I would have jeered at anyone who had prophesied that this was the beginning of a new epoch in world history.

The narrative that follows is based partly on my own observations and experiences then and in later years. However, even the most intimate episodes and reports of private conversations are grounded on documentary evidence or on statements of individuals who seemed to me thoroughly reliable.

THE DEATH OF MONEY

HEIDEN (continued)

In the summer of 1923, Hitler told a story in a large meeting: 'We have just had a big gymnastic festival in Munich. Three hundred thousand athletes from all over the country assembled here. That must have brought our city lots of business, you think. Now listen to this: There was an old woman who sold picture postcards. She was glad because the festival would bring her plenty of customers. She was beside herself with joy when sales far exceeded her expectations. Business had really been good—or so she thought. But now the old woman is sitting in front of an empty shop, crying her eyes out. For with the miserable paper money she took in for her cards, she can't buy a hundredth of her old stock. Her business is ruined, her livelihood absolutely destroyed. She can go begging. And the same despair is seizing the whole people. We are facing a revolution. . . .'

This was the story of the end of the world—seemingly the story of an old woman, but really, in seven or eight phrases, the story of the destruction of German, indeed of European, self-reliance and dignity. The truths which had seemed most certain, the multiplication table and the difference between good and evil, vanished before the eyes of the uncomprehending individual. First it was the story of the German inflation, which reduced the supposedly eternal value of the German mark from $0.24 to $.000,000,000,024; or, in other words: an object which had previously been worth twenty-four cents, now cost a sum which would formerly have equaled three times the national wealth. To a lesser degree, it was also the story of the blowing away of money in other countries, Austria, Poland, Hungary, France, Italy, Spain; and later, there were beginnings of the process in England, and even the United States. This was the twilight of the age of progress: the death of money.

On Friday afternoons in 1923, long lines of manual and white-collar workers waited outside the pay-windows of the big German factories, department stores, banks, offices: dead-tired workingmen in grimy shirts open at the neck; gentlemen in shiny blue suits, saved from before the war, in mended white collars, too big for their shrunken necks; young girls, some of them with the new bobbed heads; young men in puttees and gray jackets, from which the tailor had removed the red seams and regimentals, embittered against the girls who had taken their jobs. They all stood in lines outside the pay-windows, staring impatiently at the electric wall clock, slowly advancing until at last they reached the window and received a bag full of paper notes. According to the figures inscribed on them, the paper notes amounted to seven hundred thousand or five hundred million, or three hundred and eighty billion, or eighteen trillion marks—the figures rose from month to month, then from week to week, finally from day to day. With their bags the people moved quickly to the doors, all in haste, the younger ones running. They dashed to the nearest food store, where a line had already formed. Again they moved slowly, oh, how slowly, forward. When you reached the store, a pound of sugar might have been obtainable for two millions; but, by the time you came to the counter, all you could get for two millions was half a pound, and the saleswoman said the dollar had just gone up again. With the millions or billions you bought sardines, sausages, sugar, perhaps even a little butter, but as a rule the cheaper margarine—always things that would keep for a week, until next payday, until the next stage in the fall of the mark.

For money could not keep, the most secure of all values had become the most insecure. The mark wasn't just low, it was slipping steadily downward. Goods were still available, but there was no money; there was still labor and consumption, but no economy; you could provide for the moment, but you couldn't plan for the future. It was the end of money. It was the end of the old shining hope that everyone would be rich. The secular religion of the nineteenth century was crumbling amid the profanation of holy property.

Germany had financed her war by means of loans. The state had borrowed from its citizens approximately eighty billion marks, about a third of the so-called national wealth, and shot them into the air—without result, for the war had been lost. Every citizen had been forced to lend, even the propertyless out of their meager wages. Great fortunes and petty savings had been thrown down the gullet of war. And then, suddenly, the mark lost its value. The war loan was worth nothing. Savings of a lifetime were worth nothing. The great radical cure, ruthless equalization, was going into effect. It was a process which would affect the distant future, but most men failed even to suspect its full significance, for they saw only the beginnings, the first symptoms. The great prophecies of the nineteenth century were beginning to be fulfilled. A man who thought he had a small fortune in the bank might receive a politely couched letter from the directors: 'The bank deeply regrets that it can no longer administer your deposit of sixty-eight thousand marks, since the costs are out of all proportion to the capital. We are therefore taking the liberty of returning your capital. Since we have no bank-notes in small enough denominations at our disposal, we have rounded out the sum to one million marks. Enclosure: one 1,000,-000-mark bill.' A canceled stamp for five million marks adorned the envelope.

The state wiped out property, livelihood, personality, squeezed and pared down the individual, destroyed his faith in himself by destroying his property—or worse: his faith and hope in property. Minds were ripe for the great destruction. The state broke the economic man, beginning with the weakest.

From Russia, the explosion of 1917 had resounded throughout the world. Over one seventh of the earth's surface it had made private property questionable, and ultimately, after years of struggle and experiment, destroyed it. Like a sea, receding for a moment, then wildly surging through all dikes, a counter-movement, inspired by fear, had swept across the world. Anti-Bolshevik propaganda bureaus, clubs, newspapers were launched. Perhaps the strangest monster nurtured by this movement was *The Protocols of the Wise Men of Zion.**

Nowhere, with the exception of Russia, did the state destroy property as radically as in Germany. And it was not the workers who did it. Not the Social Democrats, who in 1918 had proclaimed the republic; or the Communists, who reviled the Social Democrats as 'traitors to the working class,' and for years kept disturbing the peace with vain, hopeless attempts at revolt. The workers had no intention at all of destroying property. Plans to this effect stood in the party programs, but nowhere else. For the proletarian is a component of the capitalist economy, and what he wishes is not to abolish exploiting capitalism, but to exploit it himself.

On November 9, 1918, Philipp Scheidemann, the Social Democratic

*[The so-called *Protocols of the Wise Men of Zion* was an anti-Semitic forgery, based on earlier satires, which purported to outline the objectives and methods of a Jewish conspiracy of world-wide subversion. The stratagems which it attributed to mysterious Jewish leaders curiously reflected the attitudes and intentions of the right-wing revolutionaries themselves. Ed.]

leader, proclaimed the republic in Berlin, saying, 'The German people has been victorious all along the line'; but a week later, the leaders of the German working-class, who had been victorious all along the line, concluded a pact with the leaders of the German employers 'for the maintenance of our economic life.' And both sides solemnly declared 'that the reconstruction of our national economy requires the pooling of all economic and intellectual forces and the harmonious collaboration of all.' It could not have been said more clearly: to save capitalism from the crushing vise of war socialism was the aim of the workers as well as the capitalists.

At this time Socialist demonstrations were swarming through the capital; as the masses passed through the Tiergarten, the great park in the middle of Berlin, a voice is said to have cried out: 'Comrades, preserve revolutionary discipline! Don't walk on the grass!' A legend, perhaps. But how apt!

Actually the leader of German capitalism after the war, Hugo Stinnes, destroyed far more private property than all the German Socialists. Mammoth industrialist with super-capitalist dreams of domination, he unconsciously sought after super-capitalist forms. Such was the magnitude of the property he amassed, and such the methods by which he amassed it, that the very concept of property burst asunder. Between 1920 and 1923, Stinnes was the most powerful man in Germany—in so far as we may speak of power in those dissolved anarchic times. By bold combination of widely ramified interests (mines, electricity, navigation, hotels, newspapers, book publishing) he exerted an influence on the whole country, financed parties and politicians, and in all his activities was guided by the feeling that Fate had called him to rebuild Germany. The first step in this reconstruction was a process of destruction. At the outset the masses misinterpreted it as nothing more than a scandalous rise in prices; only later, under the name of inflation, the process was correctly comprehended as the downfall of money.

While Walter Rathenau was still foreign minister, a group of American bankers visited Germany to study the causes of the German inflation. In some quarters it had been maintained that Germany hoped the devaluation of her currency would cause her political debts to evaporate. It is doubtful whether anyone ever cherished so naïve a hope, and surely it was never realized. In reality the inflation was largely caused by the efforts of German industry to regain its position in the world market. Rathenau and Stinnes sat down with the Americans, and Stinnes, according to his own report, gave them the following harsh explanation for the German inflation:

'I informed the gentlemen that after the lost war Germany had been obliged to develop regular working habits in the four million men who, in the army, had lost the habit of regular work; for this, I told them, raw materials and employment were necessary. In order to obtain raw materials and a market for our products, in order to preserve the life of the nation, we had been obliged to sacrifice parts of our capital; there was no other way. For if the masses had remained without employment, Bolshevism would assuredly have seized Germany. . . . I further informed the gentlemen that the weapon of inflation would have to be used further, without regard to the resultant extraordinary losses of capital, because this was the only possibility of providing the population with the ordered regular activity which was necessary to secure the life of the nation.'

The specter of Bolshevism overpowered the holiness of property. That money was obsolete could be no more dismally proved than by this suicide for fear of death. As a defense against Bolshevism, the destroyer of private wealth, private wealth was destroyed. Germany, like all countries, had been bled white by the war, and this real decline in wealth was inevitably followed by a decline in nominal titles to wealth, in the form of currency. Germany's money had been turned to cannon and hand-grenades. The grenades produced corpses, the cannon fell into the hands of the enemy, the national wealth was turned to dust. Germany had scarcely anything left.

But after the war, even the little that remained was flung away, to preserve at least political peace in the land. While Stinnes, on his royal-industrial throne at Mühlheim on the Ruhr, calmly took it upon himself to destroy private property in Germany, Hitler stamped furiously back and forth on his platform in the ill-lit beer hall and shouted: 'You had no right to make the whole economy, state as well as private enterprises, unprofitable, by overfilling them with workers at a time when the market was stagnant and there was a shortage of raw materials!' He spoke like a learned doctor of economics, and just this sounded quite incredible in his mouth; but then the beer-hall orator expressed an idea, far surpassing Stinnes in political wisdom: the chaos should have been exploited for a transformation of the German economy. He censured the government, because, 'when the soldiers streamed back from the front, it did not distribute them among much-needed projects [public works and housing], but sent them back to the places from which they had been called to the colors.'

He understood that the old *laissez-faire* economy could not be restored. He understood that the old liberal Germany could not be rebuilt. He early realized what his friend Rudolf Hess wrote, many years later:

'For Adolf Hitler the revolt of 1918 was a necessity of Fate, for, despite
its criminal leadership, it swept away many survivals of a time that was
outlived, survivals that would have created obstacles to the National
Socialist revolution.' He knew how much he owed to the chaos. At the
height of the year 1923 it was the chaos which literally fed him and his
followers; for the decay of the mark blew small financial contributions,
made in substantial foreign currency by friends in Czechoslovakia,
Switzerland, the United States, up to gigantic sums in marks; a person
could live comfortably for a week on a dollar at that time, and for a
hundred dollars one could buy a minor revolution. It was a decisive
turn in Hitler's career when his friend and admirer, Ernst Hanfstaengl,
scion of an old-established, wealthy printer's family, himself half-
American by descent, borrowed for him the fabulous sum of one thousand dollars. This money enabled Hitler to set up, in February, 1923,
the *Völkischer Beobachter* as a daily paper.

He said: 'The government calmly goes on printing these scraps,
because, if it stopped, that would mean the end of the government.
Because once the printing presses stopped—and that is the prerequisite
for the stabilization of the mark—the swindle would at once be brought
to light. For then the worker would realize that he is only making a
third of what he made in peacetime, because two thirds of his labor go
for tribute to the enemy.'

And just that made inflation a 'necessity of Fate.' It shattered public
faith in property, and nothing was more necessary for Hitler than the
shattering of this faith. And so he prophesied and described the destruction which was to pave his road to power: 'Believe me, our misery will
increase. The scoundrel will get by. But the decent, solid businessman
who doesn't speculate will be utterly crushed; first the little fellow on
the bottom, but in the end the big fellow on top too. But the scoundrel
and the swindler will remain, top and bottom. The reason: because the
state itself has become the biggest swindler and crook. A robbers'
state! . . .'

The whole demagogical debate was actually a fight between two
thieves over the corpse of the national economy. Stinnes flung away
the national wealth to banish poverty and with it Bolshevism; but Hitler
screamed: 'And what if even greater misery descended on us! Let us
have misery! . . . The greatest misfortune would be so-called prosperity. We would forget all our disgrace. If we were getting along, we
would stop hating France!' He meant it; for he went on to explain: 'In
present-day Germany, sad to say, people do not lament over the loss
of our world position and world respect, not over the loss of Alsace-

Lorraine and Upper Silesia, Schleswig-Holstein and the other ravished territories—all they complain about is the exorbitant prices. If today there were a French dictator in Berlin and the physical needs of the German people were secured by him and his officials, we may be convinced that a majority of our fellow countrymen would resign themselves to their fate. This sheds full light on the demoralization into which we have fallen, and concerning which, sad to relate, no one wastes any tears.'

Therefore, let us have misery. Therefore, chaos was a necessity of Fate; therefore, prosperity would have been a misfortune. This was the destructive, and at the same time creative, idea of a brilliant have-not, a good-for-nothing, with nothing to lose. Let us have misery! The economy is dying. Let it die, and no tears shed, for it has only plunged us into misfortune: 'The pure scientists are misled. An economy exists only because a strong national people creates it. An economy without political power is a temptation for foreign conquerors. Hence today we have a slave-economy.' The old bourgeois parties 'are to blame, for they have trained us to be merely an economic people. If economic development had gone on like that, we would have developed an innumerable mass of factory workers, crippled in body and mind'— Richard Wagner in his time had accused Germany's ruling class of letting the German worker degenerate in hunger, vice, and crime. For Hitler, Germany was stifling in the morass of peace: 'Nobody wants to die for business deals. But a man dies gladly for a political ideal!' This lost world war did Germany some good by casting it into an abyss, from which, in Hitler's opinion, it could not save itself by mere economic means: 'To liberation belongs more than economic policy; more than sweat. To make us free, we need pride, will, defiance, hate, hate, and again hate!'

And so, let us have misery! Let the people despair of the economy. Let them cease to believe in their own labor. There stood these men, pressed tightly between the tables of an overfilled beer hall. Their cheeks were sunken, their gray suits—remade uniforms—were shabby and threadbare; under their arms some held a bundle of food, arduously and illicitly acquired. The speaker fixed his eyes on one of these poverty-stricken figures and said: soon you will starve completely unless you blindly follow me, wherever I lead you. Citizens reckoning in billions, said Hitler, will die of hunger, because the farmer will stop selling his grain or butter for the worthless billions, 'with which he can paper his outhouse on the manure heap. And don't go complaining: how mean of the farmer! Will one of you step forward and say he is willing to give away his work of many months for nothing?' The money you offer the farmer 'is no longer a note on work done, it is a note on a swindling régime. And that means hunger!' On this Hitler set his great hope, on the 'revolt of starving billionaires.' The revolt against the parliamentary régime in Germany was inevitable, and hunger would bend the masses under dictatorship: 'If the horrified people notice that they can starve on billions, they must arrive at this conclusion: we will no longer submit to a state which is built on the swindling idea of the majority, we want dictatorship!'

To repeat the same in the words of the Wise Men of Zion: 'By envy and hatred, by struggle and warfare, even by spreading hunger, destitution, and plagues, we shall bring the people to such a pass that their only escape will lie in total submission to our domination.'

Adolf Hitler is a true child of the old German self-contempt. At all events, the German people was one of the first to witness the decay of those material values which a whole century had taken as the highest of all values. The German nation was one of the first to experience the death of the unlimited free property which had lent such a royal pride to modern humanity. Money had lost its value—what, then, could have any value? Of course, many were accustomed to having no money; but that even *with* money you had nothing—that was a twilight of the gods, as horrible as anything Wagner could have foreseen. When a mark was no longer a mark, the period of nihilism foreseen by Nietzsche seemed to be at hand. First the Kaiser had gone, then the silver coins with his likeness had gone, and unknown faces, sometimes distorted to frightful grimaces by eccentric artists, stared at you from worthless paper notes. The world's aim was changing. A cynical frivolity penetrated men's souls; no one knew what he really possessed and some men wondered what they really were. This could not be compared to any depreciation of currency in the past, with the assignats of the French Revolution, for example; for at that time the mass of real property was not even touched by the depreciation. But in modern times wealth largely consists of claims and credits, which have value only as long as the state protects and secures them. Men understood this with terrible clarity when the state stopped protecting and securing their wealth.

Man had measured himself by money; his worth had been measured by money; through money he was someone or at least hoped to become someone. Men had come and gone, risen and fallen, but money had been permanent and immortal. Now the state had managed to kill this immortal thing. The state was the conqueror and successor of money.

And thus the state was everything. Man looked down at himself and saw that he was nothing.

In this state of self-contempt, insults aroused the enthusiasm of the masses. 'The German people,' Hitler told them, was 'made up of children, for only a childish people would accept million-mark bills.' To hear these flattering words, the people were even willing to pay a few millions in admission. 'True, a third of the German people are heroes, but another third are fools, and the last third are cowards.' When a French firing squad in Düsseldorf shot a patriotic German saboteur by the name of Albert Leo Schlageter, Hitler cried out: 'The German people didn't deserve this sacrifice. . . . The German people of today is truly not worthy to possess a Schlageter.'

The majority of the people were 'the broad mass of the undecided, the stand-asiders, the lazy, the cowardly'; and without being dragged off the platform, he could say to a meeting of five thousand persons: 'True strength is a quality of a few men, or else we would not have the word hero. The masses consist of average men, democrats. But a hundred blind men do not make one steer, a thousand cowards do not make a hero, a hundred thousand parliamentarians do not make a statesman. Cowardly men choose the most cowardly as their leaders, so that they won't have to show courage; and they choose the stupidest among the stupid, so that everyone can have the feeling that he's a litt'e better than the leader. A people subjected to the decisions of the majority is on the road to ruin.' He wanted every single one of his listeners to feel that this applied to him, and said so plainly: 'There is a delusion in the political thinking of the broad masses. They think: anyone can govern. Every shoemaker or tailor, they think, is capable of running a state. . . .' And, slapping an intimidated audience full in the face: 'We have become so cowardly that the democratic poison threatens to penetrate everywhere. No one in the parliamentary majorities wants to accept responsibility. . . . Nations that have lost their character and honor deserve no good fortune, no happy life. . . . The German people is going the same way that the ancient peoples went: it is a people passing little by little into decay. . . . The expression, a great nation cannot go under, is nothing more than an attempt to cloak cowardice. Great nations have vanished from the surface of the earth before this, nothing has remained but ashes. . . .'

In this disorganized, drifting, doubt-torn state, Hitler tried to give the German people a new strength, which might be regarded as a substitute for the vanishing national character: that system of political

prayers, soliloquies of encouragement and command, which has been
designated by the inadequate word propaganda. It was the artificial
building of a new national character, an *ersatz* character, an attitude
created in accordance with an artificial plan. The people dream and a
soothsayer tells them what they are dreaming. This continuous, domi-
neering yet intimate conversation with the people could only have been
carried on by a man who was people and enemy of the people in one;
a torn personality who felt himself a trampled fragment of the people
in his own downtrodden miserable nonentity, and rebelled with the people against this destiny, but who at the same time was convinced of the
absolute necessity of trampling, coercing, and shaking the master's fist.
Rebellious slave and ruthless tyrant in one—there have been plenty of
slaves who would have liked to be masters; but rare are the natures
which are really both. With equal power of conviction Hitler could
summon people now to rebel, now to obey. He could deal in endless
contradictions without becoming entangled, because he was able to
put power into every contradiction. At only a few days' interval, he
could make the two following statements:

'First the Reich must be headed by heroes who carry the people
along, lash them on to resistance! Because such men were lacking, we
lost the war, and we are experiencing the same thing now. The spirit
of resistance must be kindled from above!'

And—or—but—however:

'Salvation must come from below! From above we can expect nothing. The people must redeem themselves, when the others fail!'

At first when his opponents wanted to depreciate Hitler, they accused
him of 'always saying the same thing.' When later, somewhat chastened,
they comforted themselves: oh, well, he was nothing but a propagandist, though 'a very clever one, to be sure,' then they thought they
had made a profound discovery when they declared his 'always saying
the same thing' to be the essence of his cleverness. Hadn't Hitler himself called attention to his constant repetition and 'hammering'? But
here Hitler is mistaken about himself, and his opponents, with their
sweet-and-sour praises, have misunderstood him completely. He by no
means always says the same thing. After he had mocked the masses
long enough, earned their applause by calling them inferior, cowardly,
stupid, blind, and degenerate, he suddenly changed his tune. His public
had long consisted of intellectuals or those who liked to consider themselves as such. But in the spring of 1923, a few hundred workers, driven
from the occupied Rhineland by the French military occupation, came
to Munich. Hitler tried to recruit these homeless, unemployed, uprooted

proletarians for his storm troops and did succeed in inciting them to attack Socialist newspapers and party houses. In addressing this new class of people, he slavishly adapted himself to their old habits of thought—the eternal opportunist. Yes, earlier he had boasted: 'We want no majorities. For the truth is always recognized and upheld by minorities. Every new invention has been a protest of genius against the masses'—even the style of these remarks is imitated from Nietzsche. But now: 'We are suffering from overeducation. We respect only knowledge. But the bookworms are enemies of action. What we need is instinct and will. Most people have lost both by their so-called "education." Yes, we have a class of people who are intellectually high, but they are poor in energy. If by overemphasis on mechanical knowledge we had not gone so far from popular feeling, the Jew would never have made his way into our nation. . . .' Not a word about the élite and the forceful minority, nothing about the leading rôle of the national intelligentsia, nothing about 'genius versus the mass'; no reference to the dullness and cowardice of the majority, only praise and admiration of its power. Hitler had flattered the middle class that it was the real national class, for 'those on the Left [read: workers] have been led astray by agitators.' Now, with the suppleness of an actor, he flattered those on the Left.

'Without the boundless stupidity and blindness of our bourgeoisie [formerly "national intelligentsia"], the Jew would never have become the leader of the German working-class. Stupidity was joined by pride. The "better class" thought it beneath its pride to descend to the "plebs." The millions of German fellow nationals would not have been alienated from their people if the leading classes had troubled themselves about them. Relinquish the hope that we can expect anything from above for the freedom of the German people! The most elementary requirements are lacking: the will, the courage, and the energy. Where, then, lies the power of the German people? It lies, as it always has, in the broad masses. There the energy lies slumbering, waiting for the man who can rouse it out of its slumber and hurl it into the fight for the destiny of the German race.'

What's that? Where is the power? In the 'broad mass of the undecided, the stand-asiders, the lazy, the cowardly'? In the broad mass that lives in the lunatic delusion that every shoemaker and tailor can govern? In the 'broad mass of mentally and physically crippled factory workers'? In the broad mass, two thirds of which consist of fools and cowards and which as a whole is made up of 'average men, democrats'? Yes, indeed! Only in the broad masses is there hope and power, to them alone belongs the future—once they condescend to fill Hitler's meeting halls. Then he assures them: 'It is the same as it has always been: liberation does not come down from above, it will spring up from below.' Who remembers that 'the spirit of resistance must be kindled from above'?

No, evidently propaganda is not just the trick of 'always saying the same thing'—that would be too simple. True, Hitler's adversaries thought so because they took him for a fool; he himself said so because he wanted to be taken for an iron character with immutable principles. Actually, propaganda changes and irradiates like swamp water in changing weather. The facts must constantly be interpreted, invented, falsified anew; overnight, friend must become foe; good, evil—and always the force of faith must gleam through the veil of shifting truths. Without this power of faith, the propagandist cannot make people believe even the simplest truths, much less a tissue of contradictions and lies!

A word must now be said concerning our source for these speeches. They are taken from the old issues of the *Völkischer Beobachter,* Adolf Hitler's own newspaper, edited by Alfred Rosenberg and Dietrich Eckart. The texts were examined and approved by Hitler. In 1923, Rosenberg and Eckart decided to publish the speeches in book form and entrusted Adolf Viktor von Körber, a member of the newspaper's staff, with the editorial task. Hitler told Körber certain events from his life, and Körber wrote a little biography as an introduction. At the end of 1923, he published a small volume of some one hundred and fifty pages, containing selected speeches, and entitled *Adolf Hitler, sein Leben und seine Reden* (Adolf Hitler, His Life and Speeches). Subsequently several new editions of the book appeared; and it is sometimes strange to note how the speeches changed in the course of the years.

In the *Völkischer Beobachter* text, these speeches stand before us in all their freshness, just as they were delivered. In these very words they resounded from the platform; in these very words the *Völkischer Beobachter's* reporter took them down and brought them to the printshop that very night, charged with all the power, the hatred, the self-reliance, the factual and grammatical mistakes of an agitated hour. This is what makes them such reliable testimony. Days or weeks later, the speaker re-reads his own words; he is uncertain and suspicious, as often when relaxed. Could I have said that? Perhaps Rosenberg or Körber is alarmed: the old boy has blundered again. It can't stay like this. We'll have to change it or throw it out.

Hitler has uttered a hasty word about America. The paper carries it just as it slipped out: '. . . Those phrases about reconcilation were a lie. If Wilson hadn't been a swindler, he would not have become President of America. In our country we had one of these apostles of reconciliation, Herr Scheidemann'—first premier of the German Republic. 'Today we feel the results of their pacifist activity only too clearly, though both prophets have vanished from their posts. In accordance with parliamentary custom, the peoples have to pay the bill.' In the 1923 edition the whole passage is reduced to one brief sentence: 'If Wilson hadn't been a swindler, he would not have become president of a democracy.' In the edition of 1933, the entire quotation is omitted.

Sometimes Hitler could not make up his mind whether to heap the blame for everything on France or on the Jews. So he said in one of his speeches (newspaper version): 'Between Germany and France there is a rift that cannot be leveled by pacifist telegrams or cowardly submission. The attitude of France toward the Reich is the same today as it was four hundred, three hundred, two hundred, one hundred and fifty years ago. . . . No chance to mend this rift. . . .'

But in the same speech he said (book version): 'Between Germany and France there was a fundamental rift that could not be leveled by pacifist telegrams or cowardly submission. Before the war both countries could live beside each other in arms only. True, for Germany the war of 1870 closed a century-old hostility. But in France flaming hatred against Germany was cultivated with all methods of newspaper propaganda, in textbooks, on the stage, in the movies. . . . Who croaked the ugliest calumnies? . . . All the Jewish newspapers of France. To bring about bad feeling and exploit it was, as everybody can see, the aim of World Jewry.'

Thus the prophet falsifies his own words. With the deepest conviction he contradicts his deepest convictions. It is as though the various heads of a many-headed beast were biting one another.

The truth is irremediably buried beneath these deceptions and contradictions. How, then, can the speaker expect to put through a single incisive, suitable lie, when from speech to speech, from sentence to sentence, he changes even the lies? Whom does he expect to persuade that he himself believes a single one of these mutually contradictory lies? And to what purpose does he try to spread an opinion among the people, when on the very next day he is going to sacrifice that opinion?

Such questions are asked by those who do not understand propaganda, who regard propaganda as the art of instilling an opinion in the masses. Actually it is the art of receiving an opinion from the masses.

The usual conception of the great propagandist is the commanding, purposive mind, who by magic suggestion subjects an empty animal mass to his will; Marc Antony, who in a single speech makes a thousand friends out of a thousand enemies. It is in this light that most of our contemporaries view the greatest propagandist of our day, Adolf Hitler, and this is Adolf Hitler's own idea of himself. With the authority of success, he has put over a false theory on the world: the theory that he dominates the minds of millions by tirelessly hammering the same simple statement into them. But this only shows that he never listened to himself very closely, and was never too eager to illuminate his own success. He did not hammer the same simple statement into the minds of millions; on the contrary, he played with the masses and titillated them with the most contradictory assertions. It is this art of contradiction which makes him the greatest and most successful propagandist of his time. He does not dominate the minds of millions, his mind belongs to them. Like a piece of wood floating on the waves, he follows the shifting currents of public opinion. This is his true strength.

The true aim of political propaganda is not to influence, but to study the masses. The speaker is in constant communication with the masses; he hears an echo, and senses the inner vibration. In forever setting new and contradictory assertions before his audience, Hitler is tapping the outwardly shapeless substance of public opinion with instruments of varying metals and varying weights. When a resonance issues from the depths of the substance, the masses have given him the pitch; he knows in what terms he must finally address them.

WAR IN THE RUHR

HEIDEN (continued)

On January 11, 1923, a French army occupied Germany's last and greatest coal province, the industrial heart of the Reich, the Ruhr. A war broke out between France and Germany, in so far as one can speak of war between a first-class military power and a disarmed nation. Germany waged war by falling down and passively submitting to the enemy's blows. Wherever French soldiers appeared, the trains stopped running, machines gathered rust and dust in empty factories, the coal mines were abandoned. Throughout the west of Germany, occupied by the French, life was at a standstill, excepting in the Cologne region, where the occupation was English; from near-by Koblenz, the Americans had previously departed, regretted by the population. Among the foreign conquerors they alone had given the German population the feeling that understanding was still possible between victor and vanquished, a return to peace without bitterness and vengeance.

Poincaré's France did not believe in such an understanding. Poincaré felt that Germany had not been sufficiently broken by the defeat of 1918 and wanted to break her for good. Actually Germany did have a certain power. The passive resistance to which the Cuno government summoned the Ruhr and the Rhineland was an expression of power, the standstill in western Germany was—at least in the beginning—a great political achievement. The unions gave the strike order, and everyone struck, the industrialists included. Let the conqueror find himself with a worthless country, a dead victim. The French military authorities chased thousands of inhabitants into the unoccupied territory. For Hitler it was painful and humiliating that the 'great man in the South' should also participate in the pillage, sending a company of Italian engineers after the French troops into the Ruhr; for Italy could not live without the German coal from the Ruhr. England, by contrast, was not in the least enthusiastic over the French seizure of German coal; for France had always bought a large part of the coal for her industry from England, and the English mines could not live without their French purchasers. Besides, England could not approve the establishment of French rule near the mouth of the Rhine, hard by that triangle of coasts, river mouths, seaports leading into the heart of Europe, through which one hundred and twelve years earlier Napoleon had drawn a military line extending from Cape Finisterre in Spain to Hamburg, menacing the British Isles—no, it was a cardinal principle of British policy that this coast must never belong to a single power. English banks supported the passive resistance of Germany in the Ruhr by supporting the German mark. For the strike in the western provinces was a new and even heavier drain on the mark; the strikers had to live, the employers cried out for indemnities. The campaign was financed by the Reich treasury. At the bank windows the millions were no longer counted, the piles of notes were measured with a ruler. At the beginning the mark was successfully pegged, but soon English aid proved insufficient. The mark slipped and crashed again, the passive resistance crumbled, the French held out the temptation of wages in good, solid francs, printed specially for the Rhineland. In Germany secret patriotic establishments set to work, forging masses of these Rhineland francs to make them depreciate. All to no avail. The French slowly succeeded in putting the Ruhr back to work and carrying off the coal. With her passive resistance, Germany had harmed herself more seriously than the enemy.

Nevertheless, Germany developed in this 'Ruhr War' a power which she had not shown since 1918; for a short time she had been inwardly steeled and united as she had not been since the outbreak of the World War. To be sure, she was materially paralyzed and impoverished; she was unarmed in comparison to France; but France, too, was permeated with inner conflicts, the break with England was a source of deep anxiety. With all their hearts the French people rejected the Ruhr War—like everything which in any way reminded them of war. Hitler well understood this: 'Today the disproportion between outward power and inner strength in France is greater than ever. France has only the momentary weakness of Germany to thank for her present position of power'—again the profound insight into the weakness of the enemy to which he has owed so many of his successes.

But now Germany, in the Ruhr War, developed a force of will which at the outset was highly effective. Never had Hitler been more afraid than in those days when it looked as if his 'necessary' chaos might suddenly come to an end. What if Germany should overcome her inner weakness? What if the conquered country should unite and reorganize? What if Germany should recover her power—and all this without Hitler? Here lay a true danger. If Germany should work herself out of the bloody morass of civil war and return to the solid ground of order; if the Uprooted and Disinherited should regain a hold on life; if the general ruin were halted—Hitler was lost. Consequently, the war in the Ruhr must not be won, the civil war must go on.

When the French troops moved into the Ruhr, a storm of national passion rose in Germany; the country was transformed overnight, united by a wild patriotic upsurge. But in Munich a lonely voice repeated: 'No—not down with France, but down with the traitors to the fatherland, down with the November criminals. That must be our slogan.' By the traitors against the fatherland Hitler meant the parties which were organizing strikes for the fatherland in the Ruhr. Perhaps for the first time the Nazis heard cries of shame when they approached a mass demonstration with their swastika banners. Hitler stubbornly persisted in refusing to make common front with the 'traitors,' even in the Reich's greatest need; future history must not report that he had ever forgiven them. It must go down in history that 'all these scoundrels had been called to account, that a divine judgment had broken over them which would be remembered for centuries to come.' Fear of a great national upsurge gave him the strangest ideas; he went so far as to accuse the Jews of war agitation. In his newspaper, Dietrich Eckart wrote: 'It would suit the Hebrews to lash us into an insane war against France—insane because obviously it would be lost with the swiftness of lightning.'

Hitler shouted himself hoarse for civil war and scaffold, and no one wanted to listen. And so—at the end of January, 1923—he ordered five thousand of his storm troops to Munich, ostensibly to dedicate a flag. If he spoke with this background, people would hear him. He had given his word of honor to Minister Schweyer not to make a *putsch*— why, then, this assemblage of five thousand Uprooted and Disinherited? The minister later described his own attitude: 'I attached no importance to Herr Hitler's word of honor, because, in the handling of police power, one has not business giving or accepting words of honor.' The government forbade the parade—or 'party day,' as Hitler called it—out of hand.

Hitler dashed to the police president and put on an indescribable scene; as the police chief later reported to his superiors, Hitler 'begged on his knees for approval of the parade.' When the police president, like his minister, an elderly, gray-bearded man, stuck to his guns, Hitler foamed at the mouth and cried out that he would march with his men in any case, even if the police should fire; he would march in the front rank and let himself be shot. In answer, the government forbade, not only the demonstration of the storm battalions, but also twelve public meetings at which Hitler was to speak afterward.

Who was Hitler, anyway? Did the state rise and fall with him? Was he really the most controversial person in the country, the most mysterious figure of his day—or was he just a nuisance and disturber of the peace, who could be extinguished by a touch of the trigger without any special repercussions? The question was put to the Reichswehr, for it was the Reichswehr which would have to do the firing. Lossow called his officers together and asked their opinion. Epp fumed: intolerable how the government was treating a national movement like the National Socialists. Röhm openly accused the ministers of treason against the national cause; he would not shoot at these men who were his comrades. Now a remarkable thing happened: the two conspirators encountered opposition. The captains and majors no longer agreed among themselves. A part of them already saw and sensed how the new national army was growing and coming to demand respect; they felt the magnetic force of this inwardly strong force drawing them away from the chaotic murderers' army of the Uprooted and Disinherited. 'How can you combine your attitude with your oath to the flag?' Röhm was asked. Lossow hesitated, dismissed his officers, did not object to the government's measures. The Reichwehr had let Hitler down.

Epp went back to his office, deeply depressed. Röhm, in despair, assembled a few like-minded comrades and stormed into Epp's room. He pleaded with him to gather courage and besiege Lossow again. In the end, he personally dragged the hesitant infantry leader to the supreme commander. Epp went into Lossow's study and spoke with him alone; panting and feverish, Röhm sat in the vestibule. The whole scene was not far from military insubordination. Lossow stepped to the door: 'Can you bring Hitler himself here?' 'Of course!' Röhm hurried away.

A few minutes later, Hitler and Lossow faced one another for the first time. For the first time Lossow looked into the empty, undistinguished face of the legend, faced an embarrassed, over-polite man, striving almost obsequiously to make a good impression. By the quietness of his tone, Hitler strove to convince the general that the government's fear of a *putsch* was absurd. Lossow's appraisal, as he later reported, was: 'Insignificant!' The general could not believe that this man represented a danger. But he did not wish to impair the government's authority unnecessarily. So he proposed to Hitler that he give Minister Schweyer his personal word of honor not to make a *putsch*—then he might be allowed to parade. Now, before Lossow's astonished eyes, occurred a human transformation such as few men can accomplish. Out of the embarrassed nothing there suddenly burst a volcano, filling the room with bad manners and shouting: Hitler roared that he would give Minister Schweyer no word of honor; no, never again; he had given it to him once, and one word of honor was all he had. But he would give His Excellency, the Herr General, his word, that he would make no *putsch* on January 26, 1923. He would report again to His Excellency on January 28. These, at least, were the words in which Hitler himself described the same scene later.

Lossow, again undecided, called the officers a second time and asked them if they would fire on the National Socialists if ordered to. Answer, unanimously: yes. That set his mind at rest. He commissioned Röhm to inform the government 'that in the interests of national defense, he would regret any vexation of the national elements'; he suggested that the government re-examine its decisions. And the government acceded to the armed forces. The police president again sent for Hitler and told him that the prohibition had been withdrawn; merely requested that Hitler voluntarily abandon his open-air demonstration. 'Perhaps,' said Hitler. He would see what could be done. The demonstration took place in the open.

'We have no cause to make a *putsch,*' Hitler scoffed in his speech to his troops. 'The government is so rotten and shaky that sooner or later it will collapse of its own accord.' That was his explanation for his word of honor: I will make no *putsch.* The *putsch* will make itself; assuming, of course—and again there was fear in his words—that the battle of the Ruhr should be lost and Germany collapse. 'The fight in the Ruhr must and will collapse!' he cried. Half a dozen times, in different terms, he declared to his storm troops that Germany was going under. 'Our job is to insure the success of our movement!'

But despite this seeming success, Hitler's relation to the Reichswehr had reached a strange turning point. The Reichswehr had experienced and learned to understand the problem of the proletariat in its own flesh—almost succumbing in the process. That was why the Röhms and Epps had founded their Workers' Party. Hitler was expected to bring the workers to the army—and in the spring of 1923, his employers were forced to admit that this hope had been frustrated. In its place a new hope arose. When the unions in the Ruhr, with machine-like precision, stopped the wheels of industry for the fatherland, a new road to the proletariat seemed to open. It was not Hitler's road.

General von Seeckt in Berlin made an agreement with Carl Severing, the most popular of the Social Democratic leaders, who, as Prussian Minister of the Interior, was in command of the Prussian police, an armed force second only to the Reichswehr. The two men arrived at an agreement: despite Versailles, a secret army must be set up. Severing, to be sure, did not venture to contemplate open warfare against France. The purpose of the new army should be merely to protect the eastern border against any sudden attack by Polish volunteers or similar groups. Shortly after the French invasion of the Ruhr, little Lithuania seized the German border city of Memel by force. This was done, not only against the will of the population, but also against the will of France and England; but there was no help, and Germany was unable to protect her territory against the weakest of her neighbors.

Since there was no legal remedy in the framework of the peace treaties, it would have been surprising, indeed, if no illegal remedy had been found. The 'black'—i.e., secret—Reichswehr came to life. The soldiers were ostensibly 'short-term volunteers.' Most of them were the old, familiar faces from the murderers' army, the National Socialist storm sections, the Free Corps of Ehrhardt, Rossbach, etc., and other 'defense leagues.' The Socialist leaders could not have failed to realize that they were arming and nourishing the murderers of the republic. But they thought it their patriotic duty to defend the country's borders. Also they believed that the central Reichswehr command in Berlin, by paying and arming the 'black' soldiers, might 'tie them to the crib' and thus render them harmless.

Hitler saw things in the same light, and he was embittered. Röhm—sometimes acting behind Lossow's back—calmly carried on the trade he knew so well: he amassed more and more weapons for Hitler's S.A. and raised their numbers, toward autumn, 1923, to some fifteen thousand. He thought that he was furnishing his friend with a wonderful implement of civil war. But Hitler recognized that his entanglement in the new army was destroying his political freedom, putting him back where he was before: a mere tool of the Reichswehr—yet of a Reichswehr that was cooled and strangely transformed.

There were bitter scenes, for Röhm did not understand this. Thus far the National Socialist storm troops had had their own arms, their own machine guns, and even a few cannon. In form, to be sure, these implements of murder had always belonged to the Reichswehr, but the Reichswehr, unable to store them in its own barracks for fear of the Allied control commission, had been glad to give the precious weapons to the political leagues for safe-keeping and maintenance; in fact, the leagues had been created more or less for this purpose. Little by little, they had come to regard the arms as their own property. And now came the great blow. After the outbreak of the battle of the Ruhr, the Reich had half-broken off diplomatic relations with France. In January, 1923, a control commission barely escaped murder by National Socialists in Munich, and after that the commissions ceased to function. The Reichswehr in Bavaria had no more need to hide its arms. And so the leagues were obliged to return the precious guaranty of their power, the arms with which they wanted to overthrow the republic. They received promises that the arms would be returned any time they asked for them—but these were mere promises.

This agreement had been made by Röhm. To his mind, the goal of all his desires was virtually achieved. His side had a large army for civil war; they had the power; all they needed was the will. But just this was the weak point. The will had to be aroused in the generals. And here Hitler, unlike Röhm, sensed an almost insuperable difficulty: these generals would never want civil war. Hitler was in a desperate position, requiring of them a political decision they had no intention of making, since they no longer thought it necessary. They already had their army.

In these straits, Hitler decided to employ the magnetic force of his voice on Lossow. Perhaps the general could be bewitched. Hitler called on him week after week, and in April, 1923, nearly every day. He besought him to raise the banner of civil war, to summon the entire Reichswehr to revolution, to overthrow the government in Berlin. Lossow later admitted that Hitler's eloquence made a great impression on him—though only for a time. But one thing Lossow could never deny: '. . . that in our conferences of spring, 1923, Hitler never wanted anything for himself. He wanted no position, no government post; all he wanted was to make propaganda and prepare the terrain for him who was to come. . . .'

Who was to come? Directly questioned, Hitler would have replied, perhaps with some embarrassment: Ludendorff, the great Quartermaster General of the World War. He did not yet dare to say: myself. He modestly declared that he was only a drummer who would awaken Germany. In those days Hitler always hid behind this myth of modesty when the influential leaders of the German counter-revolution began to suspect that they were nurturing their own gravedigger.

Meanwhile, in the Ruhr, little troops of men crept at night through the industrial territory. They laid dynamite on railroad trestles, bridges, and junctions. French military trains were blown up. In the canals ships sank, and for days the westward stream of coal was interrupted. The secret army had again found a task. These dynamite squads were led at night by guides who knew the country. The dynamiters were the cream of armed bohemia. The guides, however, were often even more dubious characters, who for money betrayed the men they guided to the French. In this way Albert Leo Schlageter met his death at the hands of a French firing squad, May 27, 1923—this was the man of whom Hitler said that the German people was not worthy to possess him. Before the French military court, Schlageter declared that a desire to make money had led him to dynamiting; and, involuntarily perhaps, he betrayed a number of comrades. A number of the most hideous 'Vehmic murders' were committed at just this time.*

This was not yet open warfare. But it had also ceased to be passive resistance, a war of folded arms. The unions began to protest. Severing protested to Seeckt. The Social Democrats wanted no bloodshed. Suddenly Hitler scented an opportunity for which he had no longer hoped. If the unions were against war, he would demand war. As late as the beginning of February, he had accused the 'Hebrews' of agitating for

*[The term *Vehme* referred to a German vigilante tradition which dated back to the Middle Ages. The extreme right converted this tradition to its own terrorist purposes during the Weimar period. Ed.]

war. Then he began to shift. 'Did anyone really believe,' he asked, 'that the French military machine in the Ruhr could be "idled to death"?'

He cited Georges Clemenceau, the savior of France in the World War, who had declared that he would fight the Germans before Paris, he would fight them in Paris, and he would fight them behind Paris. That was what should have been done in the Ruhr. Weapons? Technical armament? 'That is simple. Child's play. And even if at first we had nothing but our fists! If sixty million people had a single will, a fanatical national mind—the arms would spring forth from our fists!' When he was perfectly sure that no one would follow his advice, he demanded a mass orgy of dynamite; the smelting ovens might well be blown up, he said in August, 1923, when the fight was virtually over; coal mines might be flooded, houses go up in flames—if only the people were strong and unflinching, all these things would rise up again. But even these words seem cold and threadbare, compared with the same speech, when published months later in book form. Only then did he really think of all that he might have said, of the mighty, heroic impression he might have made:

> Blow up the furnaces, flood the coal mines, burn the houses to the ground—provided that behind them a nation arises, strong, unflinching, prepared for the utmost. For when the German people rise again, the rest will rise again, too. . . . The Ruhr should have become the German Moscow! . . . Behind the burning Ruhr, such a nation would have organized its resistance to the death. If this had been done, France would have proceeded with the greatest caution. And the rest of the world would have realized that Germany had recovered. A reorientation of our foreign policy would have been the first obvious consequence, a consequence welcomed in London. Not out of love for us. No, for the one aim which from time immemorial has guided England's policies: the aim of securing safety and peace, by creating an approximate balance of continental powers. . . . Cuno should have seized on the Ruhr question to harness the rising flame of our national spirit with determination and show France that a new hour was dawning. Furnace after furnace, bridge after bridge had to be blasted! France's army would not have allowed itself to be lashed into the horror of such a world catastrophe. By God, we would be in a different position today!

A speech full of decision and political boldness! It has but one failing: it was never delivered.

Forged words of flame, addressed to his officers and Communists. For this is the constant and secret sense of his propaganda: the Reichswehr is spiritually slipping out of his hands, he must refresh it and renew it constantly with the spirit of adventurism, the spirit of the extremists of Right and Left, the Uprooted and Disinherited. This must succeed in this decisive year of 1923, for thereon hangs his fate for many years to come, and perhaps for good. Germany must not return to order. The chaos must grow, there must be misery; that is a necessity of Fate: 'We have on our side historical truth and the growing misery of the people, which with natural necessity will bring a violent outbreak,' he once said to two thousand persons, by way of balm and consolation.

The possessions, hope, and faith of the German people lay in ruins. They were slipping into a night of despair, and Hitler, the shifting, restless flame, nourished by the gases of putrefaction, sent forth a fascinating glow. Hideous triumph: 'The hungry will cry out for bread, and the twenty million Germans, who, according to Clemenceau, are too many in Germany, will face a terrible destiny. And each one will have to ask himself: Will you be one of those? Hammer, Sickle, and Star, the Red Banner will rise over Germany, but France will not give back the Ruhr.'

As he wallowed in these images of terror, fear grew in him: fear that the wave which bore him might suddenly break; fear that this creeping catastrophe might end, not with a sudden plunge to ruin, but with a sudden turn for the better, a sudden mustering of energies, a sudden salvation. Hitler lived in dread of a sudden shift of fortune. What he particularly dreaded was that despite his prophecies France should give back the Ruhr.

So he looked desperately for an opportunity to force the Reichswehr into a bloody civil war, before it was too late. The opportunity seemed to come. It was May Day, 1923, 'world holiday of the proletariat.' Trade unions, Social Democrats, and even Communists planned to gather peaceably and respectably in a meadow outside Munich, listen to a few festive speeches, and sing a few of their songs—the traditional, somewhat sleepy workers' holiday as it was celebrated in most countries of the world. It was the dull demonstration of those masses who, as Hitler liked to say, were compounded of stupidity, cowardice, and laziness—of men who, 'working only with their bodies, either possess no clarity of thought, or become disinclined to all brain work. A gigantic organization of work animals, without spiritual leadership.' At all events, a peaceable herd. And just this gave Hitler courage. He called his lieutenants together and declared that under any circumstances this Red demonstration must be broken up. He, together with the leader of other 'combat leagues,' addressed an ultimatum to the government: the May Day celebration must be forbidden, or blood would flow. Leaflets were printed: Women and children, off the streets! One of the subordinate leaders promised that the Reds would be shot down like mad dogs.

But the rifles lay in the barracks. Hitler and his comrades went to Lossow and demanded them. What for? Well . . . there was danger of a Marxist *putsch*. This was a pretext, and a particularly bad one. Defense against a Marxist *putsch*, said Lossow, is something you can leave to me. Hitler grew red in the face and reminded the general of his promise to release the arms any time they were asked for. Lossow: 'As far as I'm concerned, you can call me a perjurer—I will not release the arms. And anyone creating disorder in the streets will be fired on, regardless of who it is.'

This was almost war with the Reichswehr. Hitler now ventured a desperate trick. Trucks drove up to the gates of the barracks, storm troops jumped out, the troops in the barracks didn't stir—for secretly, behind Lossow's back, Röhm had given orders to offer no resistance. The storm troopers marched into the barracks as though quite at home there, shouted a few comradely jokes at the regular soldiers, took the weapons they wanted, threw them into the trucks and drove off. A daring venture—but it exhausted Hitler's store of courage. On a meadow outside the city some thousands of Socialists stood beneath their Red banners and quietly listened to their speakers, scarcely suspecting the danger. The danger, meanwhile—stricken with indecision and discouragement—marched out the other end of the city. There Hitler assembled his followers on another meadow known as the Oberwiesenfeld, where Reichwehr troops were drilling. Hitler hoped to win them over and incite them against Lossow: the former corporal had gone far, he had lost his feeling for military discipline. With a steel helmet on his head, his Iron Cross pinned to his chest, he ran desperately from one Reichwehr officer to another, growing gloomier from hour to hour. For, as the hours passed, his hopes dwindled. Lossow had learned of Röhm's disobedience; a torrent of rage broke over the captain, and worse was doubtless in store for him. Sharp orders reached the Oberwiesenfeld. The Reichswehr drew a cordon around Hitler's troops and demanded that they lay down their arms. Hitler could only capitulate. He was granted permission to take the weapons back to the barracks himself, spared the disgrace of surrendering them in the open. Nevertheless, the whole episode was an ignominious defeat.

At the decisive moment Hitler had not shown a warrior's heart—and his men had seen this. Worst of all, the Reichswehr had not only declined to help Hitler, but had also given him an actual rebuff. More and more clearly the solid core of the army was casting off the armed adventures; they were still comrades, they still had the same past and more or less the same ideals; but their roads were beginning to part. In the beginning the split was barely visible, for the lower ranks still hung closely, intimately together; the storm troopers still were at the same time 'black' Reichswehr; Hitler still hoped to force his will one day upon the hesitant generals who could not throw him off as easily as they might have wished. But a rift there was; and less than a year later it would be an abyss.

Thus the separation between the moderates and the extremists was on the way. On September 2, the extremists, i.e., National Socialists and several other combat leagues, gathered in Nuremberg. It was a meeting of about one hundred thousand people; the origin of the 'party meetings' of later days. Hitler and Ludendorff met, almost on the same level; but still in the eyes of most Ludendorff was the real leader, Hitler only his aide and tool. The combat leagues and storm troopers formed a loosely knit union, the 'German Combat Union.' It had, in spite of strong-worded proclamations, no definite aims; it was concluded in expectation of the 'national catastrophe' which Hitler had predicted for a long time.

For in the midst of the chaos, amid the disintegration of a million fortunes and careers, Germany was gathering her strength for a new accomplishment. It had grown clear that if the Ruhr War were continued, Germany would bleed to death economically. But it was also known that the French people had no heart for this costly war in peacetime; that they dreaded any armed expedition into the heart of Germany and wanted to keep their soldiers at home; at heart they no longer supported the intransigent Poincaré. Both sides had but one desire, to end the mad struggle; and in the depths of her misery, Germany found a leadership possessing the moral courage to take the first step toward peace, a step which at first sight seemed a capitulation, but which actually led to a series of successes in the field of foreign relations, to an economic upsurge at home, and the restoration of defeated Germany to the ranks of a great power. This policy was, to a large extent, inspired by England. Lord d'Abernon, British ambassador to Berlin, was one of its spiritual fathers. In August the Reichstag overthrew the Cuno cabinet; Doctor Gustav Stresemann, a parliamentarian of the half liberal, half nationalist Right, a former chauvinist, for a time an adversary of the republic, became Chancellor; at the end of a few months he relinquished this post, but remained Foreign Minister, and for years after that remained the political leader of Germany. Stresemann wanted peace and a real *rapprochement* with the victors. To regain her strength, Germany needed peace, and to enjoy peace she would have to resign herself to certain conditions which she might consider unjust. England promised to exert a moderating influence on France; American and English banks promised a large loan to bolster up German finances, for the restoration of German economy and the stabilization of the German currency, which late in the fall of 1923 had reached the low point of 1:1,000,000,000,000. On September 24, 1923, the German government broke off the Ruhr War unconditionally.

Unconditional surrender—Hitler's triumph! His forecasts came true, the war on the Ruhr was lost; here was Germany's defeat, by Fate necessary for his victory. Everywhere in Germany the murderers' army leaped to its feet. One day after the end of the Ruhr War, Röhm proposed that the 'German Combat Union' make Hitler its political leader, and this was done. Hitler himself, as always in such crucial hours, did not make a decision immediately, but was ready to take his lead from events that seemed inevitable now. He started an extraordinary propaganda campaign; arranged, for September 26, fourteen mass meetings in Munich alone, ordered his fifteen thousand S.A. men to be ready in full strength. If public opinion was ready—and this he wanted to find out by his fourteen mass meetings—he would march; rather his masses would march and take him with them. Such was his strategy; to be led by events was what he called intuition.

But the Bavarian government parried this slowly flying thunderbolt in time. It set up its own dictator, Gustav von Kahr again, this time with the title of State Commissioner General. Kahr, a short, thickset, dark-haired man, was no inspiring personality; stubborn, but slow of decision; his limitations disappeared for a short time behind a halo of ambition and vanity. His power was greater than his ability, his popularity greater than his daring. But he started well; without hesitation he suppressed Hitler's fourteen mass meetings. In the presence of Hess, Göring, and Röhm, Hitler shrieked, he would answer by a bloody revolution immediately, but he probably knew before that Röhm would be able to talk him out of this senseless plan. Whether Kahr, by habit and tradition a somewhat soft and half-hearted counter-revolutionary and anti-Prussian, this time meant business, he probably even did not know himself; anyhow, in order not to be caught by surprise, Berlin proclaimed a state of siege for the whole Reich; and there they were. Since liquidation of the Ruhr adventure, stopping of the endless flow of money into the 'hole in the West,' and final settlement of the reparation problem and, thereby, stabilization of money were the only sensible things to do, Bavaria in all probability would have given in finally; her businessmen would have seen to that, had it not been for two circumstances.

In the Rhineland, occupied by French and Belgian forces, a movement had arisen, demanding separation of the western provinces; establishment of an independent state; and alliance with or even kind of incorporation into France. Unknown leaders suddenly had thousands of followers, dominated the streets, occupied government buildings, and declared independent governments. It goes without saying that they enjoyed the favor of the French army of occupation. The separatists were an army of the Uprooted and Disinherited, very much like the National Socialist cohorts in the south. Seemingly at one another's throats, they strove for the same aim—chaos. The separatists who then dominated the Rhineland were the same rabble who—as storm troopers —were to torment Germany in 1933. Often they were the same individuals. The danger was that even more serious people, especially businessmen, favored the idea of separation. And Rhineland was the 'heartland' of German industry.

But resistance was too strong, especially among the workers, to whom separatism smelled too much like international big business. The movement did not become really popular. Then England protested against this attempt to create a French vassal state on the Rhine, and after some weeks of seeming success, the separatist movement suddenly collapsed. Even the French army hardly dared to protect its remnants against the popular indignation. One winter's night a little group of armed civilians rowed across the Rhine and broke into a hotel in Speyer where one of the most powerful separatist leaders was dining. They turned off the lights. Shots rang out in the darkness. When the lights were turned on, the intruders had vanished and the separatist leader lay dying beside his table. In the city of Pirmasens, a crowd gathered under the eyes of the French garrison, surrounded the district office where the separatist 'government' was located; a few dare-devils climbed the roof, poured gasoline on the building, and set it on fire. Some sixty of those within met their death in the flames.

But there was more unrest in shaken Germany. A Communist wave arose; the Communist leadership saw a 'revolutionary situation' and believed it would be possible, by a clever combination of legal and illegal procedures, to seize power in at least part of Germany.

Communist-influenced and, for all practical purposes, Communist-led régimes gained power in Saxony and Thuringia, in the heart of Germany, just halfway between Munich and Berlin.

This Communist uprising was just that piece of chaos which Hitler needed in order to go on. He demanded a northward march of the Reichswehr from Bavaria, in alliance with his storm troops and the other combat leagues. First they would put down Communism in central Germany; then go to Berlin and, in collaboration with the North-German Reichswehr, overthrow the government which had permitted the existence of Communist régimes in the heart of the country. The march on Berlin became his program for the next months. Troops of the 'German Combat Union' gathered on the Thuringian frontier, ready to invade 'the enemy's country.'

Kahr, too, dreamed of seizing the Communist pretext in order to start, from Bavaria, a counter-revolution over the whole of Germany. There was, besides, a strong dose of Bavarian separatism and anti-Prussianism in his plans; an idea to restore the monarchy in Bavaria. His motives never have become quite clear, probably not even to himself. Anyhow, he induced Lossow not to obey orders from Berlin any more, but to take orders only from him, Kahr. A national split was threatened, although Kahr and Lossow went on assuring that they did not want to get 'away from Berlin'; but 'forward to Berlin.'

Kahr, von Lossow, and the commander of the Bavarian police troops, one von Seisser, formed a triumvirate with practically unlimited power in Bavaria. The three may have been uncertain for some time whether they meant to reach an understanding with the government in Berlin or overthrow it. But they were pretty well agreed as to one aim: to discipline Hitler and render him harmless. Not to destroy him entirely, but to reduce him to the level of a tool. They employed the illusory, halfway methods which have destroyed so many moderate rulers who thought they could make pacts with extremists and use them as tools. 'We always tried,' said Lossow later with childish pride, 'to bring Herr Hitler back to reality, to the realm of facts, for we had recognized the healthy core of the Hitlerite movement. We saw this core in the movement's power of recruiting the workers to a national point of view.'

Then something decisive happened: the Communist pretext disappeared. First the Communists shrank from an open uprising; they did so on orders given by the man who at that time already practically wielded the strongest influence on the international Communist machine: the secretary general of the Russian Communist Party, Josef Dugashwili Stalin. By a technical mistake there was an isolated outbreak in Hamburg (October 26); for three days the Red workers fired desperately from roofs and windows and for this folly of their inadequate leadership died in vain. Then Berlin liquidated what was left. Northern German Reichswehr marched into Saxony and Thuringia (October 29), deposed the Socialist and Communist, but nevertheless quite legal, governments by force and thus put an end to the 'Bolshevist menace.' With it disappeared Hitler's strongest propaganda weapon; and it is an irony of history that Josef Stalin had a share in this blow.

This was, for all intents and purposes, the end of the march on Berlin as the triumvirate of dictators in Bavaria soon found out. Seisser, in the first days of November, went to Berlin, talked with General von Seeckt, came back and reported that Seeckt wouldn't march. The big financial backers lost interest in the counter-revolution. These financial backers, anyway, never had been behind Hitler, but behind men like Kahr. Even a meeting between the representative of Hugo Stinnes, Minoux, and Ludendorff ended with a clash: 'you are much too economic for me,' shouted Ludendorff. Hitler's march on Berlin became a march into empty space.

Two separate worlds were at that time fighting each other: a rising world of order, still with tender membranes and limbs, easily hurt, growing and solidifying amid infinite perils—and a world of disintegration and tumult, struggling with wild outbursts against its own ruin. Hitler fought for the perpetuation of the chaos, as five years before he had fought to perpetuate the war; in both struggles he was defending his spiritual home. In a world of normalcy a Nothing, in chaos a Titan—his extraordinary powers did not develop in supporting the tottering edifice; they flowered when it came to giving it one last shove. Swimming amid wreckage, climbing over ruins; that is his gift; and seldom has a man possessed it to a greater degree. With his inner kinship to all disintegration and decay he senses the currents that lead to the abyss and in them he knows how to steer his course. But in them alone. With uncanny acuteness he guesses the hidden weakness of the adversary; but in the presence of tranquil strength his perception and understanding are dulled. All his gifts of oratory, persuasion, planning, suddenly left him once a venture proved really impossible. Unless there was something to be smashed, overturned, subjugated, this strange personality assumed the dull gray tone which continued to amaze observers even after he had achieved the summits of power. A hypersensitive nature, he reacted almost hypnotically to circumstances. This is why he responded to them so effectively. In times of calm, he was sleepy; in tormented times, he lost all restraint; like a flag, he snaps in the storm.

The Nothing put in an appearance as the chaos lifted. Those conspirators enjoying positions of power or other influence withdrew from
politics or decided to collaborate with the changed order. And now
Adolf Hitler stepped forward to show the world his empty face with
the piercing eyes of fiery revolt.

Suddenly his picture appeared on every wall. Heinrich Hoffmann,
the photographer, received an order for thousands of picture postcards
showing his face. A motion picture was made. In it, Hitler appeared
with General Ludendorff as equal beside equal, but even then it was
felt that Ludendorff represented tradition, while Hitler was youth, the
future—hence the true leader, 'Der Führer.' The term became current
at this period, and from the beginning it meant the Leader of All
Germany—at the very least.

The political problem remained as before, the problem which faces
every counter-revolution: to persuade the state power to make a revolution. The revolution from above never ceased to be the goal of Hitler's
strategy—even after the top leaders had abandoned the idea as superfluous. For Lossow, though for a time he had been driven by circumstances not of his choosing into a sort of revolt amounting almost to
mutiny against Seeckt, desired only a return to discipline and order.
Röhm resigned from the Reichswehr at the end of September, 1923.
His exact reasons are still not clear. Perhaps the accusations of armament swindling had something to do with it. In any case, his political
rôle in the Reichswehr was at an end. He now set all his hopes on a
revolution of the National Socialists, on the revolution and victory of
the creature which he had been building for five years. At about the
same time, Epp went on leave, and tendered his formal resignation a
few months later. Less courageous, less crafty than Röhm, he moved
away from the National Socialists and aimed at a political career with
the moderate bourgeois parties. He did not believe in Hitler's star.

Meanwhile, the middle officers, the captains and majors, continued
to live in expectation of the *putsch*, for they expected it to bring an
enlarged army, with magnificent posts and promotions. They saw
Ludendorff as their future general; and Hitler as the man who would
carry out the *putsch*. It was their expectations which goaded Hitler
forward. He knew that he was in a desperate way; he exclaimed: 'I
have taken this road, and I will follow it to the end, even alone and
forsaken.'

Since there was no other solution, he ran headlong into the most
insane gamble: an uprising against the Reichswehr.

He began by giving Lossow another of his words of honor not to
putsch against the Reichswehr; in order to be believed, he felt it neces-

sary to add: 'Don't think I'm stupid enough to do that!' He promised
Seisser too: no *putsch* against the police. But later he quite naïvely ex-
pounded to Lossow the crafty means by which he meant to disorganize
the Reichswehr: he had enlisted General Ludendorff to be the military
head of his uprising, and no soldier or officer would fire on Ludendorff. 'The generals, yes,' he said disparagingly to General von Lossow,
'they might want to shoot, for they cling to their swill pail, their pay-
checks; but from major down, no one will fire on Ludendorff.' When
Lossow very cautiously and coolly suggested that perhaps Ludendorff
was politically not very intelligent, Hitler apparently quite flattered,
explained that he needed Ludendorff only for the army; politically he
would have nothing to say, for politically, as Lossow couldn't fail to
realize, Hitler was for Germany what, in similar situations, Napoleon I
and Gambetta had been for France, and of course he was the German
Mussolini too.

At that very hour, unknown to Hitler, Captain Göring, supreme
leader of the storm troops, was telling a member of Lossow's staff that
of course the government must be led by Ludendorff, and 'something or
other' would be found for Herr Hitler. At the same time Göring gave
bloodthirsty commands to his lieutenants: the revolution will soon break
out; you must make yourselves respected by unprecedented terror; in
every locality, 'at least one man must immediately be shot dead, to
frighten the people.'

Germany was returning to order, but the Uprooted and Disinherited
still wanted their *putsch*. They could not yet see the beginning of
stability and were still living in absolute despair. 'If someone couldn't
get rid of his Jewish roomer, or didn't want to pay his taxes, he would
say: "I can't stand it, I'm joining the National Socialists." ' Five years
later, Hitler used these contemptuous terms to describe the men who
supported him in Germany's darkest hour. And these were not the most
desperate. Ludendorff sent for Lossow and appealed to his conscience:
better strike soon; the ranks of the National Socialist S.A. and the other
defense leagues were starving. Soon it would be impossible to restrain
them from action.

One of the lesser leaders of the S.A. was a former lieutenant, Wilhelm Brückner, who subsequently became Hitler's personal adjutant.
Brückner later gave a classic picture of the army of the Uprooted and
Disinherited in court. Officers, he related, had come to him with the reproach: 'You aren't striking! It's all the same to us. Whoever it is that
strikes, we'll go along.' And Brückner had begged Hitler to strike soon,
for 'the day is coming when I won't be able to hold the men back. If
nothing happens now, they'll run away from us.' Action at any price.

For Hitler the leap into the void became a bitter necessity. 'We had many unemployed in the S.A.,' Brückner went on, 'men who had staked their last suit, their last pair of shoes, their last cent to be trained as soldiers, and were saying: Soon things will move, we'll be put into the Reichswehr, and that will be the end of our misery.' The uprooted looked on civil war as their bread and butter and for that they drove their Leader on.

THE BEER HALL PUTSCH

HEIDEN (continued)

Hitler had hesitated until his hesitation nearly broke the movement. But then he pulled himself together. From one moment to the next he took an extraordinary decision. The task was to drive the government to revolution. But how? This time it looked as though the orders had come directly from the Wise Men of Zion.

Two refugees from Russia devised the plan, Alfred Rosenberg and his friend, Max Richter. Richter was a German from East Prussia, but he had spent a large part of his life in Russia, in the German Baltic provinces, from which Rosenberg originated. During the Russian revolution of 1905, he had belonged to one of the little private armies set up by landowners and industrialists for defense against the revolution—something on the style of the Black Hundreds. He had married the daughter of a manufacturer whose factory he had guarded. Later he had served in Turkey as a German 'diplomat,' or rather agent, and after the war, still as a German agent, he had been involved in the Russian counter-revolution. Fleeing from Russia, he had found his way to the German counter-revolution. Lossow knew him from the old days and characterized him as a man of dubious honor; Ludendorff esteemed him and vouched for his good character. Of bourgeois origin, he ennobled himself with his wife's family name, calling himself Max Erwin von Scheubner-Richter.

This political schemer of the Russian school, a craftier, more worldly man than his young friend Rosenberg, knew exactly how the Wise Men of Zion make a revolution. The revolution must be 'imperceptible,' say the *Protocols;* 'under an outward appearance of legality, the last traces of legal, constitutional life must gradually be destroyed.' At the end of September, Scheubner-Richter had provided Hitler with a lengthy plan for revolution. 'The national revolution,' he wrote, 'must not precede the seizure of political power; the seizure of the state's police power constitutes the premise for the national revolution'; one must, therefore, strive 'to lay hands on the state police power in a way that is at least outwardly legal.'

This was the type of revolution that the captains and majors had been working on for five years—revolution 'by permission of the Herr Präsident,' it was called in a secret document (one of a number that has come down to us).

In the first days of November, a great celebration, in memory of the war dead, was to be held not far from the Feldherrn Halle. According to plan, the heads of the state would stand in a short, narrow side-street, waiting for the Reichswehr troops to parade past. Kahr, Lossow, Seisser, the real rulers of Bavaria, would be there, and with them nearly all the important ministers. Also present would be Crown Prince Rupprecht, who, except for the revolution of 1918, would have been the king of Bavaria. In the war, Rupprecht had served as a field marshal and led great armies. Among the upper classes of Bavaria, whom Hitler needed, he enjoyed an almost mystical respect. Kahr, the dictator, was himself a convinced monarchist and viewed it as his life's aim some day to proclaim Rupprecht king—for these old civil servants could conceive of revolution only as a restoration of the monarchy. Hitler, it is true, despised the German princes for their cowardly flight in 1918. A few weeks previous he had informed Rupprecht through an intermediary that unless the prince did his bidding he would 'sweep him aside.' But now that the occasion offered, the king seemed to him just the right tool and very welcome.

Scheubner-Richter's and Rosenberg's plan was this: When all the notables were assembled in their little alley, but before the parading troops arrived, a few hundred storm troopers would suddenly descend in trucks, close off the street, covering the approaches with machine guns. Hitler would then approach Prince Rupprecht and Herr von Kahr and politely inform them that the German revolution was on. The overthrow of the monarchy in 1918 would be avenged, the dethroned prince recover his rights; he could then proclaim the German revolution and anything else that seemed suitable. Hitler was delighted with the idea. On the day of the celebration, Rosenberg reconnoitered the side-street in question, and was horrified to find a large and well-armed police guard. The revolution had to be called off.

But the plan was retained and carried out four days later in modified form. On the morning of November 8, Hitler made a visit to Ernst Pöhner, the former police commissioner, who had always protected him so well. Hitler told Pöhner he was going to make his *putsch* that night: 'I have great confidence in you,' he said. 'I have an important post in mind for you—will you help?' Carried away by the conspirator's lighthearted daring, Pöhner assented, and at once rendered a vital service. On the night of November 8, Kahr was to address a mass meeting, and this seemed to be the decisive opportunity to put the 'revolution with the permission of the president' through. It appears that Hitler feared Kahr might make a kind of Bavarian separatist pronunciamento—at least, this fear gave him a pretext to do what he did. All the political leaders of Bavaria—though without the prince—were again assembled in a small space. This time it was in the Bürgerbräu Keller, one of the many great halls in the city, where, in accordance with Bavarian custom, thousands of thirsty souls gathered at rough-hewn tables to drink beer out of big stone mugs. Most political meetings were held in these halls; Hitler had spoken dozens of times in the Bürgerbräu.

Kahr was to make a political speech—on a matter of little importance. Lossow, Seisser, and most of the ministers were present; and about three thousand people, who might well have been considered the leaders of the government, the army, society, and industry. The chief of the Munich police was also there, having delegated his post to a junior official, with whom we are already acquainted: Wilhelm Frick—the man who could not find the murderers. Frick was still blindly devoted and fanatically obedient to Pöhner. The Bürgerbräu, a large building surrounded by a fenced-in garden, hence easy to defend, had an ample police guard. But Frick, at the behest of his former boss, telephoned the commanding officer not to intervene in the event of disorder; but to wait and report all happenings to him.

What happened was that Hitler's armed followers captured three thousand men, representing the entire state power of Bavaria. It was many hours before the nature of the event became halfway clear to the outside world. Hitler's purpose was simply to set his gun at the heads of the dictators and force them to *putsch*. He felt sure he could carry the three thousand away by his eloquence. Six hundred of his storm troops quietly surrounded the building in the dusk. At police headquarters, Frick gave the police commissioner permission for the revolution. The president himself sat in the Bürgerbräu Keller, and Hitler took him prisoner along with the rest.

With his storm troops at their posts, Hitler, seemingly an innocent guest, stood amid the beer fumes in the crowded vestibule and whispered a command to a little middle-aged man with a pince-nez. The

little man was Scheubner-Richter. Hitler bade him drive out to Ludendorff's place in the suburbs, inform the general that the *coup d'état*
was an accomplished fact, offer him a command in the army, and bring
him to the Bürgerbräu at once. All this, of course, with the greatest
politeness—yet there was no mistaking that the unknown corporal was
giving the general orders and a job.

The trucks bearing storm troopers and machine guns rushed out of
the darkness, the illumined entrances of the building were suddenly
black with armed men. Inside, Kahr stood unsuspecting on the platform; for half an hour he had been arduously reading from his prepared manuscript. Hitler rushed into the hall, at his left side was Alfred
Rosenberg, meditating, perhaps, on the words of the Wise Men of Zion:
that the boldest and most treacherous strokes are those that gain the
admiration of the peoples. At Hitler's right side a broad-shouldered
man with a mighty mustache; this was Ulrich Graf, apprentice butcher,
an amateur wrestler and great brawler; he followed Hitler everywhere
with the loyalty of a dog, a gun always ready in his pocket. Behind
them came Rudolf Hess. Hitler jumped on a chair, while his men set
up a machine gun at the entrance to the hall; he fired a pistol at the
ceiling, jumped down, and through the sudden silence strode to the platform. A stony-faced police major, his hands in his pockets, barred the
way. Hitler, fearing a shot through the coat, quickly set his gun at the
man's head, and screamed: 'Take your hands out of your pockets!'
Another police officer pulled his arm away, but Hitler freed himself
and mounted the platform where Kahr, pale and confused, had taken
a few steps backward. Hitler cried out to the audience: 'The national
revolution has begun. The building is occupied by six hundred heavily
armed men. No one may leave the hall. Unless there is immediate
quiet, I'll have a machine gun placed in the gallery. The Reichswehr
and police barracks have been occupied, Reichswehr and police are
marching on the city under the swastika banner.' Of this last, not a
word was true.

According to a witness, Hitler had the 'expression of a madman.' His
nerves were apparently unequal to the excitement. On this point nearly
all who saw him that night were agreed. In a loud, raucous voice, he
ordered Kahr, Lossow, and Seisser to follow him. A voice in the crowd
cried out: 'Don't be cowards as in 1918. Shoot!' Little prevented Hitler
and his men from being trampled to death by the crowd. Kahr was
helpless. Lossow, who knew what a machine gun meant, held resistance
to be useless. He whispered to Seisser—as both he and Seisser later

stated: 'Put on an act!' Seisser passed the word to Kahr; amid this whispering they disappeared from the hall, led away as prisoners by the storm troopers.

What if they had refused? Today we know that Hitler's *putsch* would have instantly collapsed. But the three men were not so clear about the situation. Hitler's assertion that the Reischwehr had risen and joined him with cheers could have been true or false. Lossow, doubtless seething with rage and shame, held outward compliance to be the only way of gaining time and freedom of action.

The crowd in the hall was not so docile. Hitler left the hall with his prisoners and a sullen murmur arose. The mood grew menacing. 'Don't worry,' Göring shouted in a voice of thunder, 'we have the friendliest intentions, and anyway, you can be happy, you have your beer.'

Meanwhile, in the adjoining room—a cold, dismal place, full of beer fumes—Hitler spoke to his three prisoners · in confused, jumbled snatches. He told them that he had formed a new government with Ludendorff. This was again untrue. Ludendorff knew nothing about it. The three, he continued, had but one choice: to join him. He was the government; in a hoarse voice he stammered: 'Reich government— Hitler; National Army—Ludendorff; Police—Seisser.' Herr von Kahr could be Bavarian 'Provincial Administrator,' a post without power. Pöhner was to be premier with dictatorial powers.

No answer. All three were darkly silent. At the doors and windows stood armed bohemia, pistols at belts, rifles over their shoulders, daggers at their sides—wild men with burning eyes, the ravenous beast, sensing that the cage door is about to open. Hitler raised his pistol and cried out that he knew it was hard for the gentlemen to decide, but that anyone who did not want to collaborate in the post to which Hitler appointed him 'has no right to existence.' They had but one choice: to fight by his side and conquer, or to die. Lossow and Seisser later testified that he staggered round the room half-drunk, though he had certainly taken no alcohol. He brandished his gun in their faces: 'I have four shots in my pistol! Three for my collaborators if they abandon me. The last bullet for myself!' He set the pistol to his temple and said solemnly: 'If I am not victorious by tomorrow afternoon, I shall be a dead man.'

Meanwhile, the three had recovered their nerves. Kahr, with forced indifference, told Hitler to go ahead and shoot him: 'Dying or not dying makes no difference to me. . . .' Hitler, barely listening, roared at Graf: 'Get me a stein!' He wanted beer.

Seisser spoke. He reproached Hitler for breaking his word of honor.

Hitler suddenly grew plaintive: 'Yes, I did. Forgive me, but I had to for the sake of the fatherland.' Lossow was still silent. Kahr began to say a few words under his breath to the general. Hitler flew into a rage and interrupted: no talking without his permission. Again hostile silence.

The *putsch* was threatening to collapse. Hitler had an inspiration. He ran from the room, dashed into the hall, faced the silent, sullen gathering and announced that he had just formed a national government with the three men in the next room. Lossow would be Reichswehr minister, Seisser police minister; he himself would be political leader, while Ludendorff would lead the army. 'Tomorrow,' he repeated, 'will find a German national government in Germany, or will find us dead!'

Is the meeting agreed?—Hitler asked. When the three thousand heard that Kahr, Lossow, and Seisser were in accord with Hitler, all hearts grew light. With this lie, as a witness put it, Hitler changed the mood of the meeting 'like a glove.' Everyone cheered. Hitler returned to the adjoining room, and Kahr could hear the cheering through the open door. He was as vain as he was timid, and this made a great impression on him.

At this moment, General Ludendorff, punctually delivered by Scheubner-Richter, entered the room. He began at once to speak. He said he was just as surprised as the three gentlemen, but that this was a great national event, and he could only advise the three to collaborate. He now solemnly offered them his hand to shake. This cost Ludendorff almost as much self-control as the three. He felt that Hitler had taken him by surprise and humiliated him and that night he spoke barely five words to him. This didn't trouble Hitler at all. When Ludendorff had concluded, he cried out joyfully, almost mockingly: 'We can no longer turn back; our action is already inscribed on the pages of world history.'

Suddenly Pöhner appeared and began to argue with Kahr. The little dictator was still resisting: he was a monarchist after all and could act only in the name of his king. Pöhner, a big man, nearly a head taller than Kahr, spoke down to him. 'I, too, am a monarchist,' he declared, 'and that is exactly why I am taking part.' Meanwhile, Ludendorff stood in the middle of the room with outstretched hand; sheer respect demanded that Lossow take the hand of his general. If this was comedy, it was well played. Hitler meanwhile approached Kahr, suddenly changing his attitude. He folded his hands and assumed an unexpectedly humble tone: all he wanted was to repair the injustice suffered by the monarchy. 'If your excellency permits, I will drive out to see his majesty at once and inform him that the German people have arisen and made good the injustice that was done his majesty's late-lamented father.' In all circumstances and with all persons, he found the right words. Now Kahr, too, found his word: he was prepared to co-operate 'as the king's deputy.' He had almost forgotten that he was putting on a comedy.

The accord seemed complete. They all returned to the hall. Kahr spoke; Ludendorff spoke; Lossow spoke; Seisser spoke—the first two with emotion, the others with painful restraint. Hitler and Ludendorff celebrated the greatness of the moment: here in this hall, a German national government had been formed. Hitler repeated that he himself had undertaken the political direction of this government, thus fulfilling 'the oath I swore five years ago as a blind cripple in a military hospital.' As the historian, Karl Alexander von Müller, subsequently related, Hitler was as pleased as a child, 'beaming with joy, overjoyed at his success; he had a childlike, frank expression of happiness that I shall never forget.' Beside Müller sat Max von Gruber, professor of racial hygiene at Munich University, impassioned nationalist and scientist, uncontested authority in racial questions. As a witness, he made the following statement to the state's attorney: 'For the first time I saw Hitler at close quarters. Face and head: bad race, mongrel. Low, receding forehead, ugly nose, broad cheekbones, small eyes, dark hair; facial expression, not of a man commanding with full self-control, but betraying insane excitement. Finally, an expression of blissful egotism.'

The men on the platform all shook hands and swore loyalty to one another. The audience stood on tables and chairs and shouted, over-powered by enthusiasm. Hitler, who had threatened to shoot Kahr but a few minutes before, clasped his hand and said: 'Excellency, I shall stand faithfully behind you like a dog!'—perhaps he meant a watch-dog. Lossow and Seisser, to whom Hitler had broken his word of honor, received new oaths and new words of honor. And to the applauding, cheering throng, Hitler cried out that now there would be a march on Berlin, the 'great sinful Babel,' and there we shall establish a new Reich, a Reich 'of power and glory, Amen!'

Suddenly, amid the merry tumult, a stout, gray-bearded man stepped up to Hitler—Minister Schweyer: 'Hitler did not honor me with so much as a glance. I stepped up to him, tapped him on the chest with my finger, and said in an emphatic tone: "Now let me tell you some-thing, Mr. Hitler. Do you remember the declaration you made to me in my office a year ago, of your own free will? Do you remember?"—whereupon Hitler fell into a sort of embarrassment and gave me no answer.'

While the others were swearing oaths of loyalty and gazing into each other's eyes, Lossow, with features cast in bronze, went on with his act. Beaming with happiness, Hitler shook everyone's hand and spoke in a warm voice of Germany's dawning glory. Rudolf Hess stood at the exit with a few of his sturdy henchmen and arrested a number of ministers who tried to slip away home unnoticed. Hitler himself, despite all his apparent emotion, never let his three victims, Kahr, Lossow, and Seisser, out of his sight. He was determined to prevent them from leaving the hall. Just then news arrived of a brawl between Reichswehr men and storm troops at one of the barracks. Lossow could easily have settled this, but Hitler didn't trust him. He himself drove to the scene, leaving the beer hall in command of Ludendorff.

The crowd began to break up. The agitated human stream seeped slowly through the narrow door. Most felt exalted and happy, a few dubious and worried; all were moved by the feeling that they had experienced a bit of history behind their beer mugs. Lossow nonchalantly informed Ludendorff that he was going to his office, as there were important orders to be given. With Kahr and Seisser, he vanished in the departing crowd. 'Is it safe to let them go?' Scheubner-Richter whispered to Ludendorff. 'I forbid you to doubt the word of a German officer,' Ludendorff replied sharply. In the vestibule one of Kahr's officials approached and asked what all this meant? The little dictator replied: 'Herr Kollega, I am really despondent. You yourself saw that I was forced to give my consent. That kind of thing simply isn't done.'

Meanwhile, Berlin had learned of the *putsch*. The government met at midnight under chairmanship of President Ebert. The men in Berlin understood the problem of the hour as well as Hitler in Munich. The President asked General von Seeckt: 'Tell us, please, General, whom does the Reichswehr obey? Does it obey the laws and the government, or the mutineers?' Seeckt looked coldly through his monocle and answered: 'The Reichswehr obeys me, Herr Reichs Präsident!' This answer hit the nail on the head and meant that the Reichswehr obeys its own interests. The Munich *putsch* threatened to tear the little army asunder, and therefore had to be crushed. Seeckt's position soon became clear to the others at the meeting; the President transferred to him a sort of dictatorial power, and Seeckt wired to Munich that he would put down the *putsch* if Munich didn't do so by itself.

Munich did it. A few of Lossow's close associates, among them General von Leeb, who later became a field marshal, had no sooner received the first reports from the Bürgerbräu than they placed the troops in readiness. The man who might have prevented this—Franz von Epp—was no longer there. Kahr may have lost his head for a moment, but the generals soon set him right. One of them received the returning Lossow with the sharp question: 'All that was bluff, excellency, was it not?' By 'all that' he meant the oath to the new Germany and the handshake. No misplaced sentimentality, if you please! A civilian, a former corporal, had dragged the general and commandant out of the hall at pistol-point in the presence of three thousand people; according to the code of honor prevailing in the German Army, Lossow was under obligation to strike him down. The general called Lossow a coward, a 'sorry figure.' 'I'd shoot down these dogs with a smile,' said one of his subordinates, referring to the National Socialist storm troopers.

Hitler prided himself on his understanding of the military soul, particularly the mood among the officers from major down. Yet it seems never to have entered his head that his pistol was a bitter affront to the Army's honor.

In high good humor, he returned to the Bürgerbräu. The waitresses were removing the beer mugs from the tables. On the floor, between the table and chair legs, the storm troopers lay sleeping amid their rifles and knapsacks. In one of the smaller rooms, Hitler expected to find General von Lossow in a council of war with Ludendorff; to plan on carrying the revolution to Berlin. But no Lossow was there, nor was there any sign of Kahr or Seisser. Stunned at the blow, Hitler sank into a chair, stared at the great Quartermaster General and said nothing. He felt that his game had gone amiss, though he did not yet fully admit it to himself.

During the night of November 8, some three thousand storm troopers gathered in Munich. They had machine guns and even some cannon. But for many hours Hitler refused to believe that he would really have to fight. In that night two men were active. Röhm hurried with a small band to Lossow's headquarters where he himself had formerly worked, drew barbed wire around the building, set up machine guns in the windows, and prepared for battle. Rudolf Hess sent gangs to the homes of political opponents, rounded them up and herded them to the Bürgerbräu, aiming to intimidate Kahr and Lossow with the threat of murdering the hostages. For weeks Göring had spoken of nothing but the murder of hostages.

The night was spent in deliberation, hope, fear, hesitation. Meetings were held in the Bürgerbräu and in Lossow's offices occupied by Röhm. Hitler, Scheubner-Richter, Rosenberg, and Ludendorff examined their situation for hours. For a long time they continued to hope that Lossow or Seisser would suddenly reappear and put everything aright. They felt that a crisis, a struggle for a decision, was in progress among their adversaries. They continued to hope for a favorable turn and—partly out of pride and vanity—failed to realize the gravity of their situation. Who would dare to raise a hand against them?

'If we get through,' said Hitler darkly, 'very well; if not, we'll have to hang ourselves.' Röhm was embittered at so much inactivity and showed it. He had appeared with a fully packed soldier's kit, as though going into the trenches for weeks; he lay half asleep on the ground, his head on his knapsack, blinking at the light. Defiant and indifferent, he took no part in the deliberations. Someone suggested that perhaps the Allies, at news of the *putsch,* would send in their soldiers; particularly the Czech army was feared because of its proximity. 'There you see again,' said Hitler, 'what a worthless government we have in Berlin. They ought to have such a hold on the three million Germans in Czechoslovakia that they would rise up at the press of a button and make the whole Czech mobilization impossible.'

He began to shout at Pöhner, his new premier, that he wasn't doing enough. Patrols should march through all the streets, ring at every doorbell, and cry out: 'Hang out your banners!' The city should be bedecked with flags—'then we'd see some enthusiasm among the people.' He had a constant flow of plans with which the others were unable to keep up. Every minute he had some new idea for winning more support, for bolstering up the ruined venture. Enraged generals had decided to break him so that he would never rise up again. But Hitler and Ludendorff still believed that they could melt the souls of the opposing forces, make them open their fists, and put down their rifles.

In Munich, Hitler commanded a well-armed little troop, numerically stronger than Lossow's Reichswehr and Seisser's police; outside in the country, he could raise double, perhaps triple, the number. For a moment he thought of retreating to the open country and waging real war in his own way, rallying the peasants to his banners, morally crushing the generals, at the same time tearing the captains and majors away from them. But Ludendorff rejected the idea, and Hitler himself knew that it was not feasible. Only too well did he know his Uprooted and Disinherited who revolted to obtain bread and wages from the Reichswehr. Later he said in court: 'We had to fear that our men, who had to eat after all, would plunder.'

And then this inventive mind suddenly had a new plan—mad, desperate, magnificent in its desperation. He wanted to avoid fighting at any price. The victory which was slipping through his fingers could be salvaged only by a compromise peace—perhaps even by an apparent capitulation. Ludendorff's personal prestige had failed him. Lossow had shouted at a messenger from the general and threatened to shoot even at him. Hitler cold-bloodedly decided to drop the Quartermaster General who had proved useless. Another figure stood in the background: the pretender, Prince Rupprecht, since World War days Ludendorff's bitter personal enemy. Among the sleepy unshaved figures in the Bürgerbräu was Lieutenant Neunzert, an old armed bohemian, a good friend of Röhm's and a personal friend to the prince. In the dawn of November 9, Hitler summoned him and ordered him to Berchtesgaden, where the prince resided in a large castle. His instructions were to ask the prince to intercede with Kahr and Lossow and obtain a pardon for Hitler and Ludendorff. This would let them out of the affair without bloodshed or criminal proceedings. Hitler still hoped to win by humbling himself. An unpunished *putsch* is a victorious *putsch*. When Hitler gave Neunzert his message, Ludendorff stood by—did not speak a word.

Neunzert went—but how can petty circumstances sometimes change history! He found no car; was forced to go by train and did not reach Berchtesgaden until noon. Meanwhile, Ludendorff took the decision into his own hands. He saw his hour. There was only one way out. This band of three thousand idealists and dubious adventurers, of armed bohemians and plunderers, of believing and avid youth, must face the carbines of the Reichswehr, and the miracle must happen: the carbines must drop. Ludendorff was confident that they would if he marched in the lead. Hitler had thought so, too; but now his courage left him. While Ludendorff prepared his big act, the encounter between armed bohemia and Reichswehr, Hitler lent ear to timorous advisers who made it clear to him that the encounter would be more than an act. He hesitantly approached Ludendorff: 'They will fire on us.' The Quartermaster General replied only: 'We will march!'

Meanwhile, measures had been taken to help the miracle along. Hess packed Minister Schweyer and a second minister into the car, guarded by two sinister-looking individuals with rifles; he himself sat down beside the driver. The car sped southward, toward the mountains, where Hess appears to have had a hide-out; in any case, the two were being held as hostages for the safety of the rebel army and its leader. At a clearing in the woods Hess halted, the little company left the car and marched away from the road—things looked very much like a new forest murder. But this time it was only an act, like everything else connected with the *putsch;* after the two were sufficiently terrified, the journey was resumed. In Munich, Hitler was waiting anxiously for the saving message from the prince, and at length it came—when it was too late. Three thousand men were awaiting the order to march; the carbines that were to decide the day were already loaded. Meanwhile, in the November mist, Rudolf Hess was racing through the mountains with his two victims; more and more in sorrowful doubt whether this was the right thing to do.

The mass of hostages had been corralled in the Bürgerbräu. Göring made them join the marching columns, which in the course of the morning gathered in front of the building. He commanded one of his lieutenants, a certain Knoblauch, to keep a sharp eye on the prisoners during the march, as their life was a pledge for the safety of the whole venture. Knoblauch promised the prisoners that if anything happened to the column, he would have their skulls bashed in with rifle butts. Meanwhile, Göring and Ulrich Graf left the Bürgerbräu and went a few hundred yards toward the center of the city from which the rebels were separated by the Isar River. The bridge was closed by heavily armed police. Göring, magnificent in his black cap and black leather coat, beribboned and bemedaled, stepped up to the commanding officer, put his hand to his cap and said: 'Herr Kamerad, we are marching, and I want to tell you this: the first dead man in our ranks means the immediate death of all the hostages.' Ulrich Graf has given us a faithful picture of the whole scene. How terrible, the officer moaned, that they should begin shooting at one another. Only a little while before he and his comrades had fought shoulder to shoulder with Göring's men, and he couldn't see why they had suddenly become enemies. That, Göring replied coldly, was something he could ask von Lossow and Seisser. After much sighing on both sides the conversation ended with the following proposal from the police officer: 'Very well, Herr Kamerad, if I receive orders to move against you, I will inform you in time for you and your people to take the necessary defensive measures . . . or to withdraw if you wish to.'

At eleven o'clock the storm columns started toward the bridge. The hostages, awaiting death, stood in their ranks. Hitler passed and his eyes fell on the unfortunates. He gave orders to leave them behind—'I wanted no martyrs,' he said later. The *putsch* was three quarters lost and a massacre of these defenseless men might have cost the leaders their heads. Hitler's courage and spirit of initiative sank from hour to hour. He let himself be driven, and Ludendorff did the driving.

It was a gray November morning. The Isar River separates the quarter in which the Bügerbräu is situated from the center of the city and the government buildings. At the bridge stood the armed police squad under its benevolent commander. Göring, who for days had been possessed by blood lust, stepped forward, put his hand to his cap, and repeated: 'The first dead man in our ranks means the death of a hostage.' He thought the hostages were still in the column. At this moment the marching mass fell on the policemen, tore their carbines out of their hands, spat on them, and struck them in the face. This was no fraternization, no hopeful beginning.

In the inner city, somewhat to the north of the Feldherrn Halle, lay Lossow's headquarters, which Röhm had fortified with machine guns. Reichswehr troops had surrounded the building and set cannon in place. Neither of the two parties dared to fire. There were the closest comrades and friends on both sides. This drama had gone beyond all politics. It would have been easier for the officers to shoot into a band of unknown storm troopers. But to fire on comrades—this was hard.

And now advanced toward them, through the streets of Munich, leading three thousand more or less dubious figures, that extraordinary soldier who, to the Reichswehr, still seemed the embodiment of all military fame and greatness: the Quartermaster General of the World War. Ludendorff led his troop through the center of the city toward Lossow's headquarters near the Feldherrn Halle, apparently with the intention of liberating the besieged Röhm. He was convinced that the besieging officers and soldiers would not resist the sight of his aquiline face. When he commanded them to fraternize with their adversaries, when he commanded them to disobey Lossow, they would do so.

The column made its way into a narrow, gully-like street, opening out on the broad Odeonsplatz near the Feldherrn Halle. In the first row marched Ludendorff; to his right his personal adjutant, a former major by the name of Streck. On Ludendorff's left side marched Hitler, holding the pistol with which he had sworn to shoot himself in the event of failure. He had slung his left arm through the arm of Scheubner-Richter—an astonishing gesture of uncertainty and help-lessness. Directly ahead of Hitler marched Graf, farther to the left Göring; Alfred Rosenberg was in the second row. Dietrich Eckart, a sick man, was missing. A little to one side was a stocky, bald man with hysterically convulsed features, the anti-Semitic agitator, Julius Streicher from Nuremberg. The first ranks were followed by an auto-mobile carrying several machine guns. Then came three thousand men with shouldered rifles, some with mounted bayonets—all singing.

An armed cordon was drawn across the street where it opens into the Odeonsplatz. Perhaps a hundred men—again police and not Reichswehr—against three thousand. If the police wanted to stop the marchers, they had to do it in this narrow pass; once they reached the open square, the revolutionaries could have brought their numerical superiority to bear.

It is still not entirely clear who fired first. It would seem that Streicher leapt at one of the policemen and tried to snatch his carbine. One heard Hitler crying: 'Surrender! Surrender!' This man could bluff from the depths of his soul. At the same moment a Nazi ran forward and cried in terror: 'Don't shoot, His Excellency Ludendorff is coming!' Who can measure the effect of the fraction of a second wasted in muttering the useless word, 'Excellency'? A shot rang out and the man—probably Ulrich Graf—collapsed, wounded. A volley was fired. Göring fell, shot in the thigh. Scheubner-Richter received a fatal wound and fell. So tight was his leader's grip on him that Hitler's arm was dislocated. Hitler lay on the ground. It is not clear whether he was pulled down by Scheubner or was instinctively seeking cover. In any case, it is certain that if he wanted to cow the enemy, he had to remain on his feet.

Ludendorff remained standing. He even advanced. With Streck he passed between the rifle barrels of the police to the open square. If fifty or perhaps even twenty-five men had followed him, the day would have ended differently.

The front ranks of the three thousand returned the fire. They put their machine gun into action. Rosenberg lay on the ground near the front line. Behind him lay a National Socialist whom he did not know, shooting over him. The other side shot back; the ambassador of the Wise Men of Zion covered the unknown warrior. As Rosenberg later related, he found the man's bravery quite superfluous, and yelled at him to stop shooting in the Devil's name. The other took no heed and went on firing. Rosenberg finally crawled to one side; the firing stopped; he stood up and crept backward. Pressed against a house-wall stood Doctor Friedrich Weber, leader of the 'Oberland' Defense League allied with Hitler, weeping hysterically. Göring was carried into a near-by bank by two young storm troopers. The Jewish owner gave him first aid; this made so deep an impression on the two young National Socialists—brothers—that they soon left the party.

The whole exchange of fire had lasted less than a minute. Both sides were horrified and quickly stopped shooting. The narrow bit of street was covered with fallen bodies. Fourteen of Hitler's followers lay dead on the pavement.

Followers . . . it is noteworthy that the leaders in the first row lost only one dead: Scheubner-Richter. The other dead were unknown rank-

and-filers; one or two held respected posts in civil life, but were simple privates in the party. The leaders appear to have saved themselves by quickly throwing themselves on the ground, so that the fire passed over them into the onrushing mass, killing thirteen. Three of the police fell.

As soon as the shooting stopped, in the first seconds of stunned silence on both sides, a man rose in the front row, the first of them all to rise, the quickest, perhaps the most terrified, obeying only his instinct of self-conservation. Doctor Walter Schulz, the National Socialist physician, who had marched in the foremost ranks, later told the examining magistrate: 'I saw that Hitler was the first to stand up. Apparently wounded in the arm, he moved back. I hurried after Hitler at once and caught one of our cars which were driving at the end of the column. Hitler was taken to this car.'

Another witness, the National Socialist Doctor Karl Gebhard, mentions the rapidity with which Hitler entered the car and drove away; both stories indicate that Hitler was the first to flee.

A bystander about a hundred yards from the head of the column, not knowing that Hitler and Ludendorff were marching in the lead and certainly not suspecting that there would be shooting in a few moments, saw the following picture: The storm troopers marched in gray or yellow wind-jackets and Norwegian ski caps (from which the S.A. cap was to develop). They carried their rifles over their shoulders and sang, apparently with no thought of fighting; as on parade. Suddenly the sound of firing was heard. It was an unexpected shock, not on the program. Two, perhaps three, volleys were heard, and for a few seconds the heavy rat-tat-tat of a machine gun. The whole thing did not last much more than half a minute. Time enough for the observer to run into a house door. At the same time the long column began to halt, to break up, and to run back in leaderless flight.

Ahead of all the rest the Leader fled. The day before Hitler had taken a long chance, he had risked his head and he knew it; he had done it in high spirits and with good courage. Today he had gone into a venture, lost before it was begun. Unable to avoid it, he had staked his life on an action which he knew to be useless. Now, leaving his men stretched out on the paving stones, he stood up and ran away.

Thus did armed bohemia behave when things became serious and their lives were at stake. Walter Flex, their poet and model, once had said that a man must be capable 'of shooting at the enemy through his own body.' On November 9, 1923, there was none of this. One man who really wanted to fight was commanded by Rosenberg to stop. A few weeks before, Communist workers in Hamburg had kept on shooting; in 1919, the bloody struggles of the proletarians in Berlin had lasted for days; the same was true in Munich in April and May of 1919, in March, 1920, in the Ruhr, later in central Germany. In February, 1934, it took the Austrian Fascists with their cannon days to break the resistance of the workers—not to mention the fight which the Spanish Republicans put up for more than two years against the Fascist generals. These struggles were serious and both sides realized that their heads were at stake. But in Munich it was a different type that faced the fire. We know the professions of the men who fell. Among the sixteen there was a locksmith, a hatter, a headwaiter, and Ludendorff's servant; the others were retired officers, or 'merchants' and 'bank clerks'—in reality, retired officers, temporarily in civilian occupations: armed bohemia. When this type makes a revolution, it is by nature and plan a sham, an armed noise to drown out the whispered betrayal; the seemingly military conclusion of a business deal concluded in advance; a painless indulgence of vanity and a hoax on the audience. This time the act had been a failure, and the actors fled at once.

Two hours later, Röhm capitulated behind his barbed wire. He gave in to the persuasion of Epp, who came as intermediary and angel of peace; apparently a friend, perhaps a traitor; at all events, a faint heart and a gravedigger of the common cause. Of Röhm's men, two had fallen.

Meanwhile, a car with the two hostages was still driving about the mountain roads. Shortly after noon, the news of the collapse in Munich reached the countryside. The lonely motorists heard it while pausing for rest. Schweyer suddenly noticed that the guards had vanished. He gathered new energy and commanded the driver, who suddenly showed himself astonishingly solicitous toward the ministers, to drive them back to Munich in all haste. Rudolf Hess slipped across the border into Austria over a mountain trail.

A few days later, Hitler was under arrest. As he sat there, the German chaos came to an end, and in a pacified world, returned to normalcy, a band of aimless rebels remained behind prison gates. Six days after the shooting at the Feldherrn Halle, the German mark was stabilized; from then on, it stopped sinking and has outwardly remained one of the firmest currencies in the world. In London a committee of international financiers met and decided to help sustain the German economy. Under the guidance of the American financier, Owen D. Young, and the English banker, Sir Josiah Stamp, a plan was worked out which became known as the Dawes Plan after the chairman of the committee. Germany received an international loan of eight hundred million gold marks, secured by the German state railways. At the same time the Allied governments set an approximate limit to the German 'reparations' payments, which had been purposely left vague. The payments were to begin with half a billion marks per annum, rising, within five years, to two and a half billions. An American financier, Parker Gilbert, of J. P. Morgan and Company, was to supervise the management of German public finances and make sure the foreign capital was not misused. It was an oppressive and humiliating condition, but, in the beginning at least, understandable from the viewpoint of the creditor; for the next few years, Germany flourished under this system.

A period of prosperity, of relaxed nerves and settled living conditions began. This was the great recovery which Hitler had tried in vain to prevent with his last minute *putsch*. But the accomplices of the armed bohemians, the protectors and employers of the murderers' army, still sat in their high state positions, in the ministries and courts. It was these accomplices who were to mete out justice to Hitler.

The judges could scarcely look their victims in the eyes, the jailers did not know whether to guard or wait on their prisoners. To be sure, there were numerous conscientious officials in all departments; and among the accomplices many were enraged against Hitler for exposing them. Epp declared in no uncertain terms that Hitler had broken his word. Yet the leaders of the state were well aware that they were Hitler's accomplices and should have been on trial with him, and their bad conscience certainly weakened the prosecution. The young people who had run so fast from the fire recovered their courage in the presence of the embarrassed police inspectors and state's attorneys. They were seized with righteous indignation. They had marched out for a parade, and instead they had been forced to fight; the state which had already surrendered to them suddenly slipped away. The armed bohemians thought they were Germany; power over society was their prerogative, by virtue of their natural superiority and talents—and then they were fired upon. They were haled into court for proclaiming the violent overthrow of the government, arresting the ministers and leading officials, seizing and threatening to kill men who were totally innocent, plundering private lodgings and stealing banknotes from state printing offices. They scoffed and cursed at their judges, for daring to annoy them over such matters. Hitler in prison heard how his men had recovered their old daring and insolence; this, as he later related, considerably restored his courage. At first 'I wanted to hear nothing more of this false world'; he threatened to end his life by voluntary starvation; Anton Drexler, founder of the party, visited him, and Hitler—not too reluctantly—let himself be dissuaded.

At the end of February, 1924, he faced a special court with Luden-dorff, Röhm, Frick, and others. The trial gave him immense publicity and was a scandal in every respect. With a certain truth Hitler could declare that he had not wanted to rise against the state, for he had thought the state was with him. Gürtner, who had risen to be minister of justice, used his powerful influence to make the judges incline the scales even more than they normally would have.

In the presence of these complaisant judges, Hitler regained all his courage, and his speeches before the court are among his most impressive. He strove to prove his innocence by insisting that he had done only what Kahr, Lossow, and Seisser themselves had wanted. He attempted—and to this he attached far more importance—to explain himself to the world: 'This is my attitude: I would rather be hanged in a Bolshevist Germany than perish under the rule of French swords.' Lossow appeared as a witness and related how Hitler for months had pressed him to act, to set up a military dictatorship. 'Once we take over the government,' Hitler had said, 'the program will come of itself.' When the chairman of the court asked Hitler: 'And how did you conceive of things after that?'—the greatest propagandist of our day replied: 'I thought this: the first thing must be an inconceivable wave of propaganda. That is, a political action which would have had little to do with the other problems of the moment. . . . We would at once have approached the German nation with a great plebiscite.' But he went on to indicate that he did have at least a foreign policy: As Leader of Germany, he would have played England against France. England, he said, had the single desire to 'Balkanize' Europe in order to create a balance of power on the Continent, 'and prevent her world position from being threatened. She is not basically an enemy of Germany. . . . France, however, is Germany's explicit enemy. As England requires the Balkanization of Europe, France requires the Balkanization of Germany.' Whatever government is at the helm in France, its purpose would always be 'to exterminate twenty million Germans and break up Germany into separate states.'

He utilized the occasion to publicize himself in the presence of a hundred attentive reporters from all five continents; and in this he unquestionably succeeded. Lossow had testified that Hitler originally had only wanted to be a 'drummer'; meaning 'at that time Hitler was still modest.'

Hitler replied: 'How small are the thoughts of small men! Believe me, I do not regard the acquisition of a minister's portfolio as a thing worth striving for. I do not hold it worthy of a great man to endeavor to go down in history just by becoming a minister. One might run the risk of being buried beside other ministers. My aim, from the very first day, was a thousand times more than becoming a minister. I wanted to become the destroyer of Marxism. I am going to solve this task, and if I solve it, the title of minister will be an absurdity as far as I am concerned. When I stood for the first time at the grave of Richard Wagner, my heart flowed over with pride that here lay a man who had forbidden any such inscription as: Here lies privy-councillor, music-director, his excellency Baron Richard von Wagner. I was proud that this man and so many men in German history were content to give their names to history, without any titles. It was not from modesty that I wanted to be a drummer in those days. That was the highest aspiration. The rest is a trifle.'

In a gloomy gray suburb of Munich lay an old red-brick structure, its floors and walls in poor repair. It was an officers' training school. In one of its large classrooms the trial was held. It went on for weeks. The unknown stood up and proclaimed to the world: Make no mistake. I am the Leader.

Many times in the course of the trial he was asked directly and indirectly by what right he, a man without origins, title, or virtually any education, arrogated to himself the right to govern Germany, sweeping aside all the generals, presidents, and excellencies. Hitler replied: 'This was not overweening or immodest of me. On the contrary, I am of the opinion that when a man knows he can do a thing, he has no right to be modest. . . . In such questions there are no experts. The art of statecraft is—well, an art, and you've got to be born to it.' Here no doubt the Demon from the masses speaks more democratically than his adversaries in their gold-braided uniforms—but he is only talking. For in the last analysis he is referring only to himself; and what he has in mind is power:

'My standpoint is that the bird must sing because he is a bird. And a man who is born for politics must engage in politics whether at freedom or in prison, whether he sits in a silken chair or must content himself with a hard bench. . . . The man who is born to be a dictator is not compelled; he wills; he is not driven forward; he drives himself forward; there is nothing immodest about this. Is it immodest for a worker to drive himself toward heavy labor? Is it presumptuous of a man with the high forehead of a thinker to ponder through the nights till he gives the world an invention? The man who feels called upon to govern a people has no right to say: If you want me or summon me, I will co-operate. No, it is his duty to step forward. . . .'

In conclusion, he informed the judges that despite everything that had happened they must honor the future state power in him. With unshakable confidence he explained that despite all the moods of the historic moment, despite the temporary reinforcement of the state, despite the apparent discomfiture of the Uprooted and Disinherited by rifle fire, the Reichswehr could not permanently reject an alliance with armed bohemia. For on both sides there was the same human substance, the same ideology, the same attitude twoard social affairs; the men on both sides were and remained armed intellectuals. And if the reconciliation could be brought about in no other way, it would have to be done by war, which Hitler declared to be inevitable, necessary, an aim ardently to be desired; with his unchanged manner of speech, expressing an unchanged conviction, he called this reconciling, liberating war, this war so ardently to be hoped for, the 'great divine judgment' to come:

'I believe that the hour will come when the masses, who today stand on the street with our swastika banner, will unite with those who fired upon them. I believe that this blood will not always separate us. When I learned that it was the Green police which fired, I had the happy feeling that at least it was not the Reichswehr which besmirched itself; the Reichswehr stand as untarnished as before. One day the hour will come when the Reichswehr will stand at our side, officers and men. . . .'

Chairman: 'Herr Hitler, you say that the Green police was besmirched. That I cannot permit.'

Hitler: 'The army we have formed is growing from day to day, from hour to hour, and faster. Especially in these days I nourish the proud hope that one day the hour will come when these wild companies will grow to battalions, and battalions to regiments, the regiments to divisions; that the old cockade will be taken from the filth, that the old flags will wave again, that there will be a reconciliation at the last great divine judgment, which we are prepared to face. Then from our bones and our graves the voice of that court will speak, which alone is entitled to sit in judgment over us. For it is not you, gentlemen, who pronounce judgment upon us. The judgment is spoken by the eternal court of history which will say what it has to say concerning the accusation that has been raised against us. What judgment you will hand down, I know. But that court will not ask us: "Did you commit high treason or did you not?" That court will judge us, the Quartermaster General of the old Army, his officers and soldiers, who, as Germans, wanted and desired only the good of their people and fatherland; who wanted to fight and die. You may pronounce us guilty a thousand times over, the goddess of the eternal court of history will smile and tear to tatters the brief of the state's attorney and the sentence of the court; for she acquits us.'

The sentence of the judges was not so far from the judgment of history. Intimidated from above, tormented by the conscience of their own accomplices, in fear even of the accused, they trampled on what was most defenseless: justice. Contrary to the clear wording of the law, Ludendorff was totally acquitted. Contrary to the clear wording of the law, Hitler, despite the bloody consequences of his crime, received the mild minimum sentence of five years' imprisonment; contrary to the clear wording of the law, he was made to serve only eight and a half months of his term; contrary to the clear wording of the law, he, a foreigner, who had filled the German streets with fire and corpses, was not deported. Röhm and Frick, though formally condemned, were released at once. Göring had fled to Italy and later went to his wife's native Sweden. His unfounded fear of Munich justice kept him for nearly three years in unnecessary exile. Hess was cleverer; he returned, and an equally mild and brief sentence brought him to the same so-called 'prison' as Hitler, a sanatorium-like building in the little city of Landsberg am Lech.

Hitler's cause had collapsed more than he had at first realized. In May, the French people elected a new parliament. It was a crushing defeat for Poincaré, virtually a revolution of the French people against the war in the Ruhr, a severe condemnation of French military policy, a clear 'No' to all aspirations on the Rhine, a renunciation of the policy of adventures and conquests on German soil. The victorious parties of the Socialist and democratic Left had the power and determination to overthrow not only Poincaré but Alexandre Millerand, the President of the republic, who had favored Poincaré's policy. To be sure, elements of domestic policy were also to blame for the landslide; to be sure, the French people stood as firmly as ever for security on the Rhine. But for years to come they were to seek this security by a policy of understanding; not only with Germany, but also with England, a three-cornered relationship of peace with the foe under the aegis of a protector. After five years of vain, costly preparation, France renounced military hegemony over Europe, and withdrew to the line of security and defense. This was the clear will of the French people as expressed by the French parliamentary majority. In 1918, the 'last' of all wars had ended; this was the most sacred axiom in all French politics. When Germany bled economically as a result of the Ruhr, even when she capitulated, she had made the French military aware of the limits of their power; thus, in spite of the capitulation, the Ruhr War was the victory for Germany which Hitler had always feared, vainly prophesying that it would not come to pass.

In the summer of 1924, at a conference in London, English, French, and German statesmen met as equals for the first time in years. Stresemann, shouting and red in the face, argued with French Premier Edouard Herriot, but they arrived at an agreement. The Dawes Plan was accepted by all parties on August 16, 1924, in London, the French began to evacuate the first places in the Ruhr; the eight hundred million gold marks flowed into Germany; more hundreds of millions and ultimately billions came from England and America in the years that followed. For Germany, internally pacified, rebuilding her economy, passed now as a place where money could be invested profitably and safely. To be sure, the inflation had cost the masses a fortune which they never recovered; later it became evident that this destruction of money and hence of bourgeois self-esteem was no unique, transitory stroke of misfortune, but heralded a long wave of destruction and annihilation. But for the present, smooth, friendly conditions seemed to be returning, and hearts were filled with an illusory hope that the terrible catastrophe of 1923 would not be repeated, and should, therefore, in God's name be forgotten.

National Socialism was forgotten along with it. Impotent and embittered in his prison, Hitler laid down the leadership, broke with Ludendorff in a harsh and disrespectful manner, drew forth old sheets of manuscript on which he had begun to write in 1922, and dictated to various fellow prisoners, lastly to Rudolf Hess, the continuation of a work of monumental conception to which he later gave the title *Mein Kampf.*

Thirteen years later, Hitler spoke hard words of self-condemnation about his *putsch* of 1923. In 1922, he had given Minister Schweyer his word of honor, never to make a *putsch*. One year later, he might have had the excuse that the circumstances had been stronger than he. But in 1936, he admitted without shame: 'Today I can frankly own that in the years from 1920 to 1923 I thought of nothing else but a *putsch*.' Then he added: 'I can calmly say this: that was the rashest decision of my life. When I think back on it today, I grow dizzy. . . . If today you saw one of our squads from the year 1923 marching by, you would ask: What workhouse have they escaped from? . . . But Fate meant well with us. It did not permit an action to succeed, which if it had succeeded, would in the end have inevitably crashed as a result of the movement's inner immaturity in those days, and its deficient organizational and intellectual foundation.'

What Hitler wanted to say was that thirteen years ago he actually did not know the direction in which he was going. He hardly understood the reasons that were leading him there.